TED TURNER

TED TURNER

A Biography

Michael O'Connor

GREENWOOD BIOGRAPHIES

GREENWOOD PRESS
An Imprint of ABC-CLIO, LLC

A B C CLIO

Santa Barbara, California • Denver, Colorado • Oxford, England

Copyright 2010 by Michael O'Connor

All rights reserved. No part of this publication may be reproduced, stored in a retrieval system, or transmitted, in any form or by any means, electronic, mechanical, photocopying, recording, or otherwise, except for the inclusion of brief quotations in a review, without prior permission in writing from the publisher.

Library of Congress Cataloging-in-Publication Data
O'Connor, Michael.
    Ted Turner : a biography / Michael O'Connor.
        p. cm. — (Greenwood biographies)
    Includes bibliographical references and index.
    ISBN 978-0-313-35042-9 (alk. paper) — ISBN 978-0-313-35043-6 (ebook)
1. Turner, Ted.   2. Businesspeople—United States—Biography.   3. Sports team owners—United States—Biography.   4. Telecommunication—United States—Biography.   I. Title.
    HC102.5.T86O28   2010
    384.55'5092—dc22
    [B]   2009031625

14   13   12   11   10   1   2   3   4   5

This book is also available on the World Wide Web as an eBook.
Visit www.abc-clio.com for details.

ABC-CLIO, LLC
130 Cremona Drive, P.O. Box 1911
Santa Barbara, California 93116-1911

This book is printed on acid-free paper ∞
Manufactured in the United States of America

To my mother, Francesca O'Connor,
for her love, devotion, and perseverance.

To my wife, Renée Gelman, my perfect love and partner.

CONTENTS

Series Foreword		ix
Acknowledgments		xi
Introduction		xiii
Timeline: Events in the Life of Ted Turner		xvii
Chapter 1	Beginnings	1
Chapter 2	Poison Ivy	13
Chapter 3	Stepping Out	21
Chapter 4	Riding the Waves	31
Chapter 5	Mediated	39
Chapter 6	Oceans Away	53
Chapter 7	Into Heaven	63
Chapter 8	Atlanta Braves	69
Chapter 9	In the Cup	81
Chapter 10	News Cable	95
Chapter 11	Almost	113
Chapter 12	Stepping Up	123
Chapter 13	Reaching Out	139

Chapter 14   Getting Personal   151

Chapter 15   Color My World   163

Chapter 16   Remote Control   169

Chapter 17   Time Worn   177

Chapter 18   Synergy Crisis   189

Chapter 19   Clear Cut Reminder   203

Selected Bibliography and Further Resources   215

Index   227

Photo essay follows page 112

SERIES FOREWORD

In response to high school and public library needs, Greenwood developed this distinguished series of full-length biographies specifically for student use. Prepared by field experts and professionals, these engaging biographies are tailored for high school students who need challenging yet accessible biographies. Ideal for secondary school assignments, the length, format and subject areas are designed to meet educators' requirements and students' interests.

Greenwood offers an extensive selection of biographies spanning all curriculum-related subject areas including social studies, the sciences, literature and the arts, history and politics, as well as popular culture, covering public figures and famous personalities from all time periods and backgrounds, both historic and contemporary, who have made an impact on American and/or world culture. Greenwood biographies were chosen based on comprehensive feedback from librarians and educators. Consideration was given to both curriculum relevance and inherent interest. The result is an intriguing mix of the well known and the unexpected, the saints and sinners from long-ago history and contemporary pop culture. Readers will find a wide array of subject choices from fascinating crime figures like Al Capone to inspiring pioneers like Margaret Mead, from the greatest minds of our time like Stephen Hawking to the most amazing success stories of our day like J.K. Rowling.

While the emphasis is on fact, not glorification, the books are meant to be fun to read. Each volume provides in-depth information about the subject's life from birth through childhood, the teen years, and adult-hood. A thorough account relates family background and education, traces personal and professional influences, and explores struggles, accomplishments, and contributions. A timeline highlights the most significant life events against a historical perspective. Bibliographies supplement the reference value of each volume.

ACKNOWLEDGMENTS

I'd like to thank the inimitable Vince Burns, Executive Editorial Director at ABC-CLIO and former Editorial Director at the Greenwood Publishing Group, for first proposing that I consider doing a book. The former Vice-President of Production and Editorial at Greenwood, Gary Kuris, an intriguingly interesting and good-humored man, also played a part. My sharp and dedicated editor, Sandy Towers, who must surely have been holding her breath throughout the process, has been very highly appreciated throughout; an author could wish for none better.

Thanks go as well to Michelle Scott at ABC-CLIO/Greenwood, for overseeing the production process. The editorial staff at Apex CoVantage did a spectacular job addressing my lax and sloppy grammar.

Shout outs go to Bridget, Mark, Nicole, Barbara, and everyone else who made a successful transition from Greenwood to ABC-CLIO, as well as all those, like myself, who didn't.

I am deeply indebted to those who have written on Ted Turner in the past, especially Ken Auletta, Porter Bibb, Robert Goldberg and Gerald Jay Goldberg, Roger Vaughan, Hank Whittemore, and Christain Williams.

I also take this opportunity to thank all the institutions, educators, colleagues, novelists, friends, and family that have all left residual pieces of themselves within me. Maimonides hospital and Frankie Esposito, both in their own way, probably literally saved my life in earlier years (though no one believes my story involving Frankie).

Special mention to Elie Azenberg, Steve Zwerling, Jim Haskins, Ted Estabrook, and Alan Liss.

My mother, who held herself and the family together after my own father's suicide and has always been the rock of my life, is loved and thanked more than words could ever express. My brothers, Mark and Patrick, are and will always be the best friends I have, whether we happen to be keeping in very close contact or not. My wife, Renée Gelman, sustains and enriches my life on every level, and I will love her deeply always and forever.

And of course, Ted Turner himself, a most remarkable man and subject. Given my own father's suicide—though I was considerably younger than Ted during the experience—I feel a sort of kinship with Turner, who couldn't be more different than myself in wealth, accomplishments, and intelligence. May he live 100 years, and savor every one.

INTRODUCTION

As he stepped down from his position as Vice Chairman of AOL Time Warner in May of 2006, Ted Turner said simply, "I tried my best."

Over the past six years he had been humiliated, tied like ballast to the experimental design of a business merger that by theory was transformational but proved to be dead in the water. It was a repeat of his experience in his first attempt to defend the America's Cup nearly 30 years before, with a boat named *Mariner* and its hull with no point. He had lost all control of a media empire that he had built with tenacious determination over the first phase of his life—an empire built on the synergies that proved an impossible dream for the suits of AOL Time Warner. And he had lost most of the fortune he had planned to use to continue his efforts to improve and save the world in the second phase of his life.

After bursting onto the national consciousness in post–Watergate 1976 with his exaggerated southern drawl, his brash, boisterous, yet self-effacing endless chatter, and outsized, quirky showmanship, he had become the anti-Zelig of the 20th century, popping up everywhere and never fitting in. The yachting establishment chastised him, the baseball establishment banned him, and the media establishment ridiculed him, all to their ultimate chagrin. He proved bigger than all three.

Robert Edward "Ted" Turner III was the ultimate outsider. Shaped by a domineering, success-driven father and a childhood marked by repeated abandonment, Turner was an outsider even within his own family. Attention, any attention, became life affirming. Throughout his life he has both struggled to live up to his father's expectations and rebelled against them, while only occasionally realizing that it was his own sense of self-worth that he struggled with. He transformed himself into a carbon copy of his father, adopting his drive, his business credos, and his weaknesses as his own, more hard edged and subtly distorted than the original but softer at the core. That core though was well hidden, buried within the aching soul of a past too painful to explore.

One wonders what would have become of Ted Turner had his father stayed in the used car business and never started Turner Outdoor Advertising, the billboard business that Ted was running by the time he was 24, after his father committed suicide. When he started out, Turner was hell bent on establishing a business empire that would conquer the world as surely as his hero, Alexander the Great, had conquered his. The shape and substance of the empire itself, however, would be part happenstance, part luck, determined by his starting point. At heart, Turner was a salesman, just as his father had been; his mission was to sell advertising. Initially, television was just a better means to that end. While he quickly understood the power of the medium, it was only by working through the connections that he proved more adept at making than any other businessman of his time that he would truly make peace with the Rotarian motto that his father had often repeated, "They profit most who serve best."

By the time he walked off that stage in 2006, Jimmy Carter, Mikhail Gorbachev, and Kofi Anan had hailed him as a hero. He had been named *TIME* magazine's Man of the Year, and *Broadcasting* magazine's Man of the Century, and been named to numerous halls of fame. He had won the America's Cup and an unprecedented four U.S. Yachtsman of the Year awards. The baseball team he owned had won a World Series and an unprecedented fourteen straight divisional championships. He had received a number of honorary degrees, including one from Brown University, which he had left in his senior year after being suspended for the second time. He was collecting humanitarian and environmental awards at a rate too quick to register. He was an enduring mass draw on the lecture circuit and one of the most recognized people in the world.

While the unlikeliest of folk heroes, with a tongue set loose from his head and a penchant for making crude, biting, and ill-considered remarks, he has been well loved, though rarely completely, by far more than those who can't stand the thought of him. During his early sailing career he was feted by several crown heads of Europe as being the quintessential American, and in the sense of being self-important and selfless, arrogant and beneficent, clever and naive, I suppose it fits. A longtime member of Turner's sailing crews may have provided the best succinct description of Ted when he said, "he's an asshole, but a glorious asshole."

To understand how that day in 2006 came about we can look to the 1950s sitcoms that filled much of the airtime of his Superstation, or his favorite movie, *Gone With the Wind*, with its dashing hero whose name mimicked his own initials, RET. Deep down, Ted Turner yearns for the splendor and tranquility of a time that never was. He was cable before cable was cool, but only because he couldn't afford a network and was never able to acquire one. Like a tragedy from the classics that he loves so well, he succumbed to being the insider that this ultimate outsider always yearned to be. Those who have known him best most often cite his childlike innocence as one of his most redeeming qualities, and loyalty, honesty, and trust as being the most cherished principles passed onto him by his father. Inside a corporate boardroom, such gentlemanly ethics are for losers. In the end, the maverick that always insisted on being his own unique self was undone by a culture principally geared to looking out for yourself.

Turner still retains some bitterness over being ostracized by the lesser mortals that had conceived the shipwreck of AOL Time Warner, but for the most part he has moved on.

While he is far less wealthy than he once was, he is still quite comfortable. He continues to advocate for the causes he deems critical: environmental stewardship, nuclear deterrence, population control, sustainable energy, the eradication of poverty and disease.

He continues to find solace in land, "the only thing that lasts," owning and protecting over two million acres in the United States, much of it active ranchland dedicated to protecting and reintroducing native flora and fauna. He still has his hands in business, being the co-owner and operator of Ted's Montana Grill, serving bison burgers in a neighborhood near you. He is still contributing money to UN projects, still funding the UN Foundation, the Nuclear Threat Initiative, and the Turner Foundation. He has finally completed the autobiography he had been promising for decades.

His biggest regrets are not for the businesses or the fortune he has lost, but for his three failed marriages and the pain, particularly that most attributable to his own failings, they have visited upon his wives and children. He is still haunted by the specter of *Citizen Kane*, as he has been since first seeing it as a young adult. He is still trying his best.

TIMELINE: EVENTS IN THE LIFE OF TED TURNER

November 19, 1938	R. E. (Ted) Turner III is born in Cincinnati, Ohio, to R. E. (Ed) Turner Jr. and Florence Rooney Turner.
September 18, 1941	Ted's sister, Mary Jean Turner, is born.
1943	Ed Turner enlists in the Navy and takes his wife and daughter with him. Ted Turner, left in Cincinnati, is sent to a boarding school.
1944	Turner is sent to Sumner, Mississippi to stay with his paternal grandparents and attend public school.
1945	Turner is reunited with his family in Cincinnati.
1947	Ed Turner moves the family to Savannah, Georgia to oversee a recently purchased Outdoor Advertising plant. Ted is sent to Georgia Military Academy, south of Atlanta.
1948–49	Ed Turner purchases a yacht he names the *Merry Jane*, and hires Jimmy Brown as its caretaker. Turner is reunited with family, and attends Savannah public school.
1950–56	Turner attends McCallie Military Academy in Chattanooga, Tennessee, becoming the young-

est boarding student in its institutional history. During summers he works 40-hour weeks at Turner Outdoor Advertising, and his father charges him for room and board.

1952   Mary Jean is diagnosed with a fatal form of systemic lupus erythematosus. Opportunistic encephalitis and ensuing coma leave her brain damaged.

1955   Turner wins the Interscholastic Tennessee debating championship.

1956   Turner enters Brown University in Providence, Rhode Island, joins the sailing club, and will be named the best freshman sailor in New England.

1957   Turner's parents, Ed and Florence, divorce. Florence moves back to Cincinnati with Mary Jean.

        In December, Turner is suspended from Brown for the upcoming spring semester.

        Ed Turner marries Jane Dillard.

1958   Turner serves a six-month stint in the Naval Reserves.

1959   Turner has a personal letter from his father published in the *Brown Daily Herald*.

        Turner is named captain of the Brown varsity sailing team, and then meets Julia (Judy) Gale Nye in November.

1960   Turner is suspended from Brown for the second time and will not return.

June 22   Turner marries Judy Nye.

        Turner starts work as a salesman at Turner Outdoor Advertising.

December 15   Mary Jean dies in Cincinnati.

1961   Ted and Judy's first child, Laura Lee, is born.

        Ed Turner spends time at Silver Hill facility in New Canaan, Connecticut.

1962   Ted and Judy divorce but soon reunite.

Ed returns to Silver Hill for a brief time late in the year.

March 5, 1963 Ted's father, Ed Turner, commits suicide.

Ted, at 24, becomes president of Turner Outdoor Advertising.

Ted and Judy have a second child, Robert Edward (Teddy) Turner IV.

Ted and Judy break up for good.

June 2, 1964 Turner marries Jane (Janie) Shirley Smith.

1965 Ted and Janie have their first child, named Rhett Turner after Ted's favorite movie character.

1966 Turner wins the Southern Ocean Racing Conference (SORC) in his second year of ocean-racing.

1968 Ted and Janie's second child, Beauregard, is born.

Turner purchases his first radio station, WAPO, in Chattanooga, Tennessee.

1969 Ted and Janie's third child, Sarah Jean (Jennie), is born.

Turner Advertising is rechristened as Turner Communications Group.

1970 Turner acquires independent UHF-television station WJRJ in Atlanta and changes its call letters to WTCG.

Turner purchases a second UHF station, WCTU, in Charlotte, North Carolina and changes its call letters to WRET.

1971 Turner is named U.S. Yachtsman of the Year for 1970.

WTCG expands its schedule to 24 hours.

1972 FCC relaxes rules on cable television's importation of distant signals.

WTCG begins airing Atlanta Braves and Atlanta Hawks games.

1974 Turner is named U.S. Yachtsman of the Year for 1973.

Turner fails in a bid to defend the America's Cup.

1975   WTCG begins broadcasting *17 Update Early in the Morning.*

HBO begins satellite distribution of its signal.

1976   Turner buys the Atlanta Braves baseball franchise.

Turner signs Andy Messersmith, baseball's first free agent.

December 17   WTCG Superstation initials satellite distribution, redefining cable.

1977   Turner buys the Atlanta Hawks basketball franchise.

Turner serves as manager of the Braves for one day.

Turner is suspended from baseball for one year for tampering.

Turner wins the America's Cup.

1978   Turner wins U.S. Yachtsman of the Year for 1977.

Charlotte station WRET becomes an NBC affiliate.

1979   Turner wins the U.K.'s Fastnet race in the deadliest race in the history of yachting.

Turner Communications is rechristened as Turner Broadcasting Systems.

WTCG Superstation is rebranded as WTBS.

1980   Turner wins U.S. Yachtsman of the Year for 1979.

Turner sells WRET to Westinghouse to help finance CNN.

Turner and Reese Schonfeld launch Cable News Network (CNN), the world's first 24-hour televised news channel.

Turner fails in a bid to defend the America's Cup.

1981   Turner retires from yacht racing.

Superstation qualifies for Nielsen ratings after Turner prevails in having viewership requirements readjusted.

Turner Broadcasting sues the major networks, unions, and the White House for being denied pool coverage membership.

Superstation begins "Turner Time" programming, starting five minutes past the top and bottom of the hour.

1982   CNN2, later renamed Headline News, launches in an effort to hold off announced competition from Westinghouse and ABC.

CNNRadio launches.

CNN initiates CNN NewsSource syndication service.

Turner travels to Cuba to meet with Fidel Castro.

Reese Schonfeld is fired from CNN, and Burt Reinhardt is promoted to president of CNN.

Westinghouse/ABC co-venture Satellite News Channel launches.

1983   Turner buys out Satellite News Channel for $25 million.

1984   CNN launches International Hour.

Government's Cable Act deregulates the industry and spurs further growth.

1985   Turner creates The Better World Society.

Turner launches a hostile takeover attempt of CBS.

1986   CNN has exclusive footage of the Challenger disaster.

Turner purchases MGM film library.

Turner's Goodwill Games open in Moscow.

Turner announces plans to colorize several of his newly acquired MGM screen gems.

CNN pioneers use of "flyaway" portable satellite uplink transmitters.

Janie and Ted separate, and Ted moves in with girlfriend J. J. Ebaugh.

CNN moves into CNN Center.

Turner's son Teddy is in a serious car accident in Moscow.

1987　A group of 26 cable operators purchases 37 percent of Turner Broadcasting to save it from crushing debt. Turner cedes veto power to two of the investors.

CNN initials World Report, and opens a Beijing bureau.

Turner purchases his first Western ranch property, the Bar None in Montana.

1988　Turner Network Television (TNT) is launched.

Ted and Janie's divorce is finalized.

1989　Turner and Jane Fonda have their first date.

Turner buys a second ranch property in Montana, the Flying D, and starts building his bison herd.

Turner's bid to purchase Financial News Network is vetoed by his board.

Turner launches Turner Productions to create documentaries and docudramas for TNT and theatrical release.

CNN signal is beamed to Africa, the Middle East, India, and Southeast Asia. Coverage of Tiananmen Square wins wide acclaim.

1990　Turner starts the Turner Foundation, a conservation-minded personal trust.

Turner creates *Captain Planet and the Planeteers* animation series.

Tom Johnson, former publisher of the *Los Angeles Times*, becomes president of CNN.

1991　CNN has its "finest hour" with coverage of the Gulf War from inside Iraq.

CNN's coverage of Soviet coup attempt reaches Soviet nationals.

Turner funds Captain Planet Foundation, which is dedicated to environmental education.

Government relation of "Fin-Syn" rules signals media consolidations to come.

Turner purchases Hanna-Barbera animation studios.

December 21 Turner and Jane Fonda are married on Jane's 54th birthday.

1992 Ted Turner named *TIME* magazine's Man of the Year for 1991.

Turner's mother, Florence, passes away.

Turner considered as possible third-party presidential candidate.

Cartoon Network is launched.

Cable Television Consumer Protection and Competition Act is passed.

1993 Turner purchases New Line Cinema and Castle Rock Entertainment.

Turner Broadcasting profit is greater than that of any of the three major networks.

1994 Turner Classic Movies (TCM) is launched.

CNN profit is greater than that of any of the three major networks.

1995   Turner agrees to sell Turner Broadcasting to Time Warner.

1996 Time Warner's purchase of Turner Broadcasting is approved and becomes official.

1997 Turner pledges $1 billion in cash and stock to the United Nations, and sets up the United Nations Foundation to administer the bequest.

Turner is featured in Apple Computer's Think Different advertising campaign.

1999   Turner named *Broadcasting & Cable*'s co-Man of the Century with CBS's Bill Paley.

2000   Ted and Jane Fonda announce separation.

America Online and Time Warner announce merger plans.

Turner negotiates deal in U.S./UN dues dispute and pays the United States' $35 million shortfall in past dues.

Turner is told he will be stripped of all operating authority with the AOL Time Warner merger.

2001   Turner funds Nuclear Threat Initiative, a foundation dedicated to reducing the threat of nuclear, biological, and chemical weapons.

Merger is approved, and Time Warner becomes AOL Time Warner.

Ted and Jane Fonda's divorce is finalized.

2002   Jerry Levin resigns as CEO of AOL Time Warner.

Turner and partner George McKerrow Jr. open the first of their Ted's Montana Grill restaurants.

2003   Steve Case resigns as AOL Time Warner Chairman.

Turner resigns his post as AOL Time Warner vice chairman on the same day the company announces a net 2002 loss of $98.7 billion.

Turner becomes an outspoken critic of the Iraq war.

Time Warner drops "AOL" from its company name.

2004   Turner publishes *My Beef with Big Media*.

2006   Turner resigns from his seat on the board of Time Warner.

2008   Turner, the largest individual landowner in the United States and the owner of the world's largest herd of bison, announces that he is almost done purchasing land.

Turner releases an autobiography, *Call Me Ted.*

2009   Turner supports Ashton Kutcher's bid to gain one million Twitter followers before CNN; Kutcher pledges 1,000 nets to the "Nothing But Nets" campaign.

Chapter 1

BEGINNINGS

Robert Edward (Ted) Turner III was born at 8:50 A.M. on November 19, 1938, not in the South, but in Cincinnati, Ohio, 15 months after the wedding of his parents, Robert Edward (Ed) Turner Jr. and Florence Rooney Turner.

Ed Turner had come to Cincinnati on the promise of a sales job at Queen City Chevrolet. His own father, Robert Edward Turner, had migrated to Sumner, Mississippi in search of opportunity when the extensive landholdings of his forebears had gone barren. By the time Ed was born in 1911, his father had managed to turn a meager inheritance into a respectable holding of agricultural property while building a life as a cotton farmer, but the success would prove short lived. As his forebears had before him, he watched his harvest dwindle as this land too gave out. With his income declining, he moved the family to town, where he was an elder of the Methodist Church, and opened a general store where Ed would work as a boy. Despite and because of his reduced circumstances, Robert Edward Turner was determined that Ed would go to college, and though he couldn't afford Duke, where Ed had been accepted, the Methodist Millsaps College in Jackson seemed both appropriate and affordable. Timing would prove critical, however, as just weeks after the decision was made the stock market collapsed, initiating the Great Depression. Before long, Robert Edward Turner had to close the general store and give up his house in town, moving his remaining family back to the farm where they would be dependent on whatever income could be provided by the sharecroppers that worked his lands. Deprived of nearly all assistance from his family, Ed tried supporting himself with whatever odd jobs he could find. It wasn't enough, though, and he was forced to leave Millsaps without a degree. After wandering the South in search of a job, Ed started working for the General Outdoor Advertising Company in Memphis, Tennessee, where he worked as a "counter," standing by the side of the road and counting the number of cars and passengers that passed the company's billboards, until an acquaintance introduced him to the owner of Queen City Chevrolet.

Before leaving to go north, Ed reportedly told his parents that he would become rich and own a plantation and a yacht; whether apocryphal or not, he wasted little time in trying. Before long he was the top salesman at Queen City and his outgoing nature, Southern drawl, and good sense of humor made him a popular young man around town, especially with the ladies. He soon struck up a relationship with one of his customers, George F. Rooney Jr., who insisted he meet his sister, Florence, who had largely retreated from socializing after her fiancé had developed acute appendicitis on the eve of their planned wedding and died a few days later. George and Florence's grandfather was Henry Sicking, who had owned a chain of 20 grocery stores and a popular livery stable and is said to have been the spitting image of Ted Turner. Reportedly despondent over stock market losses, he died while absentmindedly stepping from a streetcar into the path of another, leaving behind a modest fortune. When introduced to Florence Rooney, who had lived with her mother at her grandmother's quite swanky boarding hotel since her parents' divorce, Ed Turner was immediately intrigued. Florence was tall, beautiful, refined, and surprisingly outgoing, and Ed Turner seems to have decided on the spot that he would win her hand. Florence, however, would need convincing, as would her mother, since the Rooneys were devout Catholics, with Florence having attended convent schools, while Ed, though hardly religious, still identified with his father's Methodist faith.

Ed would soon take up residence at Mrs. Sicking's hotel, where a classical ensemble performed every night and limousines lined the driveways. It may have been an extravagance, but it gave him the chance to be around Florence and her mother as often as possible. He eventually won both of them over after a weekend visit with his parents in Sumner, but not before agreeing to be married in the Catholic Church and rear his children in the faith. Once Florence was pregnant with Ted, however, Ed reneged on his promise, though in the spirit of compromise he agreed to let him be raised as Episcopalian.

Ed Turner was extremely proud of his young son Ted, the "first Turner born north of the Mason-Dixon line,"[1] and he became the center of attention. The young Turner family lived in a pleasant, middle-class neighborhood in Cincinnati, but not in domestic tranquility. Ed proved to be even more of a drinker than Florence had realized, and he tended to lose his temper when he got drunk. He also proved to be anything but completely faithful, later bragging to Ted that he had slept with 300 women by the time he was 30, including every debutante in Cincinnati save one. While successful as a car salesman, and even, according to Ted, once owning a small business called "Honest Ed's Used Cars,"[2] he eventually worked his way back to outdoor advertising at Central Outdoor Advertising. With the financial support of Florence's family, he opened his own billboard company across the river from Cincinnati in Covington, Kentucky.

Ted was a happy if rambunctious child and, always the naturalist, his first word, as reported by Ted and others, was "pretty,"[3] in response to spotting a butterfly. Things changed, however, when on September 18, 1941, his sister Mary Jean was born. The undivided attention he had enjoyed before was now very divided, and Ted started to show some of his irascible nature, acting up, destroying clothes lines, tearing ornaments off Christmas trees, and generally demanding the attention he felt to be his due. When the Japanese bombed Pearl Harbor just months after Mary Jean's birth and his advertising business started to suffer, Ed's drinking increased, his temper grew shorter, and he was particularly frustrated with his troublesome son. Ed soon decided to join the Navy, and for whatever reason or combination of reasons, Ted was sent to a boarding school in Cincinnati while Ed, Florence, and Mary Jean went off to a naval station in the Gulf.

Able to visit his grandmother only on Sunday afternoons, the four-year-old Turner couldn't make sense of his abandonment at what he recalls as a "cold, concrete dorm room and a gray gravel courtyard framed by a chain-link fence."[4] He would later tell Jane Fonda that he would have died if not for a floor proctor who "would hold me on her lap and rock me at night."[5] Somehow having been informed of just how miserable Ted was that year, his parents decided to send him south to the Turner farm in Sumner to attend kindergarten at a public school. In Sumner, Ted would take to going off on his own to explore the woods, and he became fascinated by the abundance and behavior of animals, birds, and insects. The following year, Ted would be reunited with his parents, now returned to Cincinnati, and would be sent to Lotspeich, a private school founded in 1916 with an emphasis on expanding the creativity and curiosity of its students. Still feeling starved for attention, Ted showed a bit too much creativity, constantly playing pranks on his classmates and disturbing the functioning of the school. Earlier biographies report that he was finally expelled, but Ted himself says his parents were asked to send him elsewhere for second grade, a subtle but significant difference. The next few years were ones of relative stability for Ted, attending a public school in his Avondale neighborhood, but he exhibited the same behavior as at Lotspeich. While it didn't lead to expulsion, as he told Christian Williams, "the other kids thought I was a show off and a smart ass,"[6] and he frequently found himself in fights.

Ed Turner's business was experiencing a postwar boom, but it didn't seem to quell his drinking or his temper, and his stint in the Navy had turned him into a chain smoker. While his relations with Ted do seem to have always been tempered with concern, if not a twisted sort of love, he was a firm believer in discipline and hard work. Over Florence's objections, he beat Ted often, spanking him with his hands, a razor strap, and even the occasional wire hanger, and most of these beatings were accompanied by his explanations for them or some variation on the theme that it was hurting him more than Ted. In one bizarre instance, perhaps inspired by one of the parenting books he was fond of reading, Ed told Ted, who was around seven at the time, to beat him with the strap instead. Ted ran away in tears, understandably much more scarred than enlightened, and it's a story Ted has repeatedly gone back to over the years. By the time Turner was eight, he was made to work off his summers with four hours of yard work each day, most of it pulling weeds. Turner says, "It was such drudgery that to this day I don't like to do yard work."[7] Nevertheless, each of his own children would be put to the same task.

With Ed's business continuing to prosper, his old company began to take notice, accusing him of unfair business practices. However, rather than hurt Ed's fledgling enterprise, the accusations helped assure the company's future. The ever-combative Ed Turner would win a lawsuit against Central Outdoor and receive a very generous financial settlement. Looking to the South, which had been slower to recover from the Depression and so had the bigger potential for growth, Ed used the settlement to expand his business by buying two billboard companies in Savannah, Georgia. Though he first intended to run the businesses from Cincinnati, or at least used that idea to placate Florence, Ed was soon complaining that his Savannah managers weren't aggressive enough and would wind up succumbing to the competition. Deciding that he would have a greater impact in Savannah than in Cincinnati, Ed moved the family there in 1947.

Apparently unable to find or afford a suitably sized house, as Florence would tell Roger Vaughan, the family's first purchase was only big enough for three, and the nine-year-old Ted, showing little sign of outgrowing his temperamental deviousness, was again the outcast. He was packed off to Georgia Military Academy, just south of Atlanta. It was hoped the school's reputation for handling "problem" young men would succeed in instilling Ted with the discipline that Ed, for all his trying, had been unable to impart to his son. Turner arrived at the school six weeks into the term, the youngest in his class, and standing out as a hated Northerner. The dress code at that time saw the cadets wearing Confederate gray uniforms and the pride of the South was deeply engrained in the school's culture, making Ted, now not only alone but alone in a totally foreign environment, feel all the more an outsider. "Problem" boys are by definition toughs , and the students at Georgia Military Academy were certainly no exception, but Turner was still Turner and despite the already huge target on his back, his air of superiority and a mouth that didn't know when to keep itself shut just exacerbated the problem. In remembering the experience, Turner says, "it was like Lord of the Flies."[8] With word quickly spreading that he had insulted General Robert E. Lee and Southern culture in general—

which Turner now denies—a crowd of 40 young cadets carrying a rope and intent on having themselves a lynching chased him; Ted hid in a locker for four hours. Obstinate, but never stupid, Turner realized that if this was his fate he had better get on board with this Confederate thing, and by the end of the year he was a Northerner no more.

Florence, meanwhile, had been able to find a larger house in Savannah and convinced Ed to buy it, so Ted was able to return to his family and attend a public school for what he has long said was his "happiest year so far."[9] Still generally insular, Ted took to wandering through the woods and reconnecting with nature just as he had done in the year spent with his grandparents. He would soon take up taxidermy, which he would devote a lot of attention to and was reportedly very good at. All was not exactly tranquil at home, however. Ed was involved in a war with another more established billboard company in town, and, knowing that a great part of success was making friends, Ed was actively engaged in doing just that. He quickly bought a 45-foot schooner that he named *Merry Jane*, a play on his daughter's name, which he used mainly for throwing parties and entertaining prospective clients. He was active in the local Rotary Club and joined the Yacht Club as well, where he became quite popular despite the fact that the younger set at the club took to taking bets on just when the genial Mr. Turner would become inebriated enough to get into what seemed his inevitable fights. Florence, now separated from her extended family, was increasingly concerned with his drinking, which just seemed to be getting worse and worse, and his increasingly abusive treatment of Ted was the source of many of the couple's fights. She was also more than aware that much of the time he spent entertaining "clients," was in fact spent with other women.

Shortly after acquiring the *Merry Jane*, Ed would hire Jimmy Brown, a 21-year old African American Geechee from South Carolina's Gullah islands, to take care of his boat and do general chores around the house. Jimmy Brown would become a trusted confidant to Ed, serving as everything from cook and chauffeur to a substitute father for Ted and Mary Jean, and he became an integral part of Ed's family and eventually Ted's. While he grew up in a very segregated South, where African Americans were routinely and often brutally treated,[10] Turner has rarely ever spoken about this aspect of his upbringing, favoring instead the idyllic view of his favorite movie, *Gone With the Wind*, and the heroic Rhett Butler, whose name was a homonym of his and his father's initials, R.E.T.[11]

Shortly afterward, Ed was instrumental in setting up a junior sailing program for children of the Yacht Club members, and though he used his considerable sales skills to convince others to buy 13-foot Penguin class sailboats for their children, he had to be talked into doing the same for Ted. Initially not interested in the boat, or Ed's edict that he would have to sail every weekend, once Jimmy Brown showed Ted that the boat could be used to explore an island offshore that he had always been interested in, his passion seemed to blossom. Not that he was initially very good at it. While he definitely showed an interest in competing, he didn't show the same interest in learning about his boat, and he was prone to tipping, earning him two of his earliest nicknames, "Turnover Ted" and "Capsize Kid." With Ed focused on his business, it was Jimmy who taught Ted the basics of sailing and judging winds, and as his potential started to show, John McIntosh, a friend of Ed's, also took an interest. He would soon be paired with Bunky (Carl) Helfrich, the son of another of Ed's friends at the club. Although Turner would insist on always being the captain, Helfrich would become a regular crew member on Turner's boats for years to come.[12]

After enjoying a year at home, however, Turner was enrolled at Mc-Callie Military Academy in Chattanooga, Tennessee, where he would attend school for six years beginning in 1950. Florence cried and objected, Turner refused to go, and McCallie itself had to be convinced since it had never before had a boarding student in the seventh grade. Ed's was not a mind that could be easily swayed, however, and Turner was again left to his own devices in another new environment. To Ed, Ted still needed military discipline and to get away from what he felt was Florence's coddling, and the school fit his ultraconservative political views. At the same time, it was also a show of his own new place in the world, since McCallie was the Southern equivalent of a prep school, a place where all the best young men were sent. Upward mobility was important to Ed.

One of Ed Turner's favorite lines was that insecurity breeds success, and if nothing else we have to give him his due on that. Beaten, berated, and repeatedly abandoned, Turner was by this time terribly insecure, starved for attention, and angry at the world. While naturally gregarious, he didn't make friends easily, though he certainly got attention. He excelled at practical jokes—planting clocks around the room, all set to go off at different times, letting squirrels loose in the dorm or releasing birds from beneath his desk, setting buckets of water to rain on people's heads. He climbed out windows during class and refused to polish his shoes or follow the dress standards. Collecting demerits by the dozens, he became a fixture in the "bullpen," marching with his rifle for hours on end as punishment for his infractions. The demerits were so numerous that, on any of the rare occasions when he got to go home for major holidays, he always needed a new pair of shoes, and at the end of several school terms he had to stay on longer to make up for the infractions he had yet to walk off.

In his spare time, when not on his nature watches, he would be found in the library reading everything he could find on his heroes, Alexander the Great and Admiral Horatio Nelson; military history and adventures at sea thrilled his imagination. He envisioned himself as a hero, leading his troops into battle, vanquishing the enemy, and conquering the world. He took to growing lawn grass in his room; doubtless as feed for an increasing number and variety of stray and wounded animals he was keeping there. His first friend at the school was a math teacher, Houston Patterson, who had recently learned to sail and had his boat at the school. Turner went off sailing with him as often as possible, eventually leading to the formation of a sailing club at the school. He particularly grew very close with Elliot Schmidt, his dorm master and the head of the debating team.

As the years passed, if Turner still did not establish many close relationships, he did increase his popularity. It's hard not to respect the practical joker in your midst, particularly one who doesn't try to foist the blame onto others, and Turner was always ready to accept whatever blame his escapades might bring him, and he was unfailingly forthright and honest when questioned. Though his memory and recitation of events has often been dubious, if not contradictory, that basic honesty has really been a hallmark of Turner's and a legacy from his father, who valued honor, trust, loyalty, and being true to your word as cornerstone values undergirding the achievement of success and wealth.

When he did get home for summer vacation, all was not exactly rosy. At 12 years old, Turner was now working 40-hour weeks pulling up weeds around Turner Advertising billboards. As his duties diversified and his salary increased, Ed started charging him $25 a week for room and board, and if Ted didn't like it he was free to find other lodging. It was also increasingly clear that Florence, who Ted treasured, was not about to settle into the role of the meek Southern wife that Ed demanded, and the couple's life grew ever more bitter and acerbic. He did continue to sail his Penguin at the yacht club, though, and if he was winning no championships, he was always working his way closer.

When Jimmy Brown came to pick Ted up at the end of his ninth-grade school year, he also brought word that Ted's sister, Mary Jean, had been diagnosed with systemic lupus erythematosus, a rare and fatal form of an autoimmune disease. Ed Turner tried everything he could to find a way to restore his daughter to health, but his money didn't help and with her compromised immune system, other diseases threatened. Contracting encephalitis, Mary Jean was in a coma for 12 weeks at Johns Hopkins and suffered brain damage. She returned home in deep and unrelenting pain, suffering regular seizures, and filling the house with heartrending cries of torment. Ed was devastated. He was used to being in control and didn't take well to being powerless. In one of his few earlier public comments on this time, Ted would tell Curry Kirkpatrick, "It was a horror show of major proportions. Padded rooms. Screaming at night. It was something out of Dark Shadows."[13]

Coincidentally or not, Mary Jean's illness seemed to coincide with Turner making peace with McCallie. He started taking an interest in the military aspects of the school, pressing his uniform, shining his shoes. He grew close to a religious studies teacher and was talking of becoming a missionary. In his junior year, he was voted the neatest cadet. Having performed quite poorly on the verbal portion of his College Boards, he vowed to do better and set a goal to improve his verbal score over the summer while tending to the billboards. He was voted Captain of the Corps in his senior year, and increased his score on the verbal College Boards by 162 points.

When the debating club was preparing for the Interscholastic Tennessee Championships, Turner was determined to win. The topic of the debate being whether government subsidies for higher education should be granted to deserving students according to need, Ted realized that if he could twist the topic around he could essentially quash any rebuttals to his argument. Professors at a nearby university agreed with his premise that "need," as presented in the debate topic, could be assumed to be the government's need to defeat the Soviet Union rather than the economic need of qualified students. In the finals, he left the girl set to debate him dumbfounded and in tears, and though McCallie would be viewed as somewhat unethical for distorting the debate topic, the school had won its first state championship in 30 years and Turner would be awarded the school's Holton Harris Oratorical Medal at graduation.

So, Turner, who had cried and refused to go off to McCallie, who for his first several years had to be dragged back kicking and screaming at the end of each summer, now cried at having to leave. "It was such a perfect place," he would say.[14] He would send his own eldest son there, continues to speak of its positive influence on his life, and has supported it with financial contributions ever since, though it's no longer a military academy.

As a graduation present, his father bought Turner a 19-foot Lightning class boat, but in order not to spoil him he made Ted pay half the cost, taking nearly everything Ted had managed to save from his summers working at Turner Advertising. Turner left his old Penguin to Houston Patterson to be used by McCallie's sailing club, christened his new boat *Greased Lightning*, At the end of another summer of pulling weeds he convinced two friends to accompany him on his detour from college to enter the 1956 International Lightning Regatta in Canada. Turner would jump the gun on the first day of races and at the end of the fifth day would have an overall finish in 23rd place out of 44 boats, but he was thrilled by competing on a major level and at least holding his own.

NOTES

1. Ted Turner with Bill Burke, *Call Me Ted* (New York: Grand Central Publishing, 2008), 2.

2. Ibid., 45.

3. Ibid., 1.

4. Ibid., 3.

5. Jane Fonda, *My Life So Far* (New York: Random House, 2005), 479.

6. Christian Williams, *Lead, Follow or Get Out of the Way: The Story of Ted Turner* (New York: Times Books, 1981), 21.

7. Turner, *Call Me Ted*, 5–6.

8. Ibid., 8.

9. Ibid., 9.

10. Despite that reality, whites and African Americans often interacted more in the South than they did in the North, but being "color blind," as Turner claims his father had been, is certainly no badge of honor.

11. Turner first identified his father as Rhett Butler, as he would later identify himself, even in appearance. One of his business associates once played on this, pretending to search his memory while he said Turner looked just like that character, Ashley Wilkes. In her autobiography, Jane Fonda would say he in fact identifies with Scarlett O'Hara.

12. Bunky (Carl) Helfrich would also serve as the architect of the original CNN building and several of Turner's houses, as well as vice president of planning and development at Turner Broadcasting. Ted and Helfrich remained close friends until Bunky's death in September of 2008.

13. Curry Kirkpatrick, "Going Real Strawwng," *Sports Illustrated*, August 21, 1978, 78.

14. Roger Vaughan, *Ted Turner: The Man Behind the Mouth* (Boston: Sail Books, 1978), 156.

Chapter 2

POISON IVY

Turner had had his sights set on attending the U.S. Naval Academy, but despite his father's service in the Navy and his own attendance at two military academies, Ed had other plans. Ed insisted that Ted attend an Ivy League school, and though his first choice, Harvard, turned him down given his lackluster grades at McCallie, he was accepted at the University of Pennsylvania and Brown University in Rhode Island. Ed let him decide between them. Brown won out because it had the better sailing program, and Turner started his college career there in the fall of 1956.

In a reverse from his introduction at Georgia Military Academy, Turner would now be the Southern yokel among the Northern pure-breds. In the words of Roger Vaughan, who attended Brown at the same time as Turner, "he showed up at Brown, a strange mixture of states'-rights revisionist, rebel, war lover, Dixiecrat, and humanitarian."[1] Favoring "three piece suits, bow ties, felt hats, Chesterfield coats, and cordovan shoes,"[2] Ted was the only student at Brown with his own collection of guns. He felt out of place but was ready to play his part to the hilt. In the freshman trials for the sailing team, he won every race and would go on to excel on a well regarded freshman sailing team that won every regatta it entered. Turner would be honored as the best freshman sailor in New England. While he says he studied hard that first year, his classmates say they never saw him studying at all, or even reading a book. If he would be caught reading anything it would be popular history with no direct relevance to his classes. While intelligent enough to avoid failing his classes outright, a gentleman's C seemed his highest aim. The two classmates sharing his room moved out before the end of the first semester, tired of being interrupted in their studies and subjected to Ted's unending harangues on the glory of the South and conservative views of the economy, Middle East policy, and even the redeeming values of Nazi philosophy and the leadership skills of Hitler—not to mention the glories of Turner himself. Left alone in his room, Ted turned to using BB's in his rifle to take potshots at people passing below. However, he did pretty quickly strike up a friendship with Peter Dames, another graduate from a military academy who felt equally out of place among the elite that dominated the campus.

The following summer, Ed went off to Nevada and filed for an uncontested divorce, and the often-rocky marriage of Ed and Florence Turner was officially dissolved on August 22, 1957. Ed had initiated the proceedings but didn't really seem ready to move on, so he returned to Savannah with the keys to a brand new car for Florence and a proposal that they drive it to Florida where they would be remarried. Florence was done, though. The drinking and open affairs had been bad enough, but with the never-ending battles, first over Ted and then over Mary Jean, it was just too much. As Florence told Ed, the players had changed. She took Mary Jean and moved back to Cincinnati to be with her extended family. The divorce settlement is revealing: Florence was granted full and complete custody of Mary Jean while Ed would assume absolute control over Ted, despite the fact that he was 18 at the time. Who Ed was really divorcing could be found in the fact that Florence would gain custody of Ted in the event of Ed's death, while if Florence were to die first Florence's mother would assume the care of Mary Jean. Even the *Merry Jane* was a thing of the past, having been replaced by a 54-foot motor yacht christened *The Thistle*.

Shortly after the beginning of his sophomore year, Ted neglected to send the weekly letter to his father that had been the stipulation for a $5 weekly allowance, and Ed cut him off. He took to drinking shortly after that,[3] which cost him the $5,000 Ed had promised him if he made it to 21 without drinking or smoking. His drunken boasts of being a world-class womanizer and the best sailor in the world became a regular feature in his dorm. At one point, he capped off his drinking night by singing Nazi songs in front of the Jewish fraternity, at another by posting warnings from the Ku Klux Klan outside the living quarters of the few African Americans then in attendance at Brown. These incidents would later be played up in *Sports Illustrated* and elsewhere, and they are far from being something to be proud of. Though Turner may just have been having drunken fun with his Southerner role—and the general feeling of those who knew him at Brown was that there was no serious bigotry on Ted's part—these incidents could easily have escalated.[4] Yet Ted was now gambling in every conceivable way. He played pool and poker incessantly. He bet his fraternity brothers that he could down a fifth of whiskey without stopping—though in true Turner style (and unknown to those betting against him) he had first lined his stomach by downing a near equal amount of olive oil. While women were strictly forbidden in the living quarters at Brown and having a woman in your room meant certain expulsion, Turner wasn't deterred and practically set up house with a regular girlfriend. Even in sailing, which had taken a considerable downturn in his sophomore year, he would rescue his team from defeat at the Timme Angsten Trophy Regatta with an all-or-nothing move, pulling up his centerboard and gliding right over a patch of ice that the other boats all sailed around.

The winning streak couldn't last forever, of course. After one drunken trip to Wheaton in December that involved stealing a portrait of Eliza Wheaton, smashing windows, and inscribing obscenities in the pages of one of the dorms' sign-in books, and that ended with a madcap taking to bicycles while being chased by campus police, the owner of the car in which they'd stashed the Wheaton portrait was expelled from Brown, and Turner was suspended for the spring semester.

Turner was apprehensive as he returned home that December, fearing the worst from his father, but upon arriving in Savannah he found his father had other things on his mind; Ed was about to remarry. While sitting in for a game of poker at the home of influential Savannah businessman Bill Dillard, he had met Bill's daughter, Jane. Pretty, moneyed, connected, and Southern bred, she was everything Ed needed in a wife, and the fact that she had her own young teenage son from her first marriage didn't faze him at all. Ted was no doubt of two minds on the impending marriage. While having hoped to see Ed and Florence back together again, he had to appreciate the fact that Ed was in a better state of mind to accept the heroic spin on his suspension—he had been protecting the classmates who had gotten away. Being Ed, however, he still insisted that Ted use the semester to join the Coast Guard Reserves, hoping a six-month tour of duty would instill some maturity in his wayward son and protect him from being drafted.[5]

But first there was a marriage to attend to. Ed and Jane were married at the Dillard house in late December. For their honeymoon, Ed proposed a group sail to the Bahamas on a chartered sailboat—Ed, Ted, Jane, and her son, Marshall—with Ted going off to the Coast Guard at its conclusion. The trip didn't turn out exactly as he had planned. With rough weather and heavy seas dampening the leisure and Ted keeping to himself most of the time, everyone just wanted it over. In mid-February 1958, Ted joined the Coast Guard for a six-month stint in Cape May, New Jersey. He professes to have been company commander while leading his team in a series of wins in a weekly Honor competition, but biographers who claim to have checked the records say there were no mentions of Turner having stood out at all; in any case, he was released just in time to make the fall semester at Brown. Soon after their marriage, Ed and Jane would move to Charleston, South Carolina and then to a 1,000-acre plantation just outside Charleston.

Due to the suspension, Ted started his third year at Brown still needing to complete his second semester as a sophomore. If that wasn't exactly good news for Turner, being named co-captain of the sailing team would buoy him, and the team would go on to be the best in New England. His previous suspension hadn't chastened him at all, though, and after burning down his fraternity's homecoming display (which he denies in his autobiography) he would most likely have been suspended again but for the fraternity showing some mercy in not reporting the escapade to school officials. They did, however, boot him out of the fraternity.

Given his long-standing interest in Alexander the Great and the popularity of Classics among Brown's athletes as being an easy pass, Turner decided that would be his major. He was particularly taken with Professor John Rowe Workman, who engaged his students to think for themselves and who put less of an emphasis on rote learning. Workman also collected books on disasters, and held to a theory that disasters were really the driving force of social progress. So he had a mind that Turner could appreciate—something that Turner had assessed as sorely lacking in the other professors he encountered at Brown. For his part, Workman recalled Turner as "superb in bringing out argumentative tendencies in other students. He had a Southern, postbellum way of looking at things. He would argue until the sun went down . . . he had great, fiery convictions."[6]

Informed of Ted's decision to major in Classics, Ed was beside himself. What he had most expected from Turner's college career, other than the status of an Ivy League degree, was that Ted would learn new theories of business and the economy that could have immediate impact on the billboard business. Failing that, he hoped that his son would at least learn of current events and arts that could be used in a salesman's arsenal. Instead, Ted had chosen a major that Ed saw as having no benefit whatsoever. Ed hurriedly sent off a long letter to Ted, and Ted, in response, just as hurriedly had the complete letter published, unattributed, in Brown's newspaper, *The Daily Herald*.

My dear son,

I am appalled, even horrified, that you have adopted Classics as a major. . . . I almost puked on the way home today. . . . I suppose everybody has to be a snob of some sort, and I suppose you will feel you are distinguishing yourself from the herd by becoming a Classical snob. . . . you can retire to an ivory tower, and contemplate for the rest of your days the influence that the hieroglyphics of prehistoric man had upon the writings of William Faulkner. . . . I think you are rapidly becoming a jackass, and the sooner you get out of that filthy atmosphere, the better it will suit me. . . . everybody says a college education is a must . . . everybody said the world was square, except Columbus. You go along with the world, and I'll go it alone. . . . You are in the hands of the Philistines, and dammit, I sent you there. I am sorry.

Devotedly, Dad[7]

While Turner had been angry with the letter, Ed was furious when he learned it had been published, and you can't really blame him; not many of us would want our private correspondence made so public, unattributed or not. The rebellion Turner showed in having the letter published proved short lived, though; Ted soon changed his major from Classics to Economics. Having little interest in the subject, and finding "commie professors who thought everybody ought to work for the government,"[8] Turner proved to be an even worse student under his new major and came close to failing.

If there was any lasting enmity from the letter incident, it wasn't apparent. That summer Ted again worked for Turner Advertising, saving money for the coming school year while living with his father and stepmother in South Carolina and commuting to Savannah on weekends. Father and son would go for long walks, laughing and talking about Ted's education and the future—and no doubt women, a subject on which they had little disagreement. There was no sign of tension, and Jane could see that at base the two really treasured each other's company, even if Ted was always fidgeting and hyper.

Back at Brown for the second half of his junior year, Turner was voted commodore and team captain of the varsity sailing club. It would not be one of the club's better years, but at the Timme Angsten Regatta that November, where he'd skated over the ice to victory in his sophomore year, he was paired against Northwestern and their very attractive young blonde skipper. At a party afterwards the two would dance and Ted would learn that her name was Judy Gayle Nye, daughter of one of the icons of sailing, Harry Nye. Ted was smitten, and his charm, his outspoken honesty, and the air of a lost boy that aroused her protective and rehabilitative instincts intrigued Judy. Judy visited Brown during the Christmas holidays and Turner went out of his way to make her feel special, not just one of the many conquests he made no attempt to hide. By the end of that visit, Judy virtually floated back to Illinois.

Smitten or not, Turner certainly wasn't rehabilitated, and he was soon to be expelled from Brown for being caught in his room with another young woman after apparently being informed on by an old fraternity brother from Kappa Sigma. Turner, still ceaselessly bragging, had previously recounted in amorous detail his bedding of the fraternity brother's girlfriend, compounding the injury and fostering a strong desire for revenge, which he now had. Turner contends that due to the lack of financial support from his father and his ineligibility for financial aid from the university, he was planning to leave in any case.

Somehow, Ted convinced Peter Dames, still his closest friend at Brown, that his own dismissal could not be far off. He plied Dames with plans for a grand adventure, sailing across the Atlantic in Ted's Lightning, being feted in the press, and having an endless supply of young French women. If not a sailor himself, Dames not only knew Turner's proven skills but had also been filled with Ted's own inimitable self-evaluation as the finest sailor in the world. Turner's excitement and natural sales skills were as hard to resist as the thought of being stuck at Brown without his charismatic brother-in-exile was hard to bear.

Luckily for both, Ted's boat had been severely damaged when the tree it rested under had a huge branch clipped off in a storm. So there was a slight change of plans; no glory, but the fun and sun of Florida and the fruit of its own ripe, young bikini-clad women waiting to be picked. Ted and Pete headed off to Miami in an old car Turner had bought in Providence. The reality proved far less enticing than the dream. Unable to find jobs and cut off from their allowances, the pair soon realized that it wasn't exactly romantic to live on peanut butter and ketchup, or be so poor that bathroom tissue proved an extravagant expense. And if that wasn't enough, even the women were hard to come by. Ted was depressed. He wrote several letters to Judy Nye expressing the budding idea that he'd really bungled his life and had nowhere to turn. After what may have seemed an eternity but which wasn't much more than a month, when Ed let him know that the Coast Guard was looking for Turner to fulfill a tour of duty, Ted jumped at the idea and Peter Dames returned to New York.

The tedium of his two months in the Coast Guard, with its endless drills and the ignominy of cleaning bathrooms, finally convinced Turner that rebelling wasn't about to get him anywhere. He was resigned now to crawling back to his father, taking his place at Turner Advertising, and assuming the sedate married life that society demanded. He sent a letter off to Judy Nye proposing marriage, and then headed home to South Carolina.

Happy that Turner was done with Brown and happier still that he was now settling down and ready to enter the family business, Ed, who had taken to the young man in his brief earlier visit, joined Ted in successfully lobbying Peter Dames to come back to the South and take a job with Turner Advertising. Both Turner and Dames were sent off for sales training and evaluation by Hudson Edwards, one of Ed's top salesmen in Charleston. Judy came in just after her graduation for an engagement party and within weeks, on June 22, 1960, Turner and Nye, both 21, were married at a ceremony at St. Chrysostom's on the north side of Chicago. Both Ed and Ted beamed with pride and purpose in their tuxedos and at one point, catching each other's eye, jumped up and down from the floor to a sofa while shouting with joy. Legend has it that when pronounced man and wife neither remembered to kiss, and the room Ed had booked for their wedding night, far from being a wedding suite, contained two twin beds.

NOTES

1. Roger Vaughan, *The Grand Gesture: Ted Turner, Mariner, and the America's Cup* (Boston: Little, Brown & Co., 1975), 29.

2. Ibid., 22.

3. In earlier explanations, Turner attributed his change of behavior to his father's refusal to let him accept a proffered summer job at the well-regarded Noroton Yacht Club in Connecticut.

4. Allusions to this behavior seem to have first appeared in Vaughan, *The Grand Gesture*. Specific citations of the events seem first to have appeared in Curry Kirkpatrick, "Going Real Strawwng," *Sports Illustrated*, August 21, 1978. They have since been referenced in biographies by Porter Bibb and by Robert Goldberg and Gerald Jay Goldberg, as well as numerous tabloid and Internet articles. Turner himself dismissed them as "childish pranks."

5. In *Call Me Ted*, Turner says the decision to join the Coast Guard was his own.

6. Vaughan, *The Grand Gesture*, 29.

7. The full text of this letter was originally published anonymously on the editorial page (8) of The *Brown Daily Herald*, April 15, 1959. Some part, if not the complete letter, has appeared in nearly every book and many periodical and tabloid articles and Internet pages concerning Ted Turner. Full text of the letter as reproduced in the Autolycus section of *Arion 1.1* can be accessed at http://www.bu.edu/arion/Volume1/1.1/Autolycus.pdf.

8. Janet Lowe, *Ted Turner Speaks: Insight from the World's Greatest Maverick* (New York: John Wiley & Sons, 1999), 44.

Chapter 3

STEPPING OUT

While Ed appreciated the growth his son was showing, he was still a cautious man. For the first few months of his marriage, Turner essentially continued his training, working as a salesman at a low weekly salary. Having recently bought a plant in Macon, Ed checked up on Ted's progress and had further reason to be encouraged. Turner was, as Hudson Edwards would later recount to Porter Bibb, "one of the greatest salesmen in the world . . . Just like his father . . . either one of them could charm a rattlesnake."[1] With glowing reports and solid bookings, Ed decided Turner was ready for a real test, managing the Macon plant.

Turner, determined to prove himself, would put in 15-hour days six days a week. He joined the Rotary Club, became a director of the local Red Cross, and played cards each week with his salesmen and favorite customers. A true son of his father, he also made sure to insinuate himself into the local business establishment, and the young Turner and his beautiful bride soon became one of the most popular couples in town. And with all the focus on establishing his business career, he still made time to develop what was now becoming more than a diversion, sail racing. Judy, who many thought a better sailor at the time than Ted, crewed with Turner at weekend regattas, where they won with regularity.

When not sailing, though, Judy was left to tend the house, alone with their black Labrador retriever and the variety of pets Turner always liked to have around. Her role, as Turner made clear, was to manage the house: pay the bills, cook three meals a day on the chance he might be home for one, iron all his clothes, including his socks, shine his shoes, and do all the shopping, though her own preferences didn't matter if a competing product advertised on company billboards. Turner provided Judy with a monthly stipend from which she was generously allowed to indulge herself freely with whatever remained after tending to the necessities. The reality was that she had to take a part-time secretarial job just to make ends meet.

It quickly became evident that as busy as Turner was with business, he was also continuing to indulge his urges. Within months of their marriage, the telltale signs were evident. He would arrive home late at night, drunk, his collar smeared with lipstick. It was just as evident that Judy, not unlike his own mother, was not cut in the mold of the subservient Southern wife. If anything, Judy was more headstrong than Florence had ever been, and not averse to fighting. Ed Turner would counsel Judy as he had always counseled Florence, "The provider must have his way. There is just no other way any marriage will work,"[2] but though Judy still held out hope that she could change Ted, it wouldn't be by turning the other cheek.

Less than six months after his marriage, Turner received word that on December 15, 1960, his sister, Mary Jean, had died in Cincinnati, where Florence had nursed her through her illness to the very end. She had been 19 years old, though Turner says 17 in his autobiography.

The death, a major event in the lives of both Ed and Ted Turner, came as a surprise to both Judy and Ed's second wife, Jane, neither of whom was aware that Mary Jean had still been alive. Turner has continued to say very little about Mary Jean and the impact of her illness on his own life. Although in *Call Me Ted* he does address her death more directly than ever before and acknowledges to some extent its affect on his father, it still seems curiously avoided. In Christian Williams's *Lead, Follow or Get out of the Way* (Times Books, 1981), originally intended as an autobiography, there was not so much as an index entry concerning her. In the little of what he has said, the most common comment has been that up until this point Turner had been very religious, even having been saved or reborn seven times, but he could not continue to worship a god that would put such a beautifully pure, innocent, and loving girl through such agonizing torment. These are the identical words that Ed Turner often expressed to his friends after Mary Jean's death.

No doubt there is truth to the words for both men, but for Turner, the illness and death of his sister must certainly be complicated. The arrival of siblings is always a difficult transition for children, and with Turner's virtual abandonment in Cincinnati at five years old, the separations from home that followed, the naming of Ed's first yacht as the *Merry Jane*, and the divorce of Ed and Florence, it is difficult to see how there wouldn't be a complicated mix of love, resentment, and guilt in the equation. Though Turner does hint at these more complicated emotions in *Call Me Ted*, it is the very barest of hints.

On July 23, 1961, Ted and Judy's first child, Laura Lee, was born. Turner was sailing at the time and missed the birth, and though he returned home that evening he didn't show up at the hospital until the next day. Whatever occupied Turner that night, even fatherhood wasn't changing him. His time was still consumed with the billboard business and sailing, and the signs of his extracurricular activities were now not even hidden, with love letters left around the house and panties left sitting in the glove compartment of the car. Judy would scream and fight, but that only elicited Turner's own venom as he started ridiculing her looks and the few extra pounds she'd put on since giving birth. At one point, Judy threw a well-aimed ashtray right at his head. And still, neither was ready to end the marriage outright.

Turner's performance in running the Macon plant was good enough to warrant special and unusual praise from his father, who, after visiting the plant, wrote Turner a letter saying how proud of him he was. Turner has said that "nothing he ever did before or after that day ever made me feel so good."[3] In early autumn of 1962, both Ed and Ted were excited by a move that was to raise Turner Advertising to a national powerhouse in the billboard business. General Outdoor Advertising, where Ed had first been introduced to the billboard business, had by now outgrown its ability to manage itself. Seeing opportunity, Ed Turner and a friend in the business, Bob Naegele, hatched a scheme amounting to a leveraged buyout. With a relatively small down payment, Ed could essentially become the dominant player in the South, taking over General Outdoor's plants in Atlanta, Norfolk, Richmond, and Roanoke, while Naegele would take plants in the Midwest and Northeast. The balance of the payment would be paid for with a loan secured by the assets he was acquiring. With $750,000, a good deal of that coming from selling off the old Savannah plant, Ed acquired over $4 million worth of the South's best billboard markets.

With their relationship continuing to come apart, Ted and Judy decided it was time to end the charade, and after a quick divorce Judy went off to Florida while Ed set about finding a suitable headquarters in downtown Atlanta. Given Ted's success in what was really a minor plant in Macon, Ed had decided to bring him in to Atlanta, though he wasn't ready to make him a manager at what would be the most important plant in the business. At about the same time, Judy discovered she was pregnant and she and Ted decided to try reconciliation, with Judy and Laura Lee moving back to Macon and Ted visiting on weekends when his racing schedule allowed.

By December, Ed Turner checked himself into the famed Silver Hill rehabilitation facility in New Canaan, Connecticut. He had spent a good part of the summer of 1961 at the same facility in an effort to rid himself of the demons and addictions that by that time were affecting his business and personal relationships. Since taking over the Atlanta plant, Ed had been pushing himself nonstop, intent on realizing every ounce of the potential from the plant. Turner recalled that Ed "did nothing else, thought about nothing else except working,"[4] and one night he told his father, "You're not leaving your business to me, you're leaving me to your business."[5] Continuing a grueling work schedule, Ed once again succumbed to the heavy drinking he had seemed to have under control since his first visit to Silver Hill. His cigarette smoking grew incessant, he gained weight, and he started showing signs of erratic behavior, buoyed by his acquisition one day and in a dense fog the next. He would make statements to his employees and forget having made. It was in this period that he told Ted, "Be sure to set your goals so high that you can't possibly accomplish them in one lifetime . . . I set my goals too low and now I'm having a hard time coming up with new ones."[6]

Concerned that he had been pushing himself too hard, Ed's friends were happy to see him return to Silver Hill. What no one expected was that just after the New Year, Ed would put in a near unintelligible call to Bob Naegele, expressing his fears that the deal they had pulled off was going to fail and in the process destroy all he had devoted his life to. He was convinced that economic slowdowns, increased competition from newspapers, a growing anti-billboard movement, and his own limitations all combined to point the way to failure. "It's a long way from the master bedroom to the cellar,"[7] Ed said, and not being prepared for that trip, he wanted to sell his portion of the acquisition to Naegele at the exact price he had paid. While at first reluctant, Naegele finally agreed, and even insisted that Ed take $50,000 over the original terms as profit.

When Ed returned to South Carolina early the next year, everyone could see that something was wrong. He had stopped drinking and his smoking was more under control, but Judy thought that might have only contributed to his angst. Appearing so unlike the man they knew, both Ted and Judy feared that Ed had developed a chronic illness that he didn't want to tell anyone about. Irwin Mazo, who had been Ed's accountant since shortly before his divorce from Florence and who had become one of his closest confidants, repeatedly assured him that his cash flow was fine and the debt perfectly manageable, but there seemed to be no reassurance that would calm Ed's jitters. He told Peter Dames that none of his success had been worthwhile.

Ted Turner couldn't believe that his father, the man he feared and respected more than any other, the man who had never shown fear of anything, was reduced to doubt and timidity by nothing more than his inability to accept success. In the first days of March, Ed called Ted to tell him that he was selling the General Outdoor properties. Turner tried reasoning with Ed, debating the strengths of the deal. He called his father a coward, hoping to elicit a spirited response. He begged Ed to sell the business to him rather than Naegele. But through all of the exchange the only vestige that remained of the old Ed Turner was that his mind would not be swayed. He didn't want to burden Ted with the result of his mistake, and if he himself was incapable of seeing his way through the pressures and perils of the expanded company, he certainly couldn't imagine Ted would be able to handle it.

Shortly afterward, Ed gave Jane a $50,000 check, no doubt the down payment from Naegele, and called his ex-wife Florence. He told

Florence that he'd lost face in a business deal and was contemplating suicide. Florence called Irwin Mazo, Ed's accountant, and begged him not to let Ed go through with the sale, but it was already too late. On March 5, 1963, a beautiful late winter morning in South Carolina, Ed seemed to have recovered. He was in good spirits, ate a full breakfast, and stepped out on the veranda to admire the day. He then went upstairs, entered the master bedroom, placed the barrel of a .38 caliber pistol in his mouth, and pulled the trigger. Jimmy Brown, who had prepared the breakfast, was the first to reach him. Ted received the news a short time later in a call from his stepmother.

The next day, news of Ed Turner's suicide appeared in the *Atlanta Journal Constitution*. In the same paper was a column on the Georgia State Senate holding a hearing on the environmental blight of billboard advertising. Some have seen this as a coincidence, but Ed Turner was certainly clued in enough to know of the senate hearing beforehand. By general consensus, Ed had lost his nerve in the face of levels of debt that he'd never before assumed, seeing economic slowdowns and a rising tide against billboard advertising. Haunted by the humiliations of his own father's reduced circumstances as a result of the Depression, humiliations Ed had spent his whole life overcoming, he just couldn't allow himself to drift toward those same ends. At the same time, giving in to fear and abandoning his dreams went against everything in his nature, and all he had sought to instill in Ted, and he just couldn't go on facing the son who now saw him as the coward he must surely have seen himself.

But it seems foolish to ignore the affects of Mary Jean's sickness and death on Ed's mental health and stability. By all accounts, Ed had adored his young daughter, and his inability to protect her health was the first serious blow to his sense of control over his environment. The extent to which he had to remove himself from any reminder of his having failed to protect his daughter shows just how troubling the situation was for his sense of assurance. While possibly purely coincidental, Ed's first visit to Silver Hill was approximately six months after Mary Jean's death, and his return to Silver Hill in 1962 and his initial phone call to Naegele to propose the sale almost precisely coincided with the two-year anniversary of her death.

For Turner himself, his father's suicide denied him the chance of ever coming to terms with their relationship, and especially the repeated abandonments of his early years. Throughout his life, at the moments of his biggest accomplishments, Turner has referenced his father, wishing he were there to share the moment, and several times in the 1980s he was said to have held up magazines featuring his success while asking his father if these were enough yet. For years, Turner kept in his desk drawer the gun Ed used in his suicide, the same gun he had previously used to teach Ted how to shoot. He frequently took it out and even more frequently referred casually to committing suicide himself if his plans failed to work out.

Whether Turner was in shock over his father's suicide or feeling abandoned and affronted by his father's final lack of respect in having gone ahead with the sale of the General Outdoor properties to Naegele, he did not seem overly emotional at the time, but then, there was no time for that. Almost immediately after the funeral, Ted announced to Irwin Mazo that he would not be going ahead with the sale.

It wasn't something Mazo expected to hear, and it certainly didn't sound like a good idea. While serving as the accountant for Turner Advertising and a close personal friend and confidant of Ed Turner's, Mazo had had very little direct contact with Ted. Though Turner had been managing the Macon plant and doing a credible job, everyone knew it was something of a backwater. Ed had never brought Ted into consultations and never really spoke about him in terms of the business. From what Irwin knew of Ted, he was a rambunctious young kid who took little seriously outside of sailing.

Mazo tried to talk some sense into Turner, pointing out that Ted had no credit history of his own and that an unknown and untested 24-year-old wouldn't exactly inspire confidence in the banking community. Ed's net worth at the time of his death was in the range of $2 million, and after accounting for inheritance taxes and bequests to Jane and Florence, Turner was inheriting about $1 million of that net. Between his inheritance and income from the remaining smaller, but stable, Turner Advertising, Ted would be set for life and free to pursue the interests closer to his heart. When Turner clearly wasn't swayed, Mazo tried sending emissaries that Ted might be better inclined to listen to, but Turner was serious and insistent. He was ready and eager to gamble his inheritance and his future, and he showed a much better grasp of the business than anyone would have imagined, able to reel off sales figures and potentials for each of the individual plants.

With a purchase agreement signed and Naegele's team already in Atlanta to set up transfer of the General Outdoor properties, reversing the deal seemed a long shot. Turner, though, approached the problem from every angle. If necessary, he was willing to go to court to argue that his father had made the deal while in less than full control of his faculties. He would appeal to Naegele's softer side by playing on the long and close friendship Ed and Naegele had shared. He moved the entire lease department for the Atlanta plant to the Macon operation and set his new employees to transferring all of the Atlanta leases. He threatened to start a new business in Atlanta, setting up billboards that would obscure those already in place and willing to take whatever losses were necessary to undermine the value of the original Atlanta operation.

After an initial meeting with Naegele in Palm Springs that was less than decisive, the two met again in Atlanta, with Naegele accompanied by his partners. Naegele offered Turner $200,000 to buy back the leases, or Turner could agree to pay the same $200,000 to have the sale contract voided, with the proviso that if Turner was unable to meet any and all debt payments related to the Turner Advertising business, Naegele would have the option of stepping in and assuming control. They were presenting a choice that really wasn't a choice at all, so they weren't at all prepared when Turner immediately agreed to pay them the $200,000. Without apparent reflection, without bargaining, without stalling for time to discuss the arrangements with Irwin Mazo, Turner agreed to terms that could jeopardize the futures of his entire family.

It wasn't the decision the Naegele team expected. Having come with terms designed to pressure young Turner, the thought that he would actually decide as he had was never seriously considered. As Mazo was quick to point out when Turner called to brag about his victory, Turner could barely meet payroll and had very little cash on hand, so there was no way that they could come up with $200,000, or anything close to it, within the 90 days stipulated in the agreement. However, when Naegele and his partners had had a chance to reflect on the deal, they realized that in their tax bracket in the early 1960s there would essentially be nothing left of the $200,000. Their proposal that the payments be made to their children instead of to them directly allowed Mazo and Turner some maneuvering room to negotiate and they were able to extend the payments over five years, to be satisfied with company stock rather than cash.[8]

NOTES

1. Porter Bibb, *It Ain't as Easy as It Looks: Ted Turner's Amazing Story* (New York: Crown Publishers, 1993), 34.

2. Bibb, *It Ain't as Easy as It Looks*, 36.

3. Ted Turner with Bill Burke, *Call Me Ted* (New York: Grand Central Publishing, 2008), 52.

4. Roger Vaughan, *The Grand Gesture: Ted Turner, Mariner, and the America's Cup* (Boston: Little, Brown & Co., 1975), 100.

5. Ibid.

6. Turner, *Call Me Ted*, 56.

7. Roger Vaughan, *Ted Turner: The Man behind the Mouth* (Boston: Sail Books, 1978), 173.

8. Minnesota entrepreneur Curtis L. Carlson, one of Naegele's partners, told *Fortune* magazine (Richard I. Kirkland Jr., "Should You Leave It All to the Children?" *Fortune*, September 29, 1986) that he received a call from Ted's mother, Florence, just days after Ed's death, saying she wanted Ted to have the business back. That call was followed up a few days later by a visit from Ted, who, Carlson said, "talked about how this was his one chance to get going in life." Saying Turner "can be very convincing," Carlson said he was persuaded and sold the business back to Ted. It's a much less compelling story than the prevailing version, and I haven't found it documented anywhere else, but it merits mention.

Chapter 4

RIDING THE WAVES

If still an untested young man with substantial debt, the deal gave Turner some breathing room. It also set the tone for much of Turner's negotiations and decision making in the future: making decisions seemingly off the cuff, with little apparent consideration; going against the obvious and surprising everyone involved; and agreeing to terms that would seem extravagant, even beyond his means.

In May 1963, Judy gave birth to a second child, a boy, and there was little doubt about the name, Robert Edward (Teddy) Turner IV. There were profound doubts about the marriage though. It was apparent by this time that neither Ted nor Judy was really interested in resurrecting it. Later in the year, Ted and Judy were racing against each other in a "frostbite" race on Lake Allatoona, with Judy having just made a move to put her in the lead, when Turner purposely rammed her boat. Turner's boat had the right of way, so any contact between the two would be lodged against Judy, who was disqualified.[1] The marriage that had been built on their mutual love of sailing now came to an end while sailing, with Judy realizing just how deep Turner's lack of respect really went. Her bags were packed and she was gone for good almost immediately after getting back to Macon.

Turner was churning the waters at the billboard company, giving constant pep talks to his salesmen on how the company was in danger of going under and they were in a fight against the world. He met with all of his advertisers both to assure them and find out how he could serve them better. With a looming debt payment of $600,000 just six months after assuming control of the company, Turner said, "I was sad, pissed, and determined. I was only a kid, but I had learned to hustle. I went out and convinced the employees to buy stock in the company. I sold off all the real estate that I possibly could to raise cash. I sold my father's plantation. I borrowed against our accounts receivable. I squeezed the juice out of everything."[2] While his father had largely gone it alone, Turner made a point of becoming involved with the Outdoor Advertising Association of America (OAAA), giving speeches and having them quoted regularly in its newsletter. He made sure to take prominent booths at business expositions, and he built what was then one of the largest painted billboards in the country along the Atlanta Freeway Connector.

If, in his first experience with marriage, Turner hadn't exactly distinguished himself, he was, on this front, as dependent on the institution as Ed had been, even if he didn't fully realize this himself. Shortly after Turner's divorce, Peter Dames introduced him to Jane (Janie) Shirley Smith, a pretty young blonde stewardess, at a Young Republicans' Club fundraiser for Barry Goldwater's presidential campaign, and they quickly became an item. Jane at first thought he was a bit too full of himself, but her father was very impressed with young Turner. For his part, after following in his father's footsteps with a headstrong first wife from the North, the demure and attractive Janie, born and bred in Birmingham, must have seemed exactly what he needed. They were married on June 2, 1964, just 20 days shy of what would have been his fourth wedding anniversary with Judy Nye. Ted had seemingly learned little from the failure of his first marriage, for in the course of the reception he announced to Irwin Mazo and his wife, "I didn't want to marry Janie. I said I'd marry her because she was pregnant—but don't expect me to be a good husband."[3]

Impressing his employees, his advertisers, and even the bankers with his hard work, determination, and vision, Turner was succeeding. Within little more than a year, the OAAA newsletter featured him on the cover and raved about Turner Advertising's stellar sales. Within two years, he had purchased two additional operations, giving him the best plants in Chattanooga and Knoxville. Not all bankers were impressed, but enough were to assure the continuation of the loans that Turner Advertising was dependent on for survival. The company would essentially struggle to pay its bills throughout the 1960s, but Turner's manic energy had motivated his staff, impressed the industry, and made enough believers to ensure that no one had good reason to believe that Ed's tragic end would ultimately be the end of his business. Turner, though, would take a different approach to business. He was more intent on building an empire than Ed, who was consumed with achieving the status and trappings of wealth. For Ed, there was nothing more important than business, and debt was debilitating. However, it wasn't long before Ted would be telling anyone that would listen that his business plan was to borrow as much money as he could on the theory that the more money you owed to the banks the more interested they were in keeping your business afloat. "I don't have any money . . . You know, it's like a Ponzi scheme. The whole thing is a Ponzi scheme."[4] While Turner often cites the fact that he was born to the middle class, it was comfortable middle-class, and it only went up from there. It is the great difference between father and son: one had been profoundly affected by privation, and one had never really needed to learn the value of money. Turner would fashion himself as an average guy and hero of the folk—though not quite to the extent of George W. Bush's folksiness— but only wealth and privilege could have fashioned the persona of Ted Turner.

Turner was matching his father's success, but he was doing it on his own terms. And he continued to sail throughout all the turmoil at Turner Advertising. He had won his first significant sailing championship with the Y-Flyer Nationals in 1963, with Judy crewing, at least according to the records.[5] Just five months following his father's death, Ted competed at the Atlanta Yacht Club's championship series in two different classes, Y-Flyer and Flying Dutchman, and won both, an unprecedented achievement and one made nearly impossible to duplicate when a change in the rules was made shortly thereafter.

Turner may have wanted to uphold his father's name, may have needed to prove to himself and his father that he had what it takes to be a success in business, and may have dreamed of building an empire worthy of Alexander, but there never seems to have been a complete absence of the need to escape it all, the temptation to embrace complete and utter failure, and the competing urge to blaze his own trails in the world. Sailing offered a perfect escape as well as a personal challenge. For all that Turner would accomplish in business, in his early career Ted really seemed to work at being a yachtsman, treating business as the sport and diversion.

While Turner had needed to be creative and proactive in securing the General Outdoor plants and making sure that he could cover his debt payment, it must have seemed all too easy. In Christian Williams's, *Lead, Follow or Get out of the Way*, Janie Turner was quoted as saying, "When Ted was courting me he was very bored with the office . . . And he used to sleep until ten-thirty or eleven o'clock in the morning. Sailing became everything."[6] At first, he would increase the amount of time he spent sailing at local regattas, but Turner yearned to move up to the bigger boats and ocean racing that he had been reading about. When, in mid-1964, a friend suggested they charter a boat to enter the 1965 Southern Ocean Racing Conference (SORC), a series of races established in 1961 that at the time was one of the most grueling, competitive, and prestigious set of distance races to be found, Turner was ready. Chartering a Cal-40, *Scylla*, out of North Carolina, and enlisting Jimmy Brown and Irwin Mazo among his crew, this introduction to ocean racing would prove to be a memorable learning experience, and one that would have Mazo, a naval navigator near the end of World War II, swearing, "It was the damnedest four days of my life . . . Give me a million bucks and I wouldn't go to sea with Turner again."[7]

Turner's previous experience was in boats approximately half the size of the 40-foot *Scylla*, and when it came time to take the boat south late that winter, his friend, the only one who had had some large boat experience, dropped out in favor of a race in Brazil. Shortly after leaving their berth, they took a wrong turn and wound up in the shallows, running aground on a sandbar. As the wind blew up, the temperature dropped and the pounding waves kept lifting the boat and pounding it back down against the sandbar with terrifying thuds. When they tried using their radio to call for help they found it didn't work, so there was nothing to do but hunker down to a restless and nerve-wracking night. When the storm passed and they were finally lifted from the sandbar in the morning, Turner ignored Mazo's pleas to make an unscheduled stop to fix the radio, probably correctly feeling that he would lose half his crew. He pressed on, only to sail right into a storm. Buffeted by winds of 50 miles per hour, which were far worse than anything Turner had ever experienced, it was all he could do just to keep the boat from going around in circles and losing control altogether.

When they finally put in at Charleston, Mazo and the rest of the crew, save Jimmy Brown, were off the boat as quick as their feet would take them. Turner, undeterred, rounded up another crew and again set sail for the start of the series in St. Petersburg, only to run into another storm in the Gulf of Mexico. After losing their anchor in the middle of the night and enduring a fire in the galley, Turner finally managed to compete in the series and even earned a 2nd-place finish in one of the bigger races, the Lipton Cup.

Not many would take this as an auspicious beginning, but the Savannah Yacht Club's "Turnover Ted" was convinced that ocean racing, with its dependence on leadership and motivation and its need for hard work, quick judgment, and split-second decision making, was his true calling. If there were some at Turner Advertising who already agreed with at least some of Ted's self assessment, and perhaps drawing on examples of his time at McCallie, most would have to admit that what he had exhibited so far was more of a stubborn determination than a focused, sound judgment. In today's world, the young Ted Turner would probably stand out as a poster child for Attention Deficit Hyperactivity Disorder (ADHD), for whom ocean sailing captain would not seem to be a wise career path. But, like Michael Phelps, the will to win allowed Turner to focus, and his sailing record speaks for itself.

Deciding that he needed a boat of his own, Turner ordered his own Cal-40,[8] a 39-foot fiberglass boat he received in the fall and christened *Vamp X*, after the song "Hard Hearted Hannah." Entering the SORC again in 1966, with a year of experience and a better crew, Turner would shock the sailing world by taking first place overall, and doing it by the largest margin ever. In only his second year of ocean racing, with the first cruising yacht he'd ever owned, Turner had accomplished something that most experienced sailors could only dream about, and accomplished it in part by racing every minute of the day. *Sports Illustrated* reported, "Winning the SORC in a stock boat is like buying a Buick and winning an auto race."[9] But while the tabloids and periodicals were generally enthused and somewhat amazed, Turner's win wasn't universally applauded. As Turner himself remembers, the yachting establishment was anything but amused when he was quoted as saying, "Man, we blew those other boats away."[10] True to his boat's name, Turner's comments were found to be "sweet as sour milk," and this tendency to be an ungracious winner would be something Turner would never really overcome, going a long way to establishing that most lasting of nicknames, "The Mouth."

Later the same year, Turner would win first-in-class, fourth overall, in his first transatlantic race. At the end of 1967, the boat Turner was having built was incomplete, and he wound up chartering *Bolero*, a 73-foot yawl (two-masted) out of Oyster Bay, Long Island, for his entry in the 1968 SORC. The experience would be different than that with *Scylla*, but no better. Oyster Bay was covered in six inches of ice, the crew was short-handed after a pipe burst the first night on board, and the boat sank at harbor; the deck was covered with ice, there was no heat on board, and their drinking water froze. The wood of the poorly maintained boat had been dried out and it took on water, and they wound up nearly being left on the rocks at Cape Hatteras, finally needing to be towed by the Coast Guard. In 1967 and 1968, he concentrated his efforts on 5.5s,[11] the boats then used in Olympic competition. He invested in PlasTrend, a boat works company in Fort Worth, Texas that was started by Andy Green, who had become his partner in the Olympic quest.

At home, Turner's family was growing more quickly than expected. In 1965, Janie had their first child, Rhett, named after Rhett Butler, Turner's favorite movie character. Somewhere around Christmas of 1966, when Turner's children from his marriage to Judy Nye, Laura Lee and Teddy, came to Atlanta for what was a routine holiday visit, it was clear that they had been physically abused. Later examinations showed that Teddy had suffered broken bones. Judy had remarried a weightlifter whose steroid use was affecting his mental state. When Turner told Judy that he couldn't allow his children to return to that environment, Judy, though distraught, agreed, saying she really had not expected them to return. Just about a year afterward, in January 1968, Ted and Janie's second child was born and named Beauregard (Beau), after the Confederate general who won the first Battle of Bull Run and whose aides had fired the first shots in the Civil War. Having a change of heart, Judy visited Atlanta in the spring, hoping to regain care of her children, but when her daughter refused, Judy decided that it would probably be best if they stayed with Ted and Janie permanently. When Janie discovered that she was pregnant again just four months after Beau's birth, she told Roger Vaughan, "I cried a lot when I found out. My friends thought it was vulgar. I love babies but I nearly died."[12] In February 1969, Janie gave birth to a daughter. Turner wanted to name her Scarlett, but Janie refused and she was named Sarah Jean (Jennie). With five young children at home, Janie tended to give her own children most of her attention, leaving the ever present and dependable Jimmy Brown to shoulder much of the support of, if little responsibility for, Laura Lee and Teddy. As Janie would point out, all of her children were born in the first months of the year, with Turner off sailing for each birth. With so much of Turner's non-sailing time devoted to business, and his presence at home restricted to brief visits, Teddy would come to refer to his father as "Hurricane Turner."

NOTES

1. In an interview with Roger Vaughan, Judy put this in the context of 1962 and as having precipitated the couple's divorce and her subsequent move to Florida. Turner and others have told of this as being the cause of their final breakup, after the birth of Teddy.

2. Richard Hack, *Clash of the Titans: How the Unbridled Ambition of Ted Turner and Rupert Murdoch Has Created Global Empires That Control What We Read and Watch* (Beverly Hills, CA: New Millennium Press, 2003), 77. Quoting *Advertising Age*, November 1982.

3. Robert Goldberg and Gerald Jay Goldberg, *Citizen Turner: The Wild Rise of an American Tycoon* (Harcourt, Brace & Co.), 113.

4. Goldberg and Goldberg, *Citizen Turner*, 117.

5. Judy, herself, and Roger Vaughan would date this as occurring in 1961. Judy would say she only crewed with Turner in the early years of their marriage. Given the state of their relationship described by everyone, including Turner, this earlier date would seem to make sense, but records are records.

6. Christian Williams, *Lead, Follow, or Get Out of the Way: The Story of Ted Turner* (New York: Times Books, 1981), 50.

7. Roger Vaughan, *The Grand Gesture: Ted Turner, Mariner, and the America's Cup* (Boston: Little, Brown & Co., 1975), 104.

8. The Cal-40 was one of the earliest mass-produced all-fiberglass, ultra-light sailboats, often said to have revolutionized the sport of ocean racing by spurring a trend toward lighter boats. Designed by Bill Lapworth and manufactured by Cal Yachts/Jensen Marine out of Costa Mesa, California, it appeared

on the scene in 1963 and quickly garnered many fans due to its speed and relative stability for its weight; it was particularly popular in California. While it has been out of production since the 1980s, there are still active Cal-40s that continue to perform well in the sport.

9. Hugh Whall, "The Meanest Vamp at Sea," *Sports Illustrated*, March 28, 1966.

10. Ted Turner with Bill Burke, *Call Me Ted* (New York: Grand Central Publishing, 2008), 84.

11. The 5.5-meter class is a small racing keelboat. Like the 12-meter, this class is defined by a complicated formula taking length, sail area, and displacement into consideration with the result needing to equal 5.5 meters. It became popular in Europe and was the official Olympic design from 1956 to 1968, when it was superseded due to excessive design and building costs.

12. Roger Vaughan, *Ted Turner: The Man behind the Mouth* (Boston: Sail Books, 1978), 186.

Chapter 5

MEDIATED

By 1968, Turner had decided that he had to make a change. He flirted with the idea of moving to Australia, where he could corner the market on Kentucky Fried Chicken and McDonalds franchises, but ultimately he decided selling fast food would be more boring than billboards and making millions just wasn't worth uprooting his family and moving to a foreign country. Having pondered the situation while spending more and more time sailing in the past few years, he'd come to the conclusion that, while his father may have overemphasized the threat, the growing movement against billboards on interstate highways was serious enough to warrant diversification. He had tried silk screening and direct marketing and neither seemed to be working out, and since advertising itself was unlikely to stop growing, it made sense to try to follow the money that could be lost in the event of further restrictions on the core business. The obvious answer was radio and TV.

This was nothing radical. There were already numerous companies with the same general business mix, but no one at Turner Advertising knew anything about broadcasting. Since diversification would also require funding and the banks had already made it clear that they were concerned with the company's weak management structure, any expertise he could bring in would need to be substantial enough to placate those concerns. There was only one person he knew in Atlanta that fit the bill, Jim Roddey, an impressive young guy Turner had met at advertising conventions. Roddey was serving as president of the media group at Rollins, Inc., a fully diversified corporation that had moved its headquarters to Atlanta in 1967 after acquiring Orkin Pest Control. Having started as a broadcasting company, Rollins still had a growing national presence in radio and TV stations as well as billboard plants, and they were all under Roddey's direct control. Roddey, who would later tell Christian Williams, "The first thing I learned about Ted was that he was very, very bright in addition to being completely wacko,"[1] had already had an uncomfortable experience when he once crewed for Ted on Lake Allatoona, so he had little incentive to make the move. But if Turner's animation could be rude and insensitive, it could also be quite convincing, and having identified a need he embarked on a relentless pursuit using all of his considerable charm, charisma, and enthusiasm in outlining an in-depth vision of the glories of his company's future and the fun they would have getting there. Though it would take a while, there was just no saying no, and Turner, the master salesman, finally hired Roddey as the company's first outside president while Ted became CEO.

Near the end of 1968, the perfect expansion came to light when WAPO, a radio station in Chattanooga, was put on the market. Turner had fond memories of Chattanooga from his days at McCallie Academy, and since the company already had a billboard operation there, it seemed predestined. Determined to make the acquisition, Turner grabbed Roddey and Dick McGinnis, his general sales manager for billboards, and the three drove to Chattanooga. While the station was in disarray and the asking price was low, Turner decided he could get a better price on a return visit by feigning disinterest. Returning to Atlanta fully convinced they had the station in hand, they were stunned to learn that within a half hour of their departure, someone else had gone in ready to make an offer and it had been accepted.

Furious at his own stupidity, Turner approached the new owner, who agreed to sell only if his stagnant billboard business in Norfolk, Virginia was included in the transaction. By the time it was over, WAPO not only wound up costing Ted $300,000 more than it would have, it added an unwanted Knoxville plant and terms that would involve a stock deal and some employee retention agreements. Roddey was left shaking his head and gaining some insight into how Turner had come to have a roomful of computers he had absolutely no use for.

As a radio station, WAPO was a disaster. Having no coherent format, it filled its air time with whatever it could find: an uninspiring preacher, a teenager playing his personal collection of rock albums, and live coverage of golf. Roddey had its call letters changed to WGOW at the beginning of 1969, hoping to identify it with the Go-Go boots then in fashion and the new format of Top 40 hits. Of course, Smokey Robinson and the Miracles had released the song, "Going to a Go-Go," in 1965 so the allusion may have been somewhat lame, but with new announcers and a decidedly more professional sound, at least it was no longer embarrassing. Turner also promoted the station on whatever empty billboards he had in Chattanooga, estimating that at any one time about 15 percent of the boards in a given locality were unrented and it was free advertising. He claims to have had the idea when driving by an oil refinery with an open flame on top, saying, "That bothered the hell out of me, believe it or not, that little wasted flame. You really have to be dumb to waste your resources, because you've only got so much."[2]

By mid-1969, the company, now officially called Turner Communications, owned a total of five radio stations, two in Chattanooga, two in Charleston, South Carolina, and one in Jacksonville, Florida. But while he appreciated the benefits of diversification, Ted had really shown no interest in the new acquisitions. He just couldn't get excited about radio. Frustrated with not being able to acquire a station in the prime Atlanta market, and angered when one of his new employees was arrested for transporting a young girl across state lines, all signs told him that this wasn't the business he was meant to be in.

At about this time, Turner was looking to take the company public in order to raise cash. One of the brokerage houses he approached with the idea happened to mention a TV station in Atlanta, WJRJ, that had been sinking fast since its public offering about a year before. He then noticed that the same station was advertising on one of his billboards as UHF-TV. Having no idea what that meant, he started asking around. Introduced in the earliest years of television as a means of dealing with the narrow channel capacity of VHF (Very High Frequency) in which the major networks were broadcast, UHF (Ultra High Frequency) signals carried a little more than half as far as VHF and were generally very difficult to tune properly. Virtually disappearing by the mid-1950s, few televisions included UHF tuners until the All-Channel Receiver Act of 1964 made them mandatory. By 1970, only around 15 percent of televisions in use in the United States were equipped to tune UHF stations, and the stations that remained in these frequencies were largely the jokes of the industry, usually quick to go out of business and largely educational, foreign language, quasi-professional, or akin to today's public-access channels.

WJRJ was named for its owner at the time, Jack Rice Jr., and when it began broadcasting on September 1, 1967, it was the first independent television station in the Atlanta market. With its schedule, running from 4:00 P.M. to 11:00 P.M., and its owner being largely uninvolved in its operation, spending most of his time in Palm Beach, Florida, it had lost $600,000 in 1968. When Turner first started expressing his interest in acquiring the station, he was advised by an associate that he could expect to absorb similar losses in his first two years of ownership, and that was the rosy prediction; he might just lose everything. With Turner Communications being worth approximately $7.5 million, with solid holdings and a good cash flow, few other than Ted could see any benefit in expanding into television. Fewer still seemed enticed by the idea of investing $2.5 million, a third of the company's worth, on a failing business with so little chance of success. When Jim Roddey had first come to Turner Advertising, he and Ted had discussed how to go forward. They had both agreed that television was out of the picture and beyond their means, an assessment Roddey stood by. Irwin Mazo and Tench Coxe, Turner's lawyer, both tried to convince Ted that, even as a success, the station's contribution to income wouldn't exceed anything they could achieve for less money at much lower risk.

None of this mattered to Turner. For a man who claimed to watch little or no TV at the time, he was immediately more enthusiastic about television than he had ever been about radio. If he was going to sell advertising, he would rather sell it with the most promising medium available, one that was still maturing, rather than with beleaguered billboards or reactionary radio. WJRJ wouldn't have been his first choice, but it was based in the core of his market and the $2.5 million price tag was at least doable; a VHF station would cost at least five times that. So the more he was cautioned against it, the more the challenge intrigued him; no one had ever built an empire without taking chances.

Turner worked with Robinson-Humphrey, the investment bank that was representing Rice, and together they fashioned a reverse merger scheme through which Rice would acquire Turner Communications in a stock swap that would leave Ted with 47 percent of the combined company's shares. With Turner being the largest shareholder in the company and holding voting control, Rice would then have its name changed to what would be a publicly traded Turner Communications. However, the board of the private Turner Communications, which was primarily comprised of close friends of Ted's father, would first have to approve the deal, and even Turner's powers of persuasion left the result uncertain. Approval squeaked through only when a proxy vote by one of the directors proved indecipherable, and though the vote was later determined to have been an adamant no, Turner was by that time sequestered away with Robinson-Humphrey as the deal was being completed.

While the Federal Communications Commission (FCC) reviewed and approved the transfer of ownership, everyone, including Turner, was caught by surprise when a competing UHF independent entered the Atlanta market. Owned by United States Communications, which already operated four UHF stations, the competing WATL would beat Turner to air and begin broadcasting on September 8, 1969. Some four months later, in January of 1970, Turner took control of Channel 17 and changed its call letters to WTCG (Turner Communications Group). By the following year, he would extend its programming to run 24 hours a day. This was almost unheard of at the time, when most television stations, including the major networks, went off air somewhere between midnight and 2 A.M. with the playing of the National Anthem.

In the history of Turner's business career, many have been cited as Ted's finest hours, but none were more critical than this. With no previous knowledge of television, with no reliable staff in place, armed with one of the country's tallest freestanding transmission towers but decrepit equipment and a grimy two-story cinder-block studio, Turner would somehow prevail.

In its first year, WATL invested approximately $1 million in programming, much of it quite progressive for the time. Together with reruns of the campy late-1960s series *Lost in Space* and a passel of game shows, WATL aired a slate of Japanese cartoons dubbed into English as well as the first regular broadcasts of *The Now Explosion*, an early experiment in music video. For its part, WTCG scrambled for old movies while it struggled with personnel turnover and technical problems that kept knocking them off the air, once for a full week. Turner somehow remained positive: "When you're the last-place TV station in town, you can't make a mistake. They've already been made."[3]

In the middle of the turmoil, when Lee McClurkin from Robinson-Humphrey suggested that Turner might be able to salvage some spare parts from a failing station in Charlotte, North Carolina, Ted decided he'd rather purchase the station outright. This was just six months after taking control of WTCG. Given the station's performance, there was no amount of cajoling that was going to convince his board to approve a similar purchase, so Turner bought the station himself. Paying $250,000 and assuming nearly $3 million in debt, Ted used his Turner Communications stock as collateral. He would later say, "It [WRET] was even more messed up than the last one [WTCG], but it was only losing $30,000 a month."[4]

Mazo had had enough. While he'd skirted board approval, Turner had directly placed control of the company at risk with the WRET purchase. Disgusted, and convinced that Turner was intent on destroying what Ed Turner had cobbled together, Mazo first considered a move to oust Ted from the board, but, knowing he had little chance of success, he quit instead. A frustrated Roddey, realizing that his position as president was proving totally meaningless since Turner would always do whatever he pleased, held out until the following year before he too left, returning to Rollins, Inc.

WTCG lost close to $900,000 in 1970, and the previously never unprofitable Turner Communications showed a net loss of $700,000. Being relatively trounced in the ratings by WATL, Turner was pouring every last bit of cash into WTCG and taking loans from the company to meet his obligations at WRET. Will Sanders, who was hired as vice president of finance to replace Irwin Mazo, managed to sell off the radio station in Jacksonville, Florida and the billboard business in Roanoke, Virginia, netting a healthy $2 million, but the company continued to bleed. Sanders, who would prove invaluable long past his departure nine years later, convinced Turner to finally cut his ties to PlasTrend and somehow took advantage of Turner Communications' depleted stock price to buy back enough shares to get Ted back to 55 percent ownership. But at this point no one could be faulted for asking, "55 percent of what?" When an insurance salesman called to sell Turner a policy, Turner replied, "I gotcha, but don't you understand, this is a risky business I'm in. When the elephants start fighting, the ants get stomped. Do you realize, at this very moment, you are trying to sell insurance to one of the ants that might be trampled to death tomorrow?"[5]

In desperation, he took the advice of his program manager, Sidney Pike, and held what would come to be known as the "begathon" on WRET, asking viewers for contributions to help keep the channel on the air and promising to repay all contributions with interest when the station could afford to. The gambit worked, netting $25,000–$30,000, a substantial amount given the limited penetration of UHF at the time. And though it would take three years, Turner would be true to his word, keeping the names of contributors and repaying them $1.33 on every dollar.

Somehow, Turner would manage to wrest *The Now Explosion* from WATL in his first programming coup. Though not directly related, within a few months United States Communications, having lost $50 million in trying to establish its five stations, had had enough and would suddenly close three stations, including WATL, in March of 1971. Spinning it as a victory on the field of battle, Turner insisted on thanking Atlanta for its support, running an unscripted two-hour show on WTCG that featured balloons and a live band and Ted wandering the studio to interview his embarrassed crew, many of whom had fortified themselves against such an appearance with pot.

While WTCG lost over half a million dollars again in 1971, Turner was feeling reenergized in what was now a four-station market. The longer he could survive, the larger his potential audience would become as more and more televisions were sold with UHF tuners and people became aware that the UHF channels were expanding their possible viewing choices. At one point, thinking that his audience could be larger if people only knew how to attach a UHF antenna to their television sets, Turner decided he would do a commercial demonstrating how to put one together. However, after fiddling with the pieces and searching for screws, he finally turned the box over and just let everything fall to his desk, mumbling something about all the parts being there. In any case, if you could see the commercial in the first place you had already tuned in. Restricted by limited distribution, and a paltry share of even that potential audience, Turner had little else to offer potential advertisers than his own charm and ingenuity. Trying his best to turn his weaknesses into strengths, he would claim that WTCG viewers were clearly smarter than average television viewers since they were able to tune into the notoriously fickle UHF signal in the first place, something Turner said he couldn't do himself. Since nearly all of his programming was black and white, he sold the idea that commercials in color would have a stronger impact. While it often worked, there was a limit to how often you could overcome the real numbers, and he still couldn't attract any national advertisers. In response, he hired someone to travel the country to attend product demonstration shows to find undistributed products that WTCG could offer exclusively, "available only on TV" low-budget commercials made at the station—often reusing old tape languishing in the basement. Turner fashioned deals that had a significant portion of any sale going directly to WTCG, and this strategy was one that Turner would rely on for several years as the direct response ads for fishing tackle, bamboo steamers, party rings, and of course Ginsu knives became famous in their own right. Noticing that many of the stamps on the order envelopes had never been canceled at the Post Office, he started having them removed for reuse on the station's own mail, and he would even come to use them to estimate his audience beyond Atlanta, where he had no official ratings numbers.

Turner had assembled a good management team: Sidney Pike, who had worked in television for 17 years and had helped to revamp what had become WATL, was hired as station master at WTCG; Gene Wright became chief engineer; Gerry Hogan became vice president of advertising; and R. T. Williams became producer. Nevertheless, almost all programming decisions were Turner's, even time slots. And though the schedule might have appeared overly dependent on worn out, old material, as early as 1974 he was already championing what would become the Turner ethos, "I felt people of Atlanta were entitled to something different than a whole lot of police and crime shows with rape and murders going on all over the place . . . People are tired of violence and psychological problems and all the negative things they see on TV every night."[6]

Now that they were the only independent in the area, they had their pick of old movies that the network affiliates showed little interest in, and though often chided for overpaying, Turner was getting long-term exclusive rights that he felt were a bargain. With reruns of older series being a staple of independents, he made similar long-term deals for family-friendly viewing like I Love Lucy, Leave It to Beaver, Father Knows Best, Gilligan's Island, and Petticoat Junction. He swapped the rights to Ironside and Marcus Welby for the rights to The Andy Griffith Show. This was probably a good laugh over at Cox Communications, the other party involved in the deal, but Andy Griffith would remain a huge ratings hit for many years.

Being Turner, there was no way he was going to ignore a concept named counter-programming, so he scheduled movies on Sunday mornings when everyone else was running religious programming. Despite the fact that the movies were primarily the lowest of B-grade has-beens, he would title it Academy Award Theater, and in those early years Ted himself introduced each movie while seated in a wingback armchair. This would prove to be WTCG's first hit, and with Turner away sailing most of every winter, it provided his children with a rare view of their father. When the local ABC affiliate was forced to run the network's national news broadcast at 6:00 P.M., Turner ran Star Trek against it. When the ABC affiliate counter-programmed the morning news shown on the other two network affiliates with a children's show named Tubby and Lester, Turner counter-counter-programmed by running cartoons, undercutting the Tubby audience and eventually leading to its cancellation.

Turner was having fun and was quick to take advantage of every opportunity. When four daytime network shows became available after the local NBC affiliate decided not to pick them up, Turner grabbed all four, and soon had billboards spread around Atlanta listing each one under the banner announcement, "the NBC network moves to channel 17."[7] When ABC Atlanta preempted shows for Atlanta Hawks basketball games, Turner would swoop in for the preempted shows, once even lucking in to the premiere of Brian's Song, the major made-for-TV movie

on the friendship between hall of fame Chicago Bear running back
Gale Sayers and his cancer-stricken teammate Brian Piccolo. When an
old girlfriend mentioned that the promoters of *Georgia State Wrestling*
felt that ABC Atlanta was mishandling their broadcasts, Turner stole it
away by offering a better deal. Then in 1972, while still fielding phone
calls from NBC lawyers seething over his "NBC" billboards, Turner
would make a deal to take over NBC's contract to broadcast Atlanta
Braves baseball games in what would grow to be the anchor of Turner's
television empire. Knowing that the Braves were struggling financially,
Turner had offered them three times what the NBC affiliate had been
paying for the right to broadcast 60 games, three times the number of
games NBC had carried. Cox Communications, parent of the NBC affiliate, was livid when they heard the news, calling WTCG a "Mickey
Mouse UHF station." But knowing that Turner would be prepared to
pick up every preempted show that a heavier baseball schedule would
force upon them, screaming was the only thing they could do; the deal
went through. Picking up baseball and outmaneuvering a network affiliate made Turner the belle of the ball at the next UHF station owners meeting, and Turner made a speech in front of the crowd, saying
at the end, "All you guys are comin' up and congratulatin' me on how
wonderful it is to have the Braves games, but you know, it's a lot like
gettin' married. You work so hard to do it! You really work so hard, and
then all of a sudden you wake up the morning after the wedding, and
you say, 'Gee, did I really want to *marry* this broad?'"[8] He had his arm
around his wife at the time.

When the ABC affiliate dropped Atlanta Hawks broadcasts after
seeing that WTCG was out-rating them head to head by airing the
very shows they'd preempted, Turner picked up the Hawks as well. Ratings at WTCG were on a consistent upswing. Turner was now saying
that the call letters stood for "Watch This Channel Grow," and though
WRET was lagging behind, it too showed marked improvement. In
1972, WTCG would break even by doubling its revenues. That same
year, the FCC would revise its rules in an effort to help independent stations, expanding the range to which their signals could be transmitted,
allowing cable operators to "import" more distant channels, ordering
that cable systems themselves, rather than the stations whose signals
were imported, would be responsible for any additional copyright fees

and royalties incurred by the expanded distribution, and doing away with a 1966 ruling that had frozen development of cable systems in the country's 100 largest markets. In his 1972 report to shareholders, Turner wrote, "Stations like WTCG are the ones most likely to benefit from these new [FCC] regulations."[9]

Cable television had begun in the late 1940s in several locations in the United States, but the most widely recognized as being first was in Mahony City, Pennsylvania. In 1947, the owner of an appliance store, John Walson, realized that part of the problem he had selling television sets had to do with the fact that Mahony City was located in a valley and its surrounding mountains hampered people's ability to tune in to television broadcasts from Philadelphia, some 85 miles away. To solve the problem, he decided to install an antenna on a nearby hilltop, and shortly afterward he ran a cable from the antenna to his store. Interest in and sales of televisions increased. Soon people were asking him to connect their houses to his wire, so he started improving the wire and adding signal boosters along the way, charging customers for connection and maintenance. More rural locations then started employing microwave stations to boost distant broadcast signals.

With the 1972 FCC ruling signaling a less restrictive era for the regulation of cable services, Turner, who knew of the technology but had never really paid attention to it, decided it was time to learn. He started going to meetings of the National Cable Television Association (NCTA), where he soon met Don Andersson, the NCTA's vice president of research and resident expert on microwave transmission systems, said to know the coverage of nearly every microwave relay station in the country. Andersson was quickly hired to head cable operations at WTCG and he and Turner were soon visiting cable systems in an ever-increasing ring around Atlanta. In 1973, WTCG would generate a profit of $1 million on its way to being one of the most profitable independents in the country. It had become a story that *Television/Radio Age* would say "reads more like a movie script than a prescription for success in the hard-boiled, real world of the broadcast industry."[10]

In 1974, WRET would get its own boost when televangelists Jim and Tammy Faye Bakker moved to Charlotte from California and started the *PTL Club* on the channel. WRET's Christian roots seem to have predated Turner's acquisition of it. When a few of Turner's employees were sent to Charlotte early on to get the station in shape, they reported that the manager of the station held regular prayer meetings, and its schedule included both Pat Robertson's *The 700 Club* and *The Jim and Tammy Show* prior to the Bakker's arrival in Charlotte. Once *PTL Club* was originating from WRET, however, there was more than an increase in ratings. As Turner has recounted, contributions sent in to the ministry were being delivered to a box requiring two keys, one that Turner had and one that Jim Bakker had. Since neither man trusted the other, they would get together every day and divide the money between them.

With its growing regional presence, the FCC noted that WTCG had not been meeting its required seven hours of news or public interest programming per week and ordered it to meet its obligations. Turner would hire Bill Tush (rhymes with hush), a radio personality who had moved to Atlanta from Pennsylvania as the station's first on-air personality (other than Turner's own brief appearances). In 1975, Tush would begin a 20-minute news broadcast scheduled around 3:00 A.M. called *17 Update Early in the Morning*. The show was originally designed as a "rip-and-read" recap of the news, with Tush reading from newswires or the local papers. But given the atmosphere at WTCG at the time, the show soon morphed into something else. One night, someone decided to throw a pie at Tush as he was taping and from that point on the character of the show changed forever, becoming what would essentially be the first spoof of the news on television. In addition to pie throwing, a German shepherd dressed in a shirt and tie and fed peanut butter to make it appear as if it was speaking was introduced as the co-anchor. Tush would report on Atlanta Braves games with a paper bag over his head, and would soon introduce an unknown reporter, never seen without his head in a paper bag. If Tush came upon a story he didn't like he might just crumple it up, saying he wasn't going to read it. He also had porn star Marilyn Chambers on for an interview, during which she started undressing him on the air, and he once did an entire show while wearing a Walter Cronkite mask. The show was soon famous (or infamous, depending on who was judging), and would continue to be popular until 1979. Tush himself also began introducing the Sunday afternoon movie and handling voiceovers for many of the station's direct response ads. When *17 Update* was finally put to rest, he would do a short-lived comedy show called *TUSH*, similar to *Saturday Night Live*, host a celebrity talk show named *People Now*, and host something of an *Entertainment Tonight* called *Showbiz Today*.

NOTES

1. Christian Williams, *Lead, Follow, or Get Out of the Way: The Story of Ted Turner* (New York: Times Books, 1981), 51.

2. Ibid., 55.

3. Ibid., 87.

4. Porter Bibb, *It Ain't as Easy as it Looks: Ted Turner's Amazing Story* (New York: Crown Publishers, 1993), 73.

5. Coles Phinizy, "In the Wake of the Capsize Kid," *Sports Illustrated*, July 12, 1971.

6. Tom Bradshaw, "How an Indie 'U' Made it Big with 'Good Old Days' Programming," *Television/Radio Age*, June 24, 1974.

7. Ted Turner with Bill Burke, *Call Me Ted* (New York: Grand Central Publishing, 2008), 102.

8. Hank Whittemore, *CNN The Inside Story: How a Band of Mavericks Changed the Face of Television News* (Boston: Little, Brown & Co., 1990), 7–8.

9. Bibb, *It Ain't as Easy as it Looks*, 87.

10. Bradshaw, "How an Indie 'U' Made it Big."

Chapter 6

OCEANS AWAY

After two relatively uneventful years of sailing in 1967 and 1968, Turner would kick into high gear with the purchase of *American Eagle*. Originally built as a conventional 12-meter for the America's Cup and the waters off Newport harbor, *Eagle* had competed in the Cup trials in 1964 and 1967 but failed to distinguish herself. Converted for ocean racing by her next owner and taken out for test runs against light competition on Lake Ontario, she again proved wildly unexceptional. Turner would buy her in late December of 1968 and almost immediately set off from Fairhaven, Massachusetts for the 1969 SORC, and announced that he would be entering her in the upcoming transatlantic. While other 12-meters had been converted for deep-water long-distance ocean racing, none had ever been successful. Conventional wisdom was that the design just wasn't sturdy enough for the rigors and uncontrolled conditions encountered on open ocean, and the tongues of the old guard were wagging with disbelief when she showed up for the beginning of the series. The skeptics appeared to have been right when *Eagle* was dismasted, but Turner was undeterred. Recounting similar experiences with boats deemed more seaworthy, Turner would tell *Soundings* magazine, "This reminds me of the Indian who complained that every time a white man won a fight it was a glorious victory. Every time we win a fight it's a bloody massacre."[1] By 1971, *Sports Illustrated* would say that, given his record with *Eagle* alone, Turner deserved a place in the annals of sailing as "a salvage man without peer."[2]

Eagle would shortly win the Annapolis-Newport race and place third in the transatlantic after placating the still skeptical New York Yacht Club (NYYC). Turner then decided to join the quest for the newly developed World Ocean Racing Championship (WORC). Dreamed up by the St. Petersburg Yacht Club, the WORC designated 18 races held around the globe, of which a boat would need to participate in seven of these within a three-year period, with two races being required and one needing to be at least 1,000 miles long. Within a half day of finishing the transatlantic, *Eagle* was off again for Denmark to compete in one of the WORC races, the Skaw. When pointed out as an example of trying to do too much, Turner replied, "When you are up to your rear end in alligators, it is hard to remember that your original idea was to cross a swamp."[3] Turner had planned to be picked up by plane at the end of the course so that he could be whisked off to the 5.5-meter World Championships. When conditions left him well short of the finish line within the time he had estimated, he needed to be talked out of rowing to shore in a dinghy to catch the plane. When the Skaw was finally completed, *Eagle* was again almost immediately on the move, this time to Cowes, England and its fabled Fastnet race, where she would place third in her class and fourth overall.

In 1970, the same pace continued, Turner entered the SORC and after running the first two races, winning one, flew off to Australia for the 5.5-meter Gold Cup and World Championships. By the time he arrived, he had missed the first two races in his series of three and if he didn't win at least one of the series, he would be eliminated. Although Turner had just cleared customs three hours earlier, he won the race and went on to win the Gold Cup and place second in the 5.5 World Championships. Flying back to Florida, he again was just in time for the Lipton Cup, which he won, then followed that up with two more wins, winning the SORC by the largest margin ever while accomplishing the unheard-of feat of winning four out of the five races that were counted in his score. After taking second place in two other races and fifth in another, he showed up at Newport, where he flew the Confederate flag while serving as a trial horse for *Gretel II*, the Australian boat. Just two years after the shooting of Martin Luther King Jr., Turner was making a statement as a rebel not a racist reactionary, but it was another example of the tone deafness he would frequently exhibit. The racing establishment, especially the NYYC, was disgusted, but not at the possible implications of racism. They were angered that he had aided and abetted the "enemy" Australians. It would cost him when he was blackballed in his first nomination to the NYYC, practically a requirement for competing in defense of the America's Cup, but he would still receive his first U.S. Yachtsman of the Year award for his 1970 accomplishments—narrowly beating Bill Ficker, who had skippered *Intrepid* to a victory over *Gretel II* in his own defense of the Cup.

In 1971, Turner would log over 12,000 miles in races. After an overall victory in the SORC's St. Petersburg-Fort Lauderdale race, *Eagle* would again be dismasted. By making calls to his friend Bob Derecktor in Fairhaven, Massachusetts and the Hood sail loft in Marblehead, he was ready to sail again with a new, fully outfitted mast and mainsail within six days. Perhaps more remarkably, he would well have won the series if not for the new rules that had taken effect at the beginning of the year, resulting in heavy penalties against his boat. After placing second in the Annapolis-Newport, *Eagle* went on to England, setting a new course record in the Fastnet while taking fourth place overall. From there, he had *Eagle* shipped to Australia, at severe cost, to try to salvage the WORC, and though he bombed in the Sydney-Hobart, he managed a 2nd-place finish in his very last chance in the Hobart-Auckland, taking the overall win in the first WORC. Unable to afford to have *Eagle* shipped home, he left her in Australia.

After a mostly quiet 1972, taking second in his class and fourth overall at the SORC on *Running Tide* and first in the 5.5 Nationals, he went back to Australia. He dusted off *Eagle* and nearly set a course record, finishing first in class and first overall after making a risky maneuver through some spectator boats near the start of the race that provided him with a good lead. Following this victory, Turner was quoted as saying, "This is the last picture show";[4] his legendary run with *Eagle* was over. He went on to astonish everyone at a post-race speech with an off-the-cuff paraphrasing of Conrad's *Nigger of Narcissus* and *Youth*, paying tribute to the sport, his crew, and his beloved boat. In 1973 he had a new hull, the aluminum 37-foot sloop *Lightnin'*, which he drove to ten first or second place finishes; he won the Southern

One-Ton Championships, took first in class and second overall in the SORC,[5] took first to finish, first in class, and first overall in the Montego Bay, and first in class at Annapolis-Newport. With stops in Atlanta between each, from July 13–22 he was in Oslo for the Skaw, from July 26 through August 19 he was on the Isle of Wight for the Admiral's Cup, from August 25 through September 9 he was in Sardinia for the World One-Ton Championships, and from September 28 through October 12 he was in Malta for the Middle Sea race. He won his second Yachtsman of the Year award for his efforts.

While sailing in Oslo, Turner's selection as skipper of *Mariner* in the 1974 America's Cup defense was announced. Commodore George Hinman, the manager of the Kings Point syndicate that was funding the campaign, was pure Eastern elite and a respected member of the NYYC, and after choosing Turner as his helmsman he pulled a lot of strings to get Turner elected to the club. It was a proud moment for Turner, signifying recognition in the highest echelons of the sport and making him a member in a club that his father had always spoken of with reverence. It would prove to be the highlight of the experience.

The America's Cup was named for the schooner *America*, which beat fifteen boats from Britain's Royal Yacht Squadron in an 1851 race around the Isle of Wight. The Cup itself, cast in 1848, was granted to the winner and later bequeathed to the New York Yacht Club, which had sponsored *America*'s campaign. Starting in 1870, the New York Yacht Club organized regular international challenges for the Cup, and by 1974 the boats representing the United States had won every one of the 22 challenges held since, first in the vicinity of New York and then, starting in 1930, in the waters off Newport, Rhode Island. The challenges, unlike the fleet races that were typical of ocean racing, were organized as match races, one against one. A series of trials would be held between June and August to choose a U.S. representative boat as a "defender," while another round of challenges would be held between international boats to choose a challenger. Once chosen, the challenger and defender would meet in a best four-out-of-seven series in September. While the class of boats used in the challenge has changed over time, the reigning class since 1958 had been the 12-meter. The Cup itself remained at the New York Yacht Club, inscribed with the name of each winner. As the world's longest active international sporting competition, it carried a special prestige in the yachting world, and though there was no monetary reward for winning, the amount of money spent by hopeful participants had grown exponentially. Indeed, the quest to perfect boats and sails specifically for the waters and prevailing conditions of the Challenge series had become an industry in itself.

Roger Vaughan, who was contracted to do a book about the "supergroup" that Hinman had put together for the *Mariner* campaign,[6] would sail with Turner for the Triangle Race of the 1974 SORC and painted a vivid picture of Turner as a captain. Though Turner was still not very widely known outside the sailing world, he was already a star within it, especially among reporters since he was the most colorful character around. He had already been credited with revolutionizing the sport by bringing the small-boat captain's endless concentration to the sport of long distance ocean races and never resting. Vaughan, a sailor himself, described Turner as keeping up an incredible level of concentration, considering every aspect of his boat and the position of each of his competitors at all times, even at night, while recalling a virtual database of knowledge and making over a thousand adjustments and decisions over 13 straight hours at the helm. At the same time, he would keep up a near endless verbal barrage, shouting commands to his crew and berating them mercilessly for the slightest hesitation or mistake before turning around a short time later and earnestly asking for their advice. While he never provided airfare or food allowances for his crews, they remained remarkably stable, with some, like Bunky Helfrich and Legaré Van Ness, having known and sailed with Turner since they were boys. One unnamed member of his crew provided what may well be the best summary of Turner ever: "Sure he is an asshole . . . but he is not your usual, run-of-the-mill, boring asshole. He is a glorious, totally mad, larger-than-life asshole, and besides that he has class. It's an overindulged, somewhat extreme, strange sort of class, but it's class."[7]

Britton Chance, whom Turner had worked with before, was chosen to design the syndicate's lead boat, to be named *Mariner*, while *Valiant*, a 1970 Olin Stephens design that had been badly beaten in her campaign that year, was secured as the syndicate's trial horse. Turner and Chance had had a series of run-ins over the years, and by 1974 neither thought highly of the other. Chance belittled Turner's skills as a helmsman from the beginning, calling him a one-boat wonder who had happened to stumble upon *Eagle* at the right time.

Buoyed by his success in updating the design of *Intrepid* for the 1970 Cup while Olin Stephens was busy with *Valiant*, Chance came up with a radical design for *Mariner* while working with his consultant, Pierre DeSaix, on alleviating the drag associated with the "quarter-wave," a boat's second wave formed when the initial flow of water along the hull separates from the hull. The separation of the flow and its consequent second or quarter-wave creates drag, so a goal of 12-meter design is to assure that this wave is as smooth and shallow as possible to reduce the amount of resulting drag. Chance came up with a counter-intuitive design that included a broad, underwater bulge and an abruptly cut, squared off, stair-stepped keel at the stern. The idea proved to be a marvelous success during model testing in a tank, yielding the best results and fastest design either man had ever seen. Unknown to Hinman, Chance took the liberty of equipping *Valiant* with a scaled down version of the same concept. However, while this might have provided a test of two different implementations, it effectively canceled *Valiant's* effectiveness as a reliable gauge of *Mariner's* performance.

Bob Derecktor was building the aluminum boat at his Mamaroneck, New York boatyard and had also been assigned as one of *Mariner's* crew. Turner, as captain, filled out the rest of the crew, choosing young Robbie Doyle, an assistant at Ted Hood's storied Marblehead sail loft, to be the sail trimmer and Dennis Conner, who would go on to his own America's Cup fame, to hold the important role of tactician. The rest of the crew consisted of Turner's regulars, most of whom he had sailed with for at least 5,000 miles, some for over 30,000. In a show of loyalty for which Turner is often celebrated, he even threatened not to take the helm unless one of his crew, Marty O'Meara, took part in the effort. Though it hardly seems possible, Chance was even more dismissive of the crew's skills than he was of Turner's, openly wondering why Ted had neglected to choose several people Chance thought clearly superior.

Despite the excitement of the occasion, there were signs that something was wrong from the moment the boat was put in the water as *Mariner's* wake looked unusually turbulent. In the first days of June, the NYYC sponsored an event on Long Island that pitted *Mariner* against her primary opponent in the upcoming trials, Olin Stephens's latest though largely conventional design, *Courageous*. *Mariner* lost to *Courageous* in both races, losing the second by a phenomenal eight minutes over a 16-mile course. If projected over a 24-mile course, this would be a worse defeat than the average difference in the most lopsided Challenge series in the history of the Cup.

With the exception of Chance himself, it quickly became apparent to all that his radical stern and keel were a major source of *Mariner*'s lack of speed. Legaré Van Ness, who had crewed with Turner since his Savannah days, except for the three years following his unfortunate participation in the *Scylla* experience, noted, "Even a turd is tapered."[8] Turner wanted to pull the boat and have it redesigned right away, but even when she was having a difficult time beating the undeniably slow *Valiant*, they pressed ahead. With the odd and turbulent wake that tended to suck debris in for a ride, trouble recovering from tacks that could bring the boat to a halt, steering that was difficult even for a 12-meter, and a series of engineering concerns covering everything from the mast to the winches—all of which were denied or met with derisive defensiveness from Chance and Derecktor—Turner took to muttering, "It's the Keystone Cops! 'The Keystone Cops Go Sailboat Racing.'"[9] Chance blamed everything on Turner and his crew, who in truth weren't performing very well, with Turner being erratic and the crew proving far less efficient than normal in changes of sail.

The syndicate pressed ahead to June's preliminary trials, but *Mariner* failed miserably, losing to both *Courageous* and her trial horse, the seven-year-old *Intrepid*, once by 9 minutes and 46 seconds on a 21-mile course. All had finally seen enough, and it was decided to skip the last day of the June trials and send both *Valiant* and *Mariner* back to Mamaroneck for as much rebuilding as was feasible, something that had never before happened in the history of the Cup. The plan was to have the work completed by July 17, which would be some five days into the July trials. In the America's Cup selection series, the three series of trials are of mounting importance; June is generally for feeling out your boat and the competition, July is for rounding everything into shape, and the results in August are what really count in the bid to be chosen as a defender. The work on *Valiant*, which was more dismantling than redesign, wound up being finished in time for the July trials, but she was still performing abysmally even after being returned to her more conventional lines. Chance was still hoping to preserve as much as he could of *Mariner*'s design, however. He was reluctant to give up on its "fastback," and new plans with more conventional lines wouldn't be provided to Derecktor until July 5. *Mariner* missed the entire July trials series, finally getting back in the water on August 6. There was little over a week to get a feel for what was basically a new boat and prepare for the all-important August trials. By this time, Hinman, who had been skippering *Valiant* to the growing consternation of its crew, named Conner as the skipper of the trial horse, which many took to signal concern with Turner.

Earlier in the summer, Turner had been playing a game of Pong, the first ultra-popular video game that had become a fixture in bars at the time, and had cautioned his opponent that he couldn't win if he was too worried about losing. It was a central Turner credo: losing as learning to win, losing as a builder of character—he has had innumerable variations on the theme. Others had already pointed out that Turner truly thrived on adversity, excelling most after being backed against a wall. But here he was, backed against a wall, and he seemed oddly ill at ease and worried about losing.

Mariner was proving faster in the water now that she had shed her "fastback," and the spirits of the crew were noticeably improving. But the normally loquacious Turner was now talking so much that he lost his concentration, failing to pay attention to sail changes, tacking poorly and at inopportune times, and in several pairings against Conner he had been thoroughly schooled when jockeying for advantage at the starting line. *Mariner* would win some races, but Turner was fouling Conner repeatedly, three times in one race alone. Even his own loyal crew was wondering if he should stay at the helm. Though reporters had already written off *Valiant*, she beat *Mariner* in three out of four races on August 12, splitting two with Turner steering *Mariner*, and *Valiant* winning both when Hinman decided to switch crews and tested Conner at *Mariner*'s helm. Though steering *Mariner* was still an arduous chore, and even Conner didn't look good doing it, Turner looked worse. When one of the executives from Channel 17 showed up, Turner told him, "This has been worse than when Dad died."[10] Two days later, Hinman announced that Conner would officially take over the helm of *Mariner* and Turner would be reassigned to *Valiant*.

Despite recent events, the move took almost everyone by surprise. Reporters commiserated with Turner, but they also hoped the change might finally bring him some of the humility he lacked, which, in Ted's estimation, was the one thing keeping him from perfection. Janie was upset, Turner's crew was angry; Chance was practically radiating "I told you so." On the surface, Turner took it in stride. By the second day of the official August trials, which had begun on the 15th, only the syndicate's investors held out any hope for either *Mariner* or *Valiant*; the battle for defense was clearly between *Intrepid* and *Courageous*. Turner was again embarrassed at a start against Conner, and Conner continued to excel at starts against all competition, but good start or no, neither could keep up with their rival syndicate's boats. On August 20, both *Mariner* and *Valiant* were eliminated from the trials. For his showings at starts, Conner was offered the job of handling starts at the helm for *Courageous*. The battle between *Intrepid* and *Courageous* went on until September 2, when *Courageous* was finally chosen as the defender. Conner would remain on the *Courageous* for the Challenge series, where *Courageous* would handily defeat the Australian challenger.

It was a most humiliating summer for Turner, but he won respect for his demeanor throughout the ordeal. Chance, who defended his design and still blamed Turner for the poor showing, fared much worse since everyone else acknowledged that it had been the biggest design failure in the history of the Cup. He would later be quoted as saying, "I'll say one thing: if Turner and his crew had been sailing *Courageous* they would have lost to *Intrepid*."[11] Those words would ring in Turner's ears, but for the time being he would have to be satisfied with the relief offered by Brown University, which would induct him into its Athletic Hall of Fame on November 1, 1974.

NOTES

1. Roger Vaughan, *The Grand Gesture: Ted Turner, Mariner, and the America's Cup* (Boston: Little, Brown & Co., 1975), 109.

2. Coles Phinizy, "In the Wake of the Capsize Kid," *Sports Illustrated*, July 12, 1971.

3. Ibid.

4. Hugh D. Whall, "Sailing up a Squall," *Sports Illustrated*, March 12, 1973.

5. In the last race of the series, the Lipton Cup, Turner found himself sailing into a tugboat's cable sitting high out of the water. Rather than stop or try to avoid it he decided to keep going forward and the tugboat captain, realizing that Turner had no intention of stopping, loosened the cable just in time for *Lightnin'* to sail through undamaged.

6. *The Grand Gesture*, an excellent book on a quest for the Cup.

7. Vaughan, *The Grand Gesture*, 92.

8. Vaughan, *The Grand Gesture*, 150. Turner would later be credited with the same quote, though without its alliteration and touch of decorum.

9. Ibid., 156.

10. Ibid., 263.

11. Ibid., 294.

Chapter 7

INTO HEAVEN

For the 1973 National Cable Television Association (NCTA) convention in Anaheim, California, Teleprompter set up a proof of concept demonstration of satellite distribution. Using a transmission dish in Maryland, a receiver dish provided by Sid Topol of Scientific Atlanta in Anaheim, and working with Telsat Canada's *Anik I* satellite, which had been launched in 1972, they presented a live feed of Speaker of the House Carl Albert addressing the convention from Washington. Teleprompter also organized another demonstration that same night with Jerry Levin of HBO (Home Box Office), using the same setup to transmit a heavyweight fight between Jimmy Ellis and Earnie Shavers to a hotel suite, but the fight lasted only 30 seconds and Levin himself missed it.

HBO had grown out of the partnership that started when Time Inc. bought a 20 percent share in Charles Dolan's Sterling Communications, which wired and held the franchise for the first urban cable system in the country, Sterling Manhattan Cable in lower Manhattan. When Time Inc. seemed settled on selling their stake in the venture, Dolan convinced them to change their minds by proposing a partnership in a new venture that would use the system. He wanted to create a fee-based service that would cablecast movies and sports from Madison Square Garden, originally calling it the "Green Channel" but soon changing the name to Home Box Office. At its launch in 1972, it was available only on the Sterling system in Wilkes-Barre, Pennsylvania, and it was the first programming service intended exclusively for cable delivery, using a combination of microwave and AT&T terrestrial lines, though Dolan had mentioned possible satellite delivery in his original proposal. When the service was slow to grow and losses saw Time Inc.'s equity and convertible debentures increase to 80 percent of the joint venture, Dolan swapped his shares of Sterling Manhattan and HBO for a Time Inc. cable franchise in Suffolk, New York that would eventually become Cablevision Systems. Time Inc. named Jerry Levin, a lawyer originally hired by Dolan, as president of HBO, and the New York cable system was renamed Manhattan Cable.

Western Union launched the first U.S. commercial communications satellite, *Westar I*, in April 1974 and its second, *Westar II*, in October of the same year. By mid-1974, Time Inc. was running out of patience with HBO's slow growth and lack of profit and threatened to close it down if the service didn't have 30,000 subscribers by December 31. HBO met those numbers, as long as you didn't examine them too carefully, and in early 1975, with Levin still under pressure to grow the subscriber base and show a profit, Levin proposed to his board that HBO be transmitted by satellite, where potential growth could be enormous and the costs associated with microwave relays and AT&T landlines could be avoided. On September 30, 1975, HBO delivered its first satellite-transmitted cable programming, which included two movies and the heavyweight boxing match between Muhammad Ali and Joe Frazier, billed as "The Thrilla in Manila." The transmission was made under a short-term lease of a transponder on a Westar satellite, but HBO was already in the process of signing a $6.5 million contract with RCA for a five-year lease of two transponders on its *Satcom I*, due to launch on December 13.

Reese Schonfeld, who would later become central to the launch of CNN, remembers visiting Atlanta to speak with Sid Topol of Scientific Atlanta in late 1974. In the course of the meeting, Topol mentioned that there was someone he wanted Schonfeld to meet, and he brought him to Turner's rather shabby office at WTCG. According to Schonfeld's recollection, Turner was interested in learning about communication satellites and the involved costs of using them to extend the signal of Channel 17 across the country. Schonfeld reports that he was spectacularly unimpressed with Turner and his harebrained scheme.[1] No one else seems to have a recollection of this meeting, but Schonfeld has put it in context with his own activities at the time, so it seems plausible.

Turner says he learned of satellites from a 1975 issue of *Broadcasting* magazine that reported on HBO's plan to be carried on the Westar satellite later in the year, but he already knew Sid Topol, and Don Andersson was certainly aware of satellites while still at the NCTA. Additionally, Turner had already attended NCTA conventions, and the 1974 launches of the Westar satellites had almost certainly come to his attention.

However it came to pass, in early 1975 Turner went to the New Jersey offices of Western Union and met with their vice president of marketing, Ed Taylor, who filled him in on the Westar program in terms of cost, clarity of signal, and national coverage. At about the same time, he also spoke to Jerry Levin at HBO and learned that HBO's arrangement with Western Union was in fact short term and that they would be moving to RCA's Satcom system later that year. Informed that to receive satellite signals cable systems would need to install satellite dishes costing nearly $100,000 (at that time), and that each dish could only receive signals from a single satellite, it was clear that if Ted was going to pursue satellite distribution and hope to be picked up by systems around the country, he would have to be on the same satellite as HBO.

Following the trail, Turner spoke to RCA and asked what it would take to get the WTCG signal on *Satcom I*. Already aware that he would need access to an uplink station transmitter to send his signal skyward, he learned that RCA itself had no earth stations in the South and wasn't interested in building one for a single customer, especially one that they still couldn't take very seriously. Undeterred, Turner called Sid Topol and told him that he wanted to buy an uplink station. To Topol's recollection, Ted was uninterested in seeing a proposal or even discussing it in depth; he just wanted a salesman sent over so he could buy it. At approximately $500,000 for the station and closer to $750,000 once it was fully installed, it was a major investment, but Turner saw opportunity and he wasn't about to let financial concerns get in the way. He contracted with Scientific Atlanta for the uplink station.

Only after signing the contract did Turner learn that there was one very large obstacle: a programmer could not own a transmission uplink station and become what was known as a common carrier without running afoul of several FCC restrictions. So it was that on February 1, 1975, as Ed Taylor would later recall, Turner invited Taylor and his wife to Atlanta for a weekend. Telling Taylor that it was clear that Western Union's future in the commercial communications satellite business was to be a short one, Turner wanted to sell the uplink station to Taylor for $1.00 so it could be set up as an independent corporation. With a secure and well paid if not totally fulfilling job, Taylor had his doubts, but Turner told him that he planned on charging cable systems ten cents per subscriber per month, all of which would be collected by his common carrier, and he planned on having a lot of subscribers. On the flip side, Taylor's corporation would also assume the costs for leasing the *Satcom I* transponder, estimated at approximately $100,000 per month. Taylor wound up paying his dollar and would become a wealthy man, though forming the new corporation, Southern Satellite Systems (SSS), would take over a year, with Will Sanders scrambling to find investors to help cover the leasing costs. Turner was anything but happy with the delay, but there wasn't much he could do. *Satcom I* was already in the air before Southern Satellite could even file for FCC approval.

While HBO had won FCC approval for its service, there was no guarantee that WTCG and Southern Satellite would, so all of this scrambling and expense could still prove fruitless. The FCC had established different rules for broadcasters than for pay-TV and cable-only services like HBO, which could in fact contract directly with a satellite provider without the use of an intermediary. What WTCG was seeking to do was different. While a cable system was required to make a minimal monthly payment per subscriber to its common carrier for redistributing its signal, WTCG was and would for some time continue to be considered a UHF broadcaster that happened to be transmitted via satellite. This is the idea of a "superstation," a term popularized and often attributed to Turner, though the concept and term seem to predate that popularization, even being used in relation to microwave transmissions of distant signals. In its case, though, WTCG was specifically gearing toward national distribution and, being advertiser based, it would progressively seek national advertisers. While it was abiding by the 1972 FCC regulations, it was quite evidently taking advantage of a distribution system that had not been in existence at the time. The FCC could well turn down the Southern Satellite filing based on the fact that it was too obviously over-connected with Turner Communications and WTCG, or hold it in abeyance until it could more thoroughly investigate the impact of nationwide distribution in terms of copyright fees and the stated government interest in ensuring diversity and local programming in televised communications.

Turner had already decided that his future was with cable, but if there were any doubts, they would be put to rest when he was unexpectedly called to appear before the House Subcommittee on Communications, which was then looking into the future of cable television. While cable regulations had been enacted with the specific idea of protecting UHF independents, the technology was still seen as a competitor and Turner was the only UHF operator willing to testify in support of it. Describing himself as a bumble bee that doesn't know it shouldn't be able to fly and saying that if he were smart he never would have gone into the UHF business, he promoted cable as a potential source for the diversity in communications that the government was looking to foster. He played up the fact that many communities across the country had no local independents to watch and were left to the three major networks. Diversity in programming for these communities, he argued, could not be reached if cable were to be burdened with limitations on distant signal carriage. In what would become his continuing mantra, he railed against violence on television and in the movies, citing *Taxi Driver*, which had been released earlier that year. He would continue to use *Taxi Driver* as an example of what was wrong with the status quo for years to come, saying that what America needed was a slate of the good American values represented by old movies and sports. He had made no secret that in having become a regional programmer he had acquired a wealth of sports and old movie programming, but while he said he hoped to become a superstation he never specifically raised the fact that he was currently awaiting FCC approval that would allow his wholesome programming to be distributed nationally, and while the members of the subcommittee must have known that fact, they never specifically alluded to it either.

By the end of his testimony, he had the congressmen gushing over his plain spoken intelligence and had particularly impressed Tim Wirth, a

Democrat from Colorado who would go on to become a U.S. Senator and president of Turner's UN Foundation. The UHF operators, who had feted him just a few years earlier for outsmarting a network affiliate, would now look on him as a traitor.

NOTE

1. See Hank Whittemore, CNN, *The Inside Story: How a Band of Mavericks Changed the Face of Television News* (Boston: Little, Brown & Co., 1990), 20–21.

Chapter 8

ATLANTA BRAVES

The broadcasting of Atlanta Braves games had gone a long way toward establishing WTCG as a profitable regional cable network. Turner was already planning its expansion, so a sparsely attended game in a dismal 1975 season was reason enough for concern. When informed by Dan Donahue that the team was going to be sold at the end of the year, Ted could feel his world quake. It was reasonably certain that if the Braves were to go on the market, the new owners would move the team out of Atlanta—a group in Toronto had already expressed interest—so Turner's five-year deal to broadcast Braves games, already set to expire in 1977, would stand no chance of being renewed. Still, when Donahue quickly suggested that Turner buy the team, Ted was cautious enough to ask for time to consider the offer.

The asking price was a steep $10 million, more than any acquisition in the company's history and far more than Turner could afford. Added to the fact that the team had been losing a million dollars a year, the strain on his debt load seemed onerous. But with the potential of broadcasting 162 games with an average length of 2.5 hours, a million dollars a year could prove to be the biggest bargain in programming Turner could hope for. Ted went back to Donahue and said he'd agree to the $10 million asking price if he could pay a portion up front and the remainder over 8–10 years.

Having received its asking price, the Chicago-based consortium that had owned the club since 1964 agreed to the terms, but it wanted Turner's personal guarantee for the full purchase price. Such a guarantee would essentially leave Turner back in the position he'd been in when he first took control of Turner Advertising, at risk of losing everything if things didn't work out as planned. Will Sanders, his CFO at the time, cautioned Turner not to accept the guarantee, pointing out that with attendance down and the owners having a hard time meeting payroll, a counter offer of a bit more cash up front was sure to be accepted. Turner, who'd never refused any risk out of fear of losing, agreed to the terms anyway.

After completion of the deal, Sanders found that the Braves had proceeds of just over $1 million from concession stand and season-ticket sales buried in their books, so Turner had actually purchased the team with its own money.

Holding a press conference to announce his purchase of the Braves and wearing a commemorative Hank Aaron 715 tie, Turner railed that he didn't want to see any more headlines calling Atlanta "Loserville, U.S.A"; that he was purchasing the team for Atlanta and the glory of the South, even if it was a deal that had put him in "Tap City"; and that he was thinking of changing the name of the team to the Eagles, though if they lost he might change that to the Turkeys. Having already been quoted as saying, "What is there to know about baseball? Both sides have ten guys,"[1] he admitted he didn't know much about baseball, but said he was ready to learn. Even having no specific plans on how to turn the team around, he wasn't someone who would settle for second place, and he promised a World Series title within five years.

Despite a player lockout by major-league owners at the beginning of spring training, Turner took Terry McGuirk, his vice president at WTCG, to Florida in an effort to learn the game. Turner was well aware that he had absolutely no athletic aptitude for hitting or throwing, so McGuirk's role was to take part in the informal training camp games and report back to Ted between innings. As it turned out, sharing his players' taste for chewing tobacco seems the closest he got to really learning anything that spring.

On April 10, Turner, always free with large sums of money when spent for a purpose, officially ushered in baseball's free-agency era when he signed pitcher Andy Messersmith to a three-year deal worth $1.75

million,[2] an enormous sum at the time. Messersmith, formerly of the Dodgers, and Dave McNally of the Montreal Expos, had been through a lengthy court battle against baseball's reserve clause, a rider to sports contracts that held that at the expiration of a player's contract the rights to the player were retained by the team to which he had been signed. In December of 1975, after having played a full year without a contract, an arbitrator declared the pair baseball's first free agents.[3] Though several other teams participated in the bidding, Messersmith was convinced there had been collusion among owners, but collusion or not, Turner wouldn't care; he thrived on being the outsider with something to prove, and baseball purists and establishment be damned, he had ratings on the line. Turner vowed that Messersmith would be a Brave as long as he was.

Just three days later, on April 13, 1976, Turner received a standing ovation from a crowd of 37,000 on opening night at Atlanta-Fulton County Stadium. With a pre-game sing-along of "Take Me out to the Ball Game" led by an animated Turner and a full marching band, and a rambling 25-minute "pep talk," the Cincinnati Reds, reigning World Champions and the Braves' opponent that day, were surely bemused. Taking his seat just behind the Atlanta dugout, Turner chugged beers, spit his chew juice into a plastic cup, and urged the team on as if he were any other fan. But in the bottom of the second inning, when Atlanta's Ken Henderson hit the team's first homer of the season, Turner jumped onto the field with his Braves cap and startled Henderson with a handshake as he crossed home plate. Turner was not just any fan, and wasn't about to be just any owner.

Relations with the initially adoring media hit a major bump early on when Turner fired four-foot-tall vice president Donald Davidson and demoted general manager Eddie Robinson to scouting duties after learning they had been staying in VIP suites when traveling with the team. Robinson had even been driving around in a Cadillac as a company car. The personally frugal Turner drove an aging Toyota and flew coach, and felt personally affronted by their extravagance. But both had been popular with the press, especially the diminutive Davidson, who had been with the Braves some 40 years after starting as a batboy. It didn't help that after the negative coverage of the firings, the Braves immediately went on a 13-game losing streak.

No one could deny, though, that Ted was serious about turning this moribund franchise into something to watch. He quickly installed a million-dollar video screen above the scoreboard to show instant replays, a rarity at the time. Within three months, every position player from the 1975 roster save one had been replaced with generally upgraded talent. Turner had even had a hand in redesigning the club's uniforms. And all the while, he was a fixture at games, both in Atlanta and on the road.

Always one to believe he was one of the guys as well as a master motivator, he became a fixture in the clubhouse as well, playing cards with his players, throwing parties, and affecting a Zelig-like affinity for their vernacular. His speech, always full of well trod clichés and aphorisms, was now liberally peppered with "awwright" and "not too shabby." In his mind, he was establishing a family-type atmosphere with the happiest bunch of ballplayers this side of the Himalayas. With some exceptions, the players responded to their quirky owner and generally enjoyed the atmosphere he created, though they were more comfortably amused than happy, and despite some short winning streaks, they were still losing.

The salesman in Turner wasn't about to let that stop him. He intended to make Fulton County Stadium "a fun and enjoyable place to watch a baseball game,"[4] and publicity director Bob Hope took imaginative license with that directive, creating something of an amusement park with his most salable commodity, Turner, at the center of attention. Bill Veeck, who had returned to baseball after reacquiring the Chicago White Sox and was one of Turner's few friends among baseball ownership, may have been an inspiration, but nothing Veeck did, with the exception of a 1979 demolition derby leading to a riot at Comiskey Field, would be as zany as the promotions Bob Hope dreamed up. Along with fireworks and scantily clad ballgirls sweeping the bases, there were halter-top giveaways, dollar bill scrambles, and Easter egg hunts. On a Sunday, the festivities might include a mass wedding on the field and a wrestling match sandwiched around the pedestrian ballgame. Tightrope walkers traversed the field, belly dancers bedazzled. There were college-style human mattress championships, motorized bathtub and ostrich races, and a competition involving pushing a ball from first base to home plate with your nose. There was even a tobacco juice spit off.

Turner was usually more than willing to participate. He was literally crushed in the middle of the human mattress. He was psychically crushed when he lost the ostrich race to a local reporter: "One lap? How in the hell can you determine the fastest ostrich in one lap?"[5] He was buoyed by his valiant and bloody victory against Tug McGraw in the baseball nose-push, wearing the scabs across his face as a badge of honor for weeks afterward (a picture of Turner, bloodied forehead to chin from his enthusiastic nose pushing would occupy a place in his office). He declined and was somewhat disgusted by the spit off, which was perhaps striking too close to home.

As willing a participant as he was, Turner really didn't need organized events. He would help the ballgirls sweep the bases, do a back flip, and sometimes even dance. During a losing streak, he brought in a minister to pray for the team. After further losses, he collapsed on the dugout with his hands across his chest. He kept a public announcement microphone at his seat and would regularly make announcements to the crowd, once offering everyone free tickets to the next day's game if the Braves didn't win (they didn't). He made calls to Bob Hope requesting special messages for the video board; "not too shabby" was a favorite. And he was an attraction just sitting in his seat, occasionally bare-chested, still chugging his beers, shouting encouragement, and reveling in the attention of the fans that constantly thanked him and sought his autograph.

The team got into the action as well. When Turner realized the new uniforms didn't include the players' names on the backs, he suggested they be added. Messersmith, though, pointed out that his name was too long and is said to have suggested using nicknames instead. Turner liked the idea so the team soon took the field with names like "Wimpy," "Heavy," and "Roadrunner" on their backs. Messersmith, whose assigned uniform number was 17, was "Channel," as in Channel 17.

Other owners and the league office didn't share in the amusement. The owner of the Cincinnati Reds threatened that he would have Turner arrested if he ever jumped onto the field in Cincinnati. Chub Feeney, president of the National League, quickly realized that Turner had usurped Oakland A's owner Charles O. Finley's title as the colorful scourge of baseball, and brought the title to his league. No, Turner could in no circumstance play cards or gamble with his players.

No, Andy Messersmith could not be used as a walking billboard for Turner's personal interests. No, Turner's proposed bonuses of $500 for every game the team won over 81, with an additional 5 percent of their salaries for every 100,000 in paid attendance over 900,000 were not allowable incentives.

The antagonism reached new levels when at a cocktail party following a World Series game that October, Turner approached Bob Lurie, owner of the San Francisco Giants, to invite him to a "surprise party" Turner was hosting in Atlanta that coming Saturday in honor of Lurie's not-yet-free agent Gary Matthews. Continuing on, Turner said, "When the time comes, I'm going to offer Matthews more money than the Giants will take in next year."[6] And not only did the party take place, with over 200 of Atlanta's elite attending, but Turner spent the night making sure everyone shook Matthews's hand while telling him how wonderful the city really was.

When Matthews legally became a free agent on November 4, Turner quickly offered a five-year deal worth approximately $1.5 million and Matthews accepted. Just as quickly, Lurie filed a tampering protest with Bowie Kuhn, the baseball commissioner, who had already had enough of Turner.

Whatever exchange there had been in November between Kuhn and Turner over the matter we don't really know, but at the winter meetings in Los Angeles in early December, Turner jumped onto a desk in the lobby of the Hilton screaming, "The commissioner of baseball is going to kill me! Bowie Kuhn is out to kill me. My life is over."[7] He continued with the same theme over the next several days, telling various reporters that Kuhn was going to gun him down right there in the hotel and sic baseball's private CIA agents on him, even going so far as to say (allegedly) that he was going to kill the commissioner before the commissioner could get to him. Anyone who had known Turner for a length of time would have recognized that all of this was a typical show for effect, meant to provoke Kuhn into a meeting he had thus far refused, but for other Braves officials it was more than a little scary, and from today's vantage point it's hard to understand how he escaped being arrested.

On January 2, Bowie Kuhn announced that he would be suspending Turner from baseball for a year and barring the Braves from the first round of that coming June's draft, but the Matthews signing would not be rescinded. Having made his ruling, Kuhn finally agreed to a meeting with Turner and a host of Atlanta dignitaries bearing the signatures of over 40,000 citizens of Atlanta petitioning the commissioner to drop the suspension and attesting to Turner's importance to the city. In the transcripts of the meeting, an obviously unbowed Turner was quoted making his own kind of appeal, with a lead-in styled directly on the noble Indians of the movies: "Great White Father, I am very contrite. I am very humble. I am sorry. I would get down on the floor and let you jump up and down on me if it would help. I would let you hit me three times in the face without lifting a hand to protect myself. I would bend over and let you paddle my behind, hit me over the head with a Fresca bottle."[8]

Kuhn was neither moved nor amused.

The Braves appealed the decision in March and the suspension was put on hold, so Turner was back in his box seat for the stadium's Opening Day of 1977, with the former governor of Atlanta and newly elected president Jimmy Carter throwing out the ceremonial first ball. Perhaps if Turner had actually voted for Carter things would have turned out differently, but the team continued losing. In May, with the Braves on a 16-game losing streak, Turner sent his manager, Dave Bristol, on a scouting vacation, and decided he himself would assume the role of manager. Donning uniform number 27 and looking the part, though totally ignorant of signs or strategy, Turner took to the dugout at Pittsburgh's Three Rivers Stadium for what would be the team's 17th straight loss.

While he'd officially hired himself as a coach, his tenure as manager lasted just that one game. An incensed Chub Feeney, feeling that Turner was making a mockery of the sport, pulled out obscure rule 20 (e), which stated that a manager could not have a financial interest in his team without special permission by the commissioner. Kuhn, citing Turner's lack of technical qualifications to be a manager and seeing the act as demeaning to the manager role, refused that permission. While the national press generally sided with Turner on this one and questioned the interpretation of rule 20 (e), Ted remained banned from the dugout. With Ted back in the stands, the Braves finally ended their losing streak, beating the Pirates 6-1 the following day.

Shortly afterward, on May 19, a judge ruled on Turner's suspension and in a split decision upheld the suspension but reinstated the Braves' rights to its first-round draft pick. Turner would make headlines during the hearings when, still on the stand, he threatened to punch one of Kuhn's lawyers in the nose for his aggressive questioning. The decision was significant, since Kuhn had very recently defended and won a case brought by Charles O. Finley that had essentially ruled that the commissioner had unlimited power over anything having to do with major league baseball. Finley, fearing that free agency was going to gut his ballclub while he received nothing in return, had preemptively sold the rights to Vida Blue to the New York Yankees, and had sued when, without precedent, Kuhn had canceled the transaction.

Turner lamented that he should have signed himself as a player since he then would have had the protection of Marvin Miller, head of the Major League Baseball Players' Association, saying the man people in baseball feared the most was Miller, not Kuhn. He continued to play his suspension for all of the publicity he could, portraying himself as the abused victim of an entrenched and stilted establishment, but the suspension was perfectly timed since he had plans covering the next several months anyway. Detractors would say it was perfectly timed for another reason; it was scheduled to end on the following April Fools' Day.

With so much attention focused on his baseball travails, most overlooked that somewhere around the time he was doing that crazed Tom-Cruise-on-Oprah routine at the Los Angeles Hilton, the FCC had approved satellite transmission of the WTCG signal. At 1:00 P.M. on December 17, 1976, the same day the approval was received, Turner Communications flipped a switch and "the superstation that serves the nation" had its signal, a totally uninspired B movie already in progress, relayed through the *Satcom I* satellite. That only four cable systems, two in the South, one in Kansas, and one in Nebraska actually picked up that signal belies the fact that television and communications would never again be the same. Even fewer made particular note that on January 4, 1977, just two days after Kuhn had initially announced Turner's suspension from baseball, Ted had acquired a 95 percent interest in the Atlanta Hawks basketball team for $400,000 and a promissory note.

As it turned out, Messersmith would have an injury-plagued two years with the Braves before being shipped to the Yankees following the 1977 season, longer than Turner's career as a manager but not what anyone would have thought Turner meant with the vow made at Messersmith's signing. Turner continued signing an assortment of free agents at exorbitant salaries and the Braves continued to lose. They would not win the World Series within five years. In fact, they set a record for consecutive appearances in last place in their division in Turner's first four years of ownership. In 1982, they would finally make it to the playoffs only to be swept 3–0.

Though their on-field performance was still less than spectacular, by 1982 they were officially America's team, with dedicated fans tuning in to watch their games on the Superstation in Farmington, Missouri; Sunbury, Pennsylvania; Storm Lake, Iowa; and Valdez, Alaska.

As the 1980s progressed, Turner would step back from the team in terms of operations, leaving personnel decisions to Bobby Cox, the general manager he rehired in 1985. After building a strong nucleus of young players, Cox would move to the dugout as team manager in June 1990. In 1991, the Braves would become the first team in baseball to go from "worst-to-first," storming back after the All-Star break and finally bringing a World Series to Atlanta. The series, played against the Minnesota Twins, has since been ranked as the best of all time, with five games decided by one run, four in the final at-bat, and three, including games six and seven, going into extra innings. The Braves wound up losing, but they were no longer losers.

A funny thing had happened on the way to the Minnesota Metrodome, though. In the course of the National League Championship series, the newly minted super-couple, Ted Turner and Jane Fonda, together with Jimmy and Rosalyn Carter, were pictured in the Atlanta stands doing the "tomahawk chop" while the stadium rocked with mock-Indian chants and headdress-adorned fans. Native Americans were incensed, especially with Jane Fonda, who had long supported Native American causes. By the time the World Series started in Minnesota, there was an American Indian Movement (AIM) organized demonstration outside the stadium and articles appearing in newspapers and magazines throughout the country. While Native Americans were not as upset with the name of the club as they were with names like the "Redskins," a term originally applied to scalps taken by European Americans, the cartoon stereotype of the "chop" was offensive and dehumanizing. Fonda would adopt a modified variation or demi-chop based on a Native American greeting, and Turner himself would try to avoid getting caught up in the shenanigans, but the general atmosphere and the "chop" itself would continue at Atlanta's stadium.[9]

The Braves would go on to log baseball's best winning percentage of the 1990s, with a solid team built around stellar pitching. Members of their pitching staff would win six Cy Young awards in the decade. The team itself would win an amazing 14 straight divisional championships, from 1991 through 2005 (1994, a strike-shortened season, didn't count), and return to the World Series in 1992, 1995, 1996, and 1999. Despite the phenomenal record, Turner would have to content himself with just one World Series Championship, in 1995, but he was thrilled to get it.

Unfortunately, the Braves' opponent in the 1995 series was the Cleveland Indians, with their offensive grinning-Indian logo known as "Chief Wahoo." On the eve of the series, one AIM member said, "Tomorrow, you're going to see two teams come together in the largest mass demonstration of cultural cross-dressing in this nation's history."[10]

Whether connected or not, Turner Productions would soon begin a series of Native American themed programming that included a six-hour historical documentary series called *The Native Americans* that aired on the Superstation in 1993, a 20-part series of reports on contemporary Native American issues that aired on CNN in 1994, and Superstation docudramas like *Lakota Woman*, *Geronimo*, *Tecumseh: The Last Warrior*, and *Crazy Horse*. All were roundly applauded for their general accuracy, shunning of stereotypes, airing of rarely publicized issues, and use of Native American artists and actors. But it still didn't excuse the tomahawk chop.

NOTES

1. Gary Smith, "What Makes Ted Run?: Ted Turner's Goodwill Games Are Only One Element of His Epic World Design," *Sports Illustrated*, June 23, 1986, 82.

2. Larry Foster, a Braves fan who called Messersmith's agent pretending to be Turner's representative, actually negotiated the deal. When the agent later called Turner back to accept the deal, the ruse was discovered, but Turner would agree to the terms.

3. Jim "Catfish" Hunter, a pitcher with the Oakland A's, had been declared a free agent in 1974 and signed by The New York Yankees, but that was as a result of the A's owner, Charles O. Finley, failing to make contractually obligated payments to an insurance trust for Hunter. Hunter's contract was nullified, and as a result so was the contract's reserve clause. Free agency was officially established with the elimination of the reserve clause itself.

4. "Yachtsman Turner Purchases Braves," *The New York Times*, January 7, 1976, Sports, 59.

5. Curry Kirkpatrick, "Going Real Strawwng," *Sports Illustrated*, August 21, 1978, 75.

6. Robert Goldberg and Gerald Jay Goldberg, *Citizen Turner: The Wild Ride of an American Tycoon* (New York: Harcourt, Brace & Co., 1995), 190.

7. Porter Bibb, *It Ain't as Easy as It Looks: Ted Turner's Amazing Journey* (New York: Crown Publishers, 1993), 112.

8. Janet Lowe, *Ted Turner Speaks: Insight from the World's Greatest Maverick* (New York: John Wiley & Sons, 1999), 87.

9. See Robert Lipsyte, "BASEBALL; How Can Jane Fonda Be a Part of the Chop?" The *New York Times*, October 18, 1991 and Rick Reilly, "Let's Bust Those Chops," *Sports Illustrated*, October 28, 1991.

10. Russ Jamieson, "Native Americans Plan Protests at World Series," CNN.com, October 21, 1995.

Chapter 9

IN THE CUP

One day his suspension from baseball was being reinstated, and on what seemed to be the next, there was Turner in Newport, readying for June's preliminary trials of the 1977 America's Cup, with a satellite receiver in tow so he could continue to watch his Braves games on Channel 17 (it wasn't bad marketing, either).

While you wouldn't know it from the mainstream press or the already larger-than-normal contingent of onlookers that seemed to follow Turner's every step, in the yachting world he was seen as something of a sideshow. The true competition, billed as the match of the century, pitted California's Lowell North and *Enterprise* against Massachusetts's Ted Hood and *Independence*. North and Hood were two of the top sailmakers in the world, outfitting three quarters of the worldwide yacht racing market between them. Both were also revered sailors, and both were skippering brand new boats built for speed to the latest hi-tech design standards. Turner was only there because he had taken an opportunity wrapped in what was basically an insult.

Courageous, which Hood had skippered to victory in 1974, had been secured by Alfred Lee Loomis Jr. soon after he was asked to manage Hood's 1977 campaign, but Hood wanted a new boat built to his own design. Using *Courageous* as the base for his new design, Hood would find that she was actually below legal weight for a 12-meter and would need to be modified. With costs for designing *Independence* and modifying *Courageous* starting to get out of control, Loomis approached Turner to gauge his interest in sailing *Courageous* in the spring warm-ups and making an undesignated contribution to the syndicate's coffers. There was a kicker, however; come June, Hood would choose whichever boat he preferred, leaving the slower boat for Turner. In essence, Turner was being asked to waste his time and money for a chance to revisit his humiliation of 1974.

Not one to let insult stand in the way of opportunity, or to be flabbergasted by the impudence of Northeastern elites, Turner understood that it was his money that Loomis was really after, so he upped the ante, pledging to cover nearly a third of combined campaign expenses with the understanding that *Courageous* would be his to sail no matter what happened in the warm-ups. It was an offer Turner knew Loomis couldn't refuse.

Second chances don't come frequently for America's Cup skippers, once fired they generally don't get a second chance, but then Turner never adhered to general understandings. He had been hell bent on getting that second chance and on getting *Courageous*, and both were now his. Turner had lived for three years with the echo of Britton Chance's words that *Courageous* would have lost to *Intrepid* in 1974 had Ted been at her helm. If it was widely acknowledged that *Mariner* was a slow boat and a design fiasco, there was also a growing consensus that while Turner's grit and determination made him a superb ocean racer, he lacked the skills and attention to compete at the top of closed-circuit match races like the America's Cup. That view may have flown in the face of the plaudits Turner had received in the first years of his ocean racing success, which had been attributed to the same skills he was now found to be lacking, but Ted himself had some lingering doubts. When asked in Newport why he would want to come back to the America's Cup after the ordeals of 1974, Turner replied that it was due to his "latent inferiority complex."[1]

Though he had bested both Hood and North in another match race in March, taking California's prestigious Congressional Cup for the first time in seven tries and winning by a hefty margin, no one expected that that would have any relevance in Newport. The Cal-40 boats used in the Congressional Cup were assigned by a drawing of lots, and Turner was acknowledged as an excellent skipper of second-hand and unfamiliar rigs. Things would be different in the America's Cup, where both opposing skippers would have the chance to become familiar with their new boats, built specifically to be faster than *Courageous*, whose added weight would tend to make her slower in light to moderate winds though faster in heavier gusts. Of course, Turner preferred the low pre-race expectations and being considered the underdog. As one writer in *Sports Illustrated* had put it, "He loves to battle with his back against a wall. If there is no wall close by, he will go miles out of his way to find one."[2] It also allowed him to inspire his troops with one of his patented us-against-the-world speeches that he had used with the billboard company, Channel 17, and even the Braves. On this occasion, he suggested that his crew of well-heeled, ivy-league educated, experienced sailors were blue-collar toughs who would rely on their street smarts to overcome the professional technicians of the opposing teams.

But the crew had as much to prove as Turner did. Gary Jobson, the tactician—basically the in-race strategist who watches conditions and competing boats and relays instructions to the skipper—was a little known 27-year-old from Toms River, New Jersey. More than half of the rest were retreads from the *Mariner* campaign, people who had been crewing with Turner for years and who had met with even greater, if less vehement, disdain from Britton Chance in 1974. It didn't hurt either that Loomis was proving to be overbearing, looking to restrict the press and crowds that flocked around Turner, curtailing visitors from the clubhouse where Turner and the crew slept, and missing no opportunity to make it clear that *Courageous* was the second-class boat.

Though he stayed away from bars and struggled mightily to stay out of trouble, Turner found his own cauldron-stirring issue over a problem with sails. Over the objection of Loomis, who had wanted *Courageous* fully equipped with Hood-manufactured sails, Turner made a deal with Lowell North to be supplied with some sails from his lofts. In Turner's view, he was upholding the amateur tradition in yacht racing. Loomis gave in, but at the beginning of June, North told Turner that he couldn't keep his word since his syndicate, which had financed his latest sail designs, had refused to make them available to the competition; he could provide sails made to his 1974 designs, but not the newest ones. Though Turner was having trouble getting sails from his own syndicate as well, and would finally have to rely on crew member

Robbie Doyle to pull some strings at the plant to finally get the sails delivered, North bore the brunt of his scorn.

Whatever other faults he might have, Ted had been taught by his father that a man needed to be true to his word, and nothing angered him more than someone breaking that commandment. That Turner saw the issue as an example of the encroachment of commercialism on the sport that he loved stoked the fires even deeper. Seemingly obsessed, he harangued anyone he could corner about the unfairness of it all, swearing that he would never again buy North's products and would do all in his power to ruin him. In an otherwise routine visit to the *Enterprise* in mid-June with Gary Jobson, Turner suddenly unleashed a sustained and butchering verbal attack on North that left North dumbfounded and Jobson shivering with regret. Turner's anger was again evident at a party held for the two syndicates, and he seemed on the verge of going physical until a young woman wanting to meet North stepped between the two. In a Turner-focused *60 Minutes* segment done by Walter Cronkite in July, Ted could be heard saying of North, "If they're beating us at the end I might have to sink him . . . that would be unsportsmanlike conduct, I'm sure."[3] Such comments would continue throughout the summer.

When the preliminaries finally got under way on June 17, the extent of Turner's investment in his performance was revealed when he threw up three times on the way to his first start. Once on the water, however, it was Hood and North who appeared sick. *Courageous* won seven of eight races for the month, with her one loss to *Independence* being by seven seconds. In contrast, Lowell North would win just 4 of 10 races, making some uncharacteristically poor tactical decisions in the process and having a series of mishaps with his sails. Hood and *Independence* fared even worse, taking just two of eight races. No one was underestimating Turner anymore; the match of the century clearly had a third opponent.

It was the best start since *Intrepid*'s 10 years before, but Turner wasn't celebrating anything yet and neither Hood nor North was capitulating. Despite the lopsided win totals, most of the races were won narrowly, and the top boats had a history of rounding into shape by the time the critical August trials came around. Turner was unusually demure in his post-win press conferences. In fact, the one time he appeared to be genuinely happy was when he'd actually lost a race. Maybe it was the discomfort of performing so well so early in the game, but if Turner was trying to be low key, the ever-expanding number of onlookers and television crews was anything but.

Turner had owned the Braves for a year and a half at this point and still couldn't tell you just exactly what a balk was, and to the uninitiated, and particularly from any distance, yacht racing appears to be a slow, silent Philip Glass ballet. As one Braves player admitted, it was impossible to understand just exactly what all that tacking was for. Still, while yacht racing had never been high on the list of favorite sports of the American folk, if it was on the list at all, the country seemed ever more riveted if no less mystified than the brave Brave. Maybe it was a reaction to his run-in with Bowie Kuhn, or just a perfect post-Watergate aperitif, but the irascible Turner was becoming the folk hero he had long fashioned himself.

The combustive qualities of mixing Turner with close attention by the press soon became apparent. Due to a misunderstanding, Ted and Janie had accepted an invitation to a party at a private club at Bailey's Beach that was being thrown by a wealthy Atlanta couple they didn't know. The hostess had Turner autograph about 15 copies of the July *Sports Illustrated* that featured Turner on the cover, and dragged both Ted and Janie around to introduce them to everyone as if they were best friends. According to Turner, they shot about two rolls of film that pictured Ted with one or the other of them and showed off other pictures of themselves with famous people. Turner, feeling used and out of place among a roomful of people he had no desire to associate with, noticed a young, attractive woman with a companion in his mid-sixties. When her companion turned away, Turner remembers saying, "'What are you doing with someone so much older than you?' She said she enjoyed spending his money. And I said, 'Do you get enough lovin'?' And she said, 'From that old prune? I'm horny as hell.' And I said, 'Well, maybe we could arrange to have something done about that.' Or words to that effect."[4] At some point soon after this conversation, Ted had a few words with the hostess about the couple, excused himself to go to the bathroom, and slipped out of the party unannounced.

The full truth may have been somewhere in between Ted's account and the accounts that would appear elsewhere and make their way around Newport almost instantaneously. In any case, Loomis, who had been keeping Turner on an increasingly short leash, lashed out in rage when he heard some of the second-hand accounts of the incident.[5] He threatened to fire Ted and at one point said he wished Turner were a dog so he could beat him. Understanding just how close he was to losing his chance for America's Cup redemption, Turner accepted his punishment as he had accepted the punishments from his father, even writing a letter of contrition to the owner of the Bailey Beach club when Loomis demanded he do so. The incident lost some of its venom when the club owner returned a gracious note that said he had had no complaints whatsoever in regard to the party in question, or Turner's behavior at it. He then made reference to Lincoln's legendary quote that if Grant drank too much they should find out what brand it was so that the rest of his generals could drink it, and said both Ted and Janie would always be welcome at the club.

In his later follow-up with Roger Vaughan, Turner would say, "I am always unhappy to make someone unhappy, but they had made me unhappy. I mean, if I had committed murder don't you think it would have been judged justifiable homicide after three and a half hours?"[6] Still, Turner was chastened, and he redoubled his efforts at what one newspaper termed his generally "monklike" behavior: "I do what I'm told and keep my mouth shut, and I find both very difficult."[7]

When the July trials came around, *Courageous* again seemed to be dominating the field, taking three of her first four races, with the one defeat coming on a disqualification after being first across the finish line. Then everything seemed to fall apart. On the fourth day, she was hammered hard by *Enterprise* in two races, losing one of those by the widest margin of the summer so far, 2 minutes and 46 seconds. After barely squeaking out two victories against *Independence*, now recognized as the slowest of the three boats, she would again lose two straight races to *Enterprise*.

Turner agonized, Jobson assumed blame, saying tactics had been watered down, and Doyle worked feverishly every night to retrim the sails. In the midst of it all, Turner was dining at one of Newport's better restaurants when he noticed another guest wearing a button that the *Enterprise* syndicate had printed up. It read, "Beat the Mouth," and displayed an unmistakable mustache above a large oval. Enraged, Turner went up to the man's table and tore the button from his lapel, offering to meet the man in the parking lot if he really wanted to beat the mouth. Frustration was building, and Turner had certainly heard the rumors that Loomis himself had been spotted pinning one of the buttons to a *Courageous* poster.

Tensions were eased somewhat when in their last head-to-head matchup of July, *Courageous* came from behind three times to beat *Enterprise*. But on the eve of the all-important August trials, the battle for defense of the Cup was wide open. No one knew what to make of the July results, with *Enterprise* beating *Courageous* five times out of seven, *Courageous* beating *Independence* in five of six races, and *Independence* beating *Enterprise* in four of six. While the general rule is that an early lead generally wins the day, in more than half of the races so far, 19 of a record 32, the lead had changed, and in eight of these it had changed more than once. Nineteen races were decided by one-minute margins, with the margin in 11 of those being less than half a minute.

The final trials in August would prove anticlimactic. Whatever the trouble had been with *Courageous* in July, there was no evidence of it now. Turner blew everyone out of the water, winning five straight races before suffering what would be the only loss of the month. In one race against *Enterprise* about four days into the trials, with a wind that would be too light for an official Cup race, North reverted to some of the poor tactical decisions he had made in June and *Courageous* wound up winning by more than eight minutes. A few days later, North was fired and Malin Burnham replaced him as official skipper of the *Enterprise*. A few days after that, Hood and *Independence* were eliminated by the selection committee. It was all but official and everyone knew it. While *Courageous* readied for another match against *Enterprise*, crowds packed around the dock and Turner preened for the photographers who had managed to slip past the Loomis blockade. As *Courageous* was being towed out for the start, Turner noticed *Australia*, the aluminum 12-meter that had handily beaten the French and Swedish boats earlier in the month to become the most feared official challenger in memory. Having *Courageous* pulled up beside her, Turner led his crew in an honorary serenade of "Waltzing Matilda." With *Courageous* taking the start and *Enterprise* again being plagued by several mishaps with her sails, Turner won easily and was now 9–1 for the month.

After the race, *Enterprise* was officially eliminated in the middle of a violent thunderstorm that passed just as the selection committee readied to board *Courageous*. When it was announced that Turner and his crew had been selected as the defenders of the America's Cup in the 23rd Challenge Match, cheers rang out from crowded streets and rooftops, champagne was popped, and the crew of *Courageous* tumbled joyfully into the waters of Newport harbor. At the end of the day, when the *Enterprise* crew readied to leave a party thrown by the selection committee on Goat Island, Turner rousted up a few of his crewmates for their second and more barbed serenade of the day, "California Here I Come." The normally placid North, who had laughed off most of Turner's earlier theatrics over the sails by declaring them great publicity, would later reveal the depth of his animosity when he told a reporter for the *East Windsor Press* that he hoped "the Australians beat Turner and take the Cup home with them."[8]

While North was falling from grace, Ted seemed to be ascending to it. Though he was obviously thrilled with the victory, telling the *Providence Journal-Bulletin*, "There will never be a time in my life as good as this time,"[9] there were few overt signs of Turner's gloating. When asked about the possibility that his head could wind up under glass at the New York Yacht Club, the conjectured fate of the first American skipper that might, as North wished for Turner, lose the Cup to a foreigner, a relaxed Turner replied, " . . . even if I lose I don't think they'd take my head. They don't allow mustaches yet down at the New York Yacht Club."[10]

While certainly not dismissing his own part in the win, he praised the teamwork and attitude of his crew, the skillful tactical work by Jobson, and, most of all, the brilliant job Doyle had done with the sails. The entire *Courageous* crew would have enthusiastically agreed; Doyle's sails outperformed those on *Independence* and *Enterprise*, and *Courageous* would not have won without them.

A few days later, Turner and Janie received invitations to a special dinner at the White House to be held on September 7 in celebration of the recently signed Panama Canal treaties. While he had long been on a first-name basis with kings and had even taken his Braves and WTCG staffers to Plains, Georgia to play a softball game against Jimmy and Billy Carter late in 1976, this was the White House, with a guest list that included Gerald Ford, Lady Bird Johnson, Coretta Scott King, and Muhammad Ali, so it was a particular honor. Not only did he attend, but he received an introduction from the President himself, who cited his representation of the United Sates at the America's Cup while chiding the less stellar performance of the Atlanta Braves. Not at all shabby, though he didn't have a chance to send Bowie Kuhn an autographed copy of the guest list to follow up on the cover story from the July issue of *Sports Illustrated* he'd sent him earlier.

Back in Newport, there was still sailing to do, but Turner was showing no sign of the anxiety that had been obvious before the June trials. Having dinner at a Chinese restaurant with Alan Bond, manager of the Australian syndicate, he said, "I'll show you how hot I am," and cracked open a fortune cookie containing the message, "A precious possession will soon be yours."[11] Gary Jobson, seeming equally relaxed, laid out a detailed account of how each boat would handle itself in the upcoming challenge; it would prove remarkably prescient.

In the first race on September 13, which both boats handled very conservatively, *Australia* seemed to take the lead at the start and held the more advantageous position. At the first mark, however, *Courageous* was ahead by as much as a minute and would hold the lead to win by one minute, 41 seconds. Gary Jobson aptly summed it up: "They aren't slow. They aren't fast either."[12]

On September 16, *Courageous* took the second race by one minute and three seconds, with *Australia* having closed a wider gap near the end. After the race, Turner, saying he was having a nicotine fit, asked the gathered media for a cigar or some chewing tobacco and gave the clearest signal yet that he considered the outcome a foregone conclusion when he referenced his father, as he so often did at his proudest moments: "I wish he could come back and see me, you know? Like in Carousel? The dead father, when he comes back to see his daughter at graduation? Damn! We were good friends."[13]

The following day, *Courageous* won again, beating *Australia* by the widest margin yet, two minutes and 32 seconds. When a reporter asked whether the results would be the same if the boats were switched, Turner, thinking it the height of stupidity, said, "We're used to our boat [. . .]. Noel is used to his. It's like asking [. . .] what would happen if we switched wives. Noel is used to his wife and he likes her better than mine. And I like mine better than his." He then added with perfect comedic timing, "She ain't much, but she's all I got."[14] It didn't seem to matter to him that Janie was in the room; he enjoyed it, and more importantly so did his audience. Janie herself didn't laugh.

In the final race on September 18, everything followed form; Turner would take a substantial lead within the first 2 miles of the 24-mile race, and hold it until the end, winning by two minutes and 25 seconds. As *Courageous* crossed the finish line, cannons boomed, a raucous cheer went up from the crowd, and horns from the largest spectator fleet ever to witness the America's Cup blared continuously. Turner raised his arms in triumph and lit a cigar as *Courageous* was taken under tow in the middle of a wild swell of boats that followed as closely as they could, one throwing a few cases of beer onto *Courageous*'s deck. With fireboats sending streams of water into the air and the Goodyear blimp descending close overhead, the crew hugged and started gulping beers. More than once, Turner raised his shirt to young women on the accompanying boats and shouted, "Show me your tits!" a phrase that would become synonymous with the post-victory celebration and Turner himself.

Within the hour or so it took to tow *Courageous* into Bannister wharf, two-drink Turner got drunk. When the boat was docked at the wharf, the crowds surged all around and Loomis jumped aboard *Courageous* with champagne, followed by wives, lovers, and sordid hangers on, who all—even a reluctant Turner—tumbled into the harbor. Janie watched from the dock as Turner called to her while clutching wet-shirted buxom young beauties at either side of him. The Swedish team shoved a bottle of Aquavit into Turner's hands to help him celebrate. Somehow, Turner, with both Jobson and Janie now by his side, waded through the dense and boisterous crowd that pressed around him as he made his way down Thames Street toward the post-race press conference. Entering the huge wooden shed behind the National Guard Armory, where hundreds of reporters and an equal number of photographers and television crews awaited, Turner was greeted with thunderous applause, which he accepted as if he were Caesar himself. When Ted was finally seated beside Jobson, each lit a victory cigar as the Australians sang a spirited rendition of "Dixie." As Alan Bond, the manager of the *Australia* syndicate, began to speak and the cameras whirred, Ted noticed someone stashing his Aquavit below the table. He blurted out, " . . . give me that you dumb [. . .],"[15] and proceeded to slide under the table to retrieve it. Turner's head soon bobbed up again, plastered with a wide, self-satisfied grin, and followed by the source of his pride, a bottle of Aquavit in each hand. Pleased with his rescue mission, he took a long chug from one of the bottles.

When he finally had a chance to speak, Turner struggled to keep his eyes open and stay on his feet as he searched through his mind for words: "I never loved sailing against good friends any more than the Aussies. I love 'em. They are the best of the best. The best . . . of the best."[16] After getting some direction from Gary Jobson, who was in nearly as bad shape, Turner soon thanked his crew, who took the opportunity to hoist him on their shoulders with a cheer and carry him triumphantly from the room. Once outside, Turner bolted through the streets of Newport on his way back to the dormitory, where Carl Helfrich, an old friend of Ted's father, helped Janie put him to bed. His last words of the evening before falling into a deep sleep were, "Wouldn't the old man be proud of me tonight?"[17]

The entire scene proved every fear that Turner's detractors had of him and set their stiff upper lips quivering with embarrassment. To journalists, however, Turner was a pleasant dream in the midst of an event that was normally as exciting as watching grass grow. Better yet, the whole act had been caught on camera. By morning, Captain Courageous, the moniker Turner had chosen for himself and emblazoned on buttons and t-shirts following his victory in the trials, had been usurped in newspapers throughout the country with what would prove a more lasting nickname, Captain Outrageous.

Turner wasn't apologizing. He claimed that in the excitement of winning he had forgotten about the press conference and asked what state people think Super Bowl champions are in three hours after a win. In any case, no coverage is bad coverage, and as he had been quoted earlier, "If being against stuffiness and pompousness and bigotry is bad behavior then I plead guilty."[18] Detractors could say what they would, but he had upheld the tradition of amateurism in yachting and won the Cup with what would prove to be the last amateur crew in the history of the event, and he did it convincingly, in any and all conditions. Noel Robins, the skipper of *Australia*, went so far as to say,

"I think we were up against the best defender that's ever been given the job of defending the Cup."[19] If his victory wouldn't silence all of the critics of his sailing skills, it at least quelled his own self-doubts, and surely no less important in Turner's eyes, it expanded his stage and firmly established him as an American icon. Maybe he just could be elected president after all.

There were signs, though, that even reaching this pinnacle failed to provide him the expected sense of accomplishment. Turner was soon saying it was just a boat race and was not as if he had won the World Series. As he would tell Roger Vaughan, "I don't know what to do with the rest of my life. Sailing has gotten so professional I don't even like it anymore."[20]

NOTES

1. Roger Vaughan, *Ted Turner: The Man behind the Mouth* (Boston: Sail Books, 1978), xvii.

2. Coles Phinizy, "Staging a Battle Royal on the Briny," *Sports Illustrated*, July 4, 1977.

3. *60 Minutes*, Walter Cronkite, July 24, 1977, http://www.cbsnews.com/video/watch/?id=4578655n.

4. Vaughan, *The Man behind the Mouth*, 23.

5. Some of the comments had him leaving with the young woman in question, making rude remarks to the hostess, and offering to have sex with several of the older women in attendance. Turner was most upset with the last, and pointed out that anyone who knew him would know that wasn't true.

6. Vaughan, *The Man behind the Mouth*, 24.

7. Steve Cady, "A Brash Captain Courageous," *The New York Times*, September 19, 1977, Sports, 60.

8. Robert Goldberg and Gerald Jay Goldberg, *Citizen Turner: The Wild Rise of an American Tycoon* (Harcourt, Brace & Co.), 203.

9. Ibid., 211.

10. Ibid., 213.

11. "Defending the America's Cup," *TIME*, September 19, 1977.

12. Ibid.

13. Curry Kirkpatrick, "Going Real Strawwng," *Sports Illustrated*, August 21, 1978.

14. Vaughan, *The Man behind the Mouth*, 201.

15. Christian Williams, *Lead, Follow, or Get out of the Way: The Story of Ted Turner* (New York: Times Books, 1981), 152.

16. Vaughan, *The Man behind the Mouth*, 207.

17. Goldberg and Goldberg, *Citizen Turner*, 217.
18. "Defending the America's Cup," *TIME*.
19. Goldberg and Goldberg, *Citizen Turner*, 216.
20. Vaughan, *The Man behind the Mouth*, 33.

Chapter 10

NEWS CABLE

In the late 1970s, Ted Turner was a journalist's dream, a colorful, boisterous, good-time redneck providing an endless array of great copy. But
the idea of Ted Turner being associated with serious news would have
been the basis of a good stand-up comedy routine. His Superstation
was still serving the nation with the FCC minimum of 40 minutes of
news per day, with 20 minutes of that being Turner's own production of
Bill Tush's irreverent *17 Update Early in the Morning*; "no news is good
news" was practically its motto. As Turner had told Roger Vaughan in
1974, "The news is the biggest rerun on TV anyway. Which would you
rather watch? Alfred Hitchcock or the news?"[1]

Actually, Turner Communications was producing an honest-to-
goodness local news show in 1978, since they had somehow managed to
make WRET, their all but overlooked Charlotte, North Carolina UHF
station, the local NBC affiliate. Turner himself says he had first thought
of doing cable news before he even had the Superstation on a satellite
in late 1976. Few remember his ever mentioning the notion in that
time frame, but Harold Rice of RCA Americom, who had worked out
the deal for Turner's lease of a transponder on *Satcom I*, said Ted had explained his plans for a news network at that time, and Legaré Van Ness,
a longtime crewmember on Turner's boats, mentioned Turner talking
about doing news even earlier with some crown heads of Europe that
he knew from sailing competitions.[2]

The idea of round-the-clock television news itself seemed pretty laughable at the time. The broadcast networks had budgets of over $200 million a year to produce a half-hour news show each day and maybe a news/talk show in the morning, and extrapolating from that made the idea daunting to say the least. Then you had delivery. There wasn't enough VHF bandwidth to build a separate news network. In 1978 there were approximately 200 UHF stations nationally, but many of those were clustered and patches of the country had none. Even if you chose to go that way you would have to do an awful lot of underwriting to get the independents switched over to 24-hour news, and you would still be left with the frustratingly fickle reception problems. Cable was in a maximum of 13 million homes nationwide, virtually none in major cities, and it wasn't Nielsen rated. The idea was a non-starter. Jerry Levin at Time Inc.'s HBO division is said to have considered the idea in 1977 and come to that very conclusion, HBO itself was still not showing an annual profit in 1977, so what Levin may have been investigating seems a mystery; a pay-per view news channel? HBO was running a 70-hour-per-week schedule of sports and movies at the time, so maybe he thought of filling the downtime with news and hoping that would attract additional subscribers.

As Turner had said in 1976, if he was smart he never would have bought a UHF station in the first place. Scorning research, seeing televised news dominated by the broadcast networks, and focused on growing cable as a technology, cable news seemed a good idea that no one else was pursuing. With his raw idea known by only a select few at Turner Communications, Ted decided to call Reese Schonfeld to explore what might be involved. Schonfeld had worked in news since 1956 and was currently running what had been his own creation, the Independent Television News Association (ITNA), which provided and shared world and national news among a small but growing number of independent television stations across the country. Over the past several years, Schonfeld had occasionally pitched to Turner and his head of programming the idea of joining the association, only to be rebuffed. He also remembered meeting Turner in 1974 while he was in Atlanta to speak with Sid Topol at Scientific Atlanta about an earlier venture he had inadvertently been involved in. His prevailing impression of Turner was that he was more than a touch unbalanced. Still, when Schonfeld received a call from Turner in September of 1978, he had already laughed off Ted's idea to make the rinky-dink UHF Channel 17 a national network. Yet Turner had done just that, and by this time the channel was received in two million cable-equipped homes. To a man who lived and breathed news, the possibility of a 24-hour news channel was the opportunity of a lifetime, and since he figured you would have to be at least partly crazy to entertain financing the idea in the first place, Schonfeld decided he would at least fly to Atlanta at his own expense to see where it might lead.

At their first exploratory meeting, Turner told Schonfeld he had already decided on Cable News Network (CNN) as the name of the venture, since it would both promote the medium and lead to subscriber expectations of receiving the station as part of their service. In Turner's original vision, the channel was to have four half-hour blocks—news, sports, finance, and women's issues—that would rotate throughout the day. But Schonfeld wasn't interested in that; there was nothing wrong with the content of the blocks, but he wanted live news and a flexible schedule. Turner agreed. As was typical for the always rushed Turner, it took about 15 minutes to discuss the basics: whether the news channel could be based in Atlanta, the number of satellite dishes and other equipment needs, and possible headline talent. With that out of the way, Turner placed calls to both Jerry Levin at Time Inc. and Russ Karp at Teleprompter, the two biggest cable systems in the country at the time, offering each of them one third of the network; both declined. To the initially skeptical Schonfeld, it was clear Turner was serious, but it was also clear that Turner was in a fact-finding stage, preparing for the upcoming Western Cable Association show in December where he would float the idea and gauge interest. Nevertheless, Schonfeld was ready to cast his lot with someone who had been a total blank at the mention of one of the brightest stars in the news industry, Dan Rather at CBS.

When word of Turner's plans got around to the staff at Turner Communications, most were incredulous. They knew Turner enough to know his plans were serious, but like Mazo and Roddey at Ted's initial foray into television, they thought the chances for success were negligible. One day a sign appeared on Turner's desk. It read, "please, Ted! don't do this to us! if you commit to a venture of this size you'll sink the whole company."[3] Ted left the sign on his desk and went on with his business.

With Terry McGuirk accompanying him, Turner went off to Anaheim, site of December's cable show. While he knew that the network would need to be a basic cable service, Turner had decided that he would need to charge 15 cents per subscriber per month if it was to have any chance of surviving. While cable had been growing steadily over the previous few years, its penetration amounted to about 18 percent of total television homes. In 1980, the year Turner was planning to launch the network, the only borough of the prime New York market receiving cable was Manhattan, with the other boroughs still mired in various stages of planning. Given his presumed monthly operating expenses, CNN could break even by reaching 8 of the 13 million existing cable homes and selling $800,000 in advertising, both ambitious targets.

With McGuirk armed with contracts and a letter stating that once they had commitments for 500,000 of their target subscription base the Cable News Network would be primed for launch on January 1, 1980, Turner made his pitch to the NCTA board. After he'd explained his plans, the reaction of the board was generally encouraging. But when he had McGuirk distribute the contracts and insisted everyone sign on the spot, the atmosphere changed. In response to them joking that they hadn't even read the contract yet, Turner said, "*Take* a minute or two, but I need an answer before you walk out of here."[4] Still, few were ready to sign on to a half-baked idea that stood a better-than-even chance of never materializing, so Turner tried again, saying, "If it doesn't work, we'll go out of business and you can quit without paying us."[5] By the end of the conference, he had received very few signed contracts, and a dejected Turner, disappointed at failing to sell a product that should have sold itself, called Schonfeld and told him the idea would have to be shelved.

In early 1979, RCA announced plans to launch a new satellite, named *Satcom III*, to address the burgeoning cable market; the launch was scheduled for December 10 of that year. With interest in satellite programming at a fever pitch, if Turner failed to act soon he risked losing the chance at securing a transponder that could carry the CNN signal. However, without subscribers, even Turner was hesitant to move ahead. As a hedge, Turner put WRET on the market. He had already determined that any hope of financing his news venture would require selling the Charlotte station, now an NBC affiliate, and since he now solidly identified himself with cable, it would make sense to sell it in any case.

But subscribers weren't his only worry. While there may have been relatively little fanfare at the launch of Turner's WTCG Superstation, by April of 1979 it was available in 46 states and had nearly five million subscribers, with 400,000 added in April alone. At the same time, the clamor of complaints from baseball, Hollywood, and the big three broadcast networks about the effects of cable, and particularly superstations like Channel 17, had reached a fevered pitch. Claiming copyright violations, all were lobbying heavily for a form of "retransmission consent" that would essentially be an end run around the 1976 Copyright Act, stipulating that before cable operators or a superstation could transmit distant signal programming to new markets, they would first need to obtain permission from local broadcasters and the owners of the content being transmitted. If retransmission consent were to be adopted, owners were unlikely to give consent to Turner's Superstation or any cable operators without extracting usurious fees. As Turner said at a news conference in Washington, adoption of the proposals would "Wipe us out. I mean it would be a complete wipeout,"[6] and he didn't mean Channel 17 but the whole of the still nascent basic cable industry.

At the same news conference held on April 23, Turner also announced that his Superstation would begin airing adult prime-time programming consisting primarily of PBS retreads as well as similar quality commercial-free children's programming each morning and afternoon. Saying that as of April 30, Channel 17 would cut commercial time by 21 percent, he went on to make it clear that the event itself was something of a commercial for his side of the retransmission debates, saying, "The networks have had 30 years to upgrade television and haven't done it yet. They need competition to make them better, and I promise to provide that competition."[7] For the first time in public, he would mention his plans for a news venture that he assumed would be at least a year away. Just two days later, the FCC proposed rules that would end limits on importation of "distant" signals by cable operators, signaling their rejection of the calls for retransmission consent. Robert L. Schmidt, president of the Cable Television Association, termed it "a major victory for the viewing public,"[8] but the fight was far from over. Congress, spearheaded by California's Lionel Van Deerlin, chairman of the House Subcommittee on Communications, had proposed rewriting the Communications Act of 1934, and retransmission consent was a major point of focus.

While Turner had gone public with a vague reference to his Cable News Network, he had yet to get back to Schonfeld and was still reticent to commit. In early May, 43-year-old Bill Lucas, vice president of player personnel and effectively general manager of the Atlanta Braves, the highest ranking African American official in baseball, suffered an unexpected cerebral hemorrhage. Stunned by the news, Turner decided he had done enough stalling and in a phone call to Schonfeld later that same day, he said, "None of us are going to live forever. Let's do this f[. . .]ing thing."[9]

A few days later, Schonfeld signed an agreement to become CEO and president of CNN. He had six months remaining on a new contract he had signed with ITNA while awaiting Turner's decision, but Ted wasn't concerned. Rushing him over to the WTCG building, Turner waved the signed agreement in the air and shouted, "I want y'all to meet Reese Schonfeld. . . . He's gonna be the president of CNN! And I'm gonna be the most powerful man in America! . . . the *two* of us."[10] With inertia behind him, Turner was ready to push ahead. He wanted Schonfeld to accompany him to the National Cable Show in Las Vegas, which was starting on May 20 in less than two weeks. There, they would announce that CNN was a reality, and Turner thought it would really be good if they could introduce a "name" anchor at the same time. ITNA contract or not, Schonfeld was now on Turner time.

One week later, Turner was in Washington to appear as a witness before the House Subcommittee on Communications. In 1976, he had angered broadcasters with his vigorous endorsement of cable, but charmed the committee members. History doesn't always repeat itself.

Things got off to a bad start when the always-moving Turner was left sitting hour after hour as the representatives of the forces allied against cable testified about the dire consequences that would surely ensue should Congress not restrict cable. Jack Valenti, president of the

Motion Picture Association, decried the disparity between what cable had been paying for programming and what the networks paid, flipping Turner's cherished big-guys argument by citing several conglomerates highly invested in cable systems. "I don't think we need to have welfare programs for companies like G.E. and Times-Mirror," he would say.[11] Norman Lear, creator of the sitcom hit *All in the Family*, argued that transmission of syndicated reruns to every market in the country undercut producers' ability to make independent syndication deals with each of those markets, contending that the proceeds from those deals were what made producing the shows viable in the first place. The commissioners of baseball, basketball, and hockey claimed that the transmission of "distant" games was undercutting gate receipts and destroying their product by making sports commodity viewing. "Let's not wait for the autopsy, the threat of bankruptcy is real,"[12] averred Bowie Kuhn.

By the time he was finally called, it was nearly 4:00 P.M., and as a dour Turner took his place at the witness table, he realized that there were few members of Congress left in the room. Now openly fuming, Turner's delivery dripped with disdain as he commented on how the empty room had been full for his opposition's statements. Just then the committee members filed back in from a roll-call vote on the House floor. Thrown further off stride, Turner tried to assume the mantle of a protector of decency and the downtrodden little guy who was fighting the organized purveyors of filth, violence, and mindless garbage like *The Newlywed Game*. But with a tone devoid of any hint of his natural ebullience, he wasn't winning anyone over. He hinted that retransmission consent had been added to the subcommittee's agenda by an agent of the broadcasters and said that the subcommittee should leave all these matters to the FCC, which knew what it was doing, implying that Congress did not. When he was asked about running his news program at 3–4:00 A.M., he replied, "That's accurate. We have a hundred percent of the audience then."[13] But while the audience laughed, Turner uncharacteristically ignored them, reinforcing the sarcastic contempt that had run through all of his testimony.

On May 20, Turner flew to Las Vegas for the start of the cable show. A press conference to announce CNN was scheduled for the next day. Schonfeld would be arriving with Daniel Schorr, the "name" anchor

Turner wanted on hand for the announcement. A longtime news veteran, Schorr had worked for *The New York Times* and CBS, where he had been a protégé of Edward R. Murrow, and had gone on to win three Emmys, open the CBS Moscow bureau, and serve as the network's senior Watergate correspondent. He'd resigned from CBS after refusing to divulge his sources for a report on covert activities at the CIA and FBI, feeling the network had given him little support, and had since been working with Schonfeld at ITNA. Turner had spoken with Schorr's agent but had yet to meet Schorr in person and he was relying on Schonfeld's judgment that he was the right person for the job. While interested, Schorr had yet to sign a contract and knew little about Turner or cable television, but he had heard about Bill Tush's tongue-in-cheek news show and still had some misgivings. Schorr wanted assurances that he would not be asked to do commercials or forced to do or say anything that would compromise his journalistic integrity. He also wanted to know if he would have the right to resign if Turner himself said anything that Schorr found embarrassing. Between running in and out of the room and being constantly interrupted by phone calls, Turner seemed to respect Schorr's concerns, saying, "Look, I have a news conference at four o'clock this afternoon, at which I'm going to announce that starting June first of next year I'm going to start the operation of Cable News Network. If you will appear with me, if you want to work with me, let's sign something, anything."[14] Telling Schorr to write down anything he felt necessary as an addendum to the contract, Turner assured him he would sign it. Schorr would make history twice that day, with the announcement that he was the first official full-time employee of what would be the world's first 24-hour televised news network and with the most unique contract ever drafted.

At the news conference the next day, Turner touted cable as the medium of the future and CNN as a venture that would change the face of American journalism. Introducing future president and CEO Reese Schonfeld, as well as Daniel Schorr, who had signed a two-year contract as chief Washington correspondent, Turner went on to cite several names already signed up to do commentary: Roland Evans and Robert Novak, Dr. Joyce Brothers, astrologer Jean Dixon, Bella Abzug, Phyllis Schlafly, and medical reporter Dr. Neil Solomon. With a plan to charge 15 cents per subscriber per month for cable systems also carrying his Superstation and 20 cents for those systems carrying only CNN, cable systems would also receive two minutes of commercial time per hour, allowing them to sell local advertising. Schonfeld said that by its launch date of June 1, 1980, CNN planned on having 10 domestic bureaus as well as sources from around the world and at least 200 employees, 50 of whom would be reporters or anchors. Specifics on what would fill all those hours of news time were sketchy, but he mentioned live feeds and the heart of the day being a two-hour newscast scheduled from 8:00–10:00 P.M. Eastern Time, followed at 11:00 P.M. with a half hour of sports news. Schorr expressed excitement for the budding venture, faith in both Schonfeld and Turner, and faith in the future of CNN. Now that it was more than a notion, many more cable operators were willing and eager to sign on.

Within a week or so, Turner was back in Washington to appear before the Subcommittee on Communications of the Senate Committee on Commerce, Science, and Transportation, chaired by Senator Ernest Hollings of South Carolina. After squandering his opportunity before the House, Turner made sure to listen to his lobbyists this time as they prepped him for his appearance. On the rare occasions that Turner tries to follow a script, he tends to be terribly wooden, so he was provided a set of talking points that could be included in a free-flowing exchange. Advised that the Senate setup would be different than that in the House, with three witnesses seated together at one table, he was told to avoid the center seat, since that position would always be addressed second and tended to get the least attention. Turner made sure he was the first person at the table and grabbed the chair at the right, usually the last position in order of testimony, giving its occupant the best opportunity to rebut previous responses. Seated in the middle seat was Gene Jankowski, president of the CBS Broadcast Group, and on the far left, Henry Geller, Assistant Secretary for Communications and Information and Administrator of the National Telecommunications and Information Administration (NTIA), the leading proponent of retransmission consent.

Geller started by positing retransmission consent as nothing but the free marketplace and that cable had been benefiting under a government-imposed unfair advantage that undermined the concept of free market capitalism. He argued that making cable operators deal directly with program owners would impose nothing more than payment of a fair price for their programming. Jankowski intoned the virtues of American television, which offered wide and varied choices in entertainment, and underscored Geller's point that there was a basic unfairness in broadcasters bearing significant rights fees while cable operators paid a minimal application of charges as outlined in the 1976 Copyright Act.

When Turner's time came, it was immediately obvious that his recent House experience was behind him. He cited the huge pretax profits the networks were experiencing, the movie industry's record box-office receipts, and the 50 percent increase in pretax income being enjoyed by the eight major production companies. He had been able to grab the big-guy argument and demonstrate that cable was apparently having none of the negative effects its opponents had been screaming about, a point he would later lure Jankowski into admitting. Summing up, Turner said, "What alarms me most is that when a small businessman comes in, works hard, plays by Mr. Ferris's [Charles Ferris, Chairman of the FCC] rules and has a few successes, the first thing these huge organizations do is try to use their power and influence to change the name of the game."[15] As usual, after backing himself into a corner, Turner was on his game.

With the senators already seeming to favor Turner's views, both Geller and Jankowski made statements that undercut their own arguments. Geller mentioned that the networks were currently reaching 98 percent of American homes and then elicited a discussion that Jankowski felt disparaged the content of network programming. There was nothing Turner would have preferred to rebut, saying that the networks programmed "lowest-common-denominator junk . . . They'll cover . . . a Senator getting into trouble, but they don't cover the good Senators. They don't cover the good things."[16] He wasn't missing a beat. When the opposition said the existing broadcast news system was one reason the country was as strong as it was, Turner replied that the country was in fact weaker than it had been for at least 40 years, asserting, "I think it's the networks' poor treatment of the national news they spend twenty-two minutes a day covering. I've already announced starting a twenty-four-hour-a-day satellite cable news network . . . and we're going to give you gentlemen an opportunity to really air your views."[17] Scorning what he portrayed as mindless network fare, praising the benefits of cable and its capacity to carry an ever increasing number of networks devoted to serious and special interest programming, and warning of the joined powers of the networks, Turner said, "I hope that the American people have a lot more choice, because—I mean it would be a horrible country if there were only three magazines, wouldn't it, gentlemen?"[18]

The Senate subcommittee would never add retransmission consent to its proposed bill; within weeks, the House subcommittee would remove it from its own proposal.[19]

Buoyed and victorious, Turner returned to Atlanta. On June 2, as Ted and Janie celebrated their 15th wedding anniversary, Turner enlisted Bunky Helfrich, his longtime friend and crewmate, to the CNN cause. Bunky was a successful architect, and Turner wanted his help in developing a headquarters for his growing cable empire. Later in June, after having negotiated to sell WRET to Group W, the broadcasting arm of Westinghouse Electric Company, for $23 million, Will Sanders announced that after nine years he would be leaving Turner Broadcasting. While he was a close confidant of Ted's, being a chief financial officer for Turner was akin to being a pinball bouncing from crisis to crisis. However, the timing of the decision would indicate that he, like Mazo before him, thought Ted's newest adventure would destroy the company. Bill Bevins, an accountant from Price-Waterhouse, would replace him as Chief Financial Officer

In early July, Turner called Bunky and wanted to meet to look at the Progressive Club on Techwood Drive, formerly a country club. It was a 21-acre property with a horseshoe driveway that led to a 90,000-square-foot redbrick mansion fronted by a portico with tall white columns. From the front, it was a two-story building, but there was a full basement and the property sloped downward so the windows on the back wall of the basement looked out on a green lawn and well landscaped grounds with trees and gardens. Turner wanted the top floor to serve as office space, with the first floor for the Superstation and the basement for CNN, with six to seven receiving dishes placed on the back lawn. Altering it from its present condition to something that could serve as television space would require massive demolition work and rewiring, but there were just 11 months before the scheduled launch and Turner had not yet even made an offer on the property; Bunky could see the potential, but it wasn't going to be easy.

Turner would be in and out of Atlanta throughout the rest of July as he spent time with his family and did some sailing. Near the end of the month, in the middle of planning an undertaking that was certain to be a financial drain for at least the next three years, Turner bought St. Phillips Island, a 5,000-acre marsh island just off St. Helena Island in Beaufort County, South Carolina for $2 million. At the beginning of August, he was off to the village of Cowes on England's Isle of Wight, site of Cowes Week, a series of ocean races leading up to the 605-mile Fastnet Cup race named for Fastnet Rock off the southern coast of Ireland, which boats round for the return to Plymouth on the British mainland. With over 300 yachts competing in Fastnet, it is arguably the most prestigious prize in yachting. Turner had broken the course record with *American Eagle* in the 1971 Fastnet race, but he had wound up taking fourth place on corrected time. He really wanted to win this one.

Schonfeld was proving to be not only as driven as Turner, but also as indefatigable. He had finally come to an agreement that would let him out of his contract with ITNA on August 1. By July 1 he had already enlisted an old boss, Burt Reinhardt, to join the effort as vice president of CNN, and he was actively searching for additional staff while pushing for his "open newsroom" vision. He wanted CNN not just to present the news but to show news as a dynamic organism, with background staff scurrying around, phones ringing, and teletype machines and printers whirring. It had never really been done before and no one else thought it would work, but Schonfeld was adamant. With Turner away in England when Schonfeld finally got to Atlanta in August, one of the first things he did was take Bunky Helfrich, who had never designed for television before, to Vancouver, Canada to show him a small working newsroom that was as close to his idea as he could get.

On the Isle of Wight, Turner and his crew of 19, including Gary Jobson, Turner's 16-year-old son Teddy (in his first year of ocean racing), and Christian Williams, who was in the process of writing an autobiography of Turner,[20] manned Turner's 61-foot *Tenacious*. Winning her class in the overnight kickoff Channel Race, *Tenacious* continued her success in the remaining days of races in the swift-flowing Solent channel that separates the Isle of Wight from the island of Great Britain.

The last of the Cowes Week races, the New York Yacht Club Challenge Cup was named in honor of the schooner *America*, which had bested the Royal Yacht Squadron in the Solent 128 years before, establishing the since unbroken string of American victories in the America's Cup. As the race got underway, the wind picked up and the sea heaved. *Tenacious* was nearly capsized when it was broadsided by a massive wave, but her spinnaker ripped apart instead and the boat righted itself. Thirty of the 52 boats starting the race failed to complete the course. Despite the fright and the disappointing finish in that final race, *Tenacious* was awarded the Queen's Cup as the best performing boat of the week.

Two days later, on Saturday, August 11, Fastnet was underway. The 303 competing yachts started in shifts, the smallest first, with *Tenacious*, being one of the larger boats, getting off about 1:30 P.M. Though the crew had split into groups that would take rotating shifts of four hours on and four hours off, with Turner and Gary Jobson as the helmsmen, all were on deck to experience the spectacle of the large fleet. Conditions were near idyllic, with a good moderate breeze and little rain, and by evening *Tenacious* had caught and passed the smaller boats and was sailing at the head of the fleet with the five maxi-yachts in the race. By Sunday evening, they reached Lands End and headed into the Irish Sea. By Monday, *Tenacious* sailed alone and an unusually quiet Turner was apparently feeling very good about his chances at winning and perhaps even breaking his own course record. At about 6:30 P.M. that evening, *Tenacious* was rounding Fastnet Rock in a light rain when Peter Bowker, the navigator, received weather reports of a heavy overnight storm that was approaching. The storm had Force 8 winds (39–46 mph) that were expected to increase to Force 9 (47–54 mph). Bowker reported the news, saying, "My goodness, I guess we're going to have a lot of breeze."[21]

Gale force winds are always a concern, but in the shallow depths of the Irish Sea, waves tend to build steeper and higher than they do in deeper waters, so everyone knew that this bit of breeze was going to mean a rough time ahead. In *Call Me Ted*, Turner reports that after thinking about the large number of small boats in the race he predicted to his crew that 20 men would die that night.[22] Jobson took over the helm at 8:00 P.M. as the winds grew and the sea turned turbulent. At midnight, Turner was back at the helm and the winds had climbed to

Force 10. Waves were 20–25 feet high and the boat listed and heaved while the decks were hit by two-foot walls of water. As the night progressed, the waves reached closer to 30 feet, but the crew's true fear was of rogue waves, at least one of which should form each hour according to statistics, at heights twice that of the prevailing average.

Having rounded Fastnet Rock, *Tenacious* was racing upwind, a much more enviable position than the smaller boats that were struggling with it, but she was carrying too much sail and in danger of being dismasted or worse, so the crew needed to unclip from the relative safety of their harnesses to wrestle the mainsail down and replace it with a small triangular storm sail. Though the sail change helped, the seas were still growing, pounding the boat, lifting and dropping her, and slewing her upwind and down while Turner struggled to keep some semblance of control and continue racing. When the running lights of the smaller boats were soon seen blinking from red to green in front of them, it was obvious they were having an even harder time maintaining control, but there was little *Tenacious* could do but hope to avoid ramming one. Trying to get a reading on the Scilly Isles, which lay off the southwesternmost tip of Great Britain and were a graveyard for ships, Bowker took his radio direction finder (RDF) on deck, where he hoped there would be less interference, only to be thrown sideways when a huge wave hit, slamming him into the steering wheel with enough force to knock it several inches out of line and losing the RDF overboard while he himself came within inches of doing the same.

At 4:00 A.M. on Tuesday, August 14, Jobson again took the helm as the crew started hearing slivers of radio reports on the unfolding tragedy happening around them. By 6:00 A.M., conditions in the Irish Sea, where the smaller boats were, grew even worse as gusts reached 90 mph, and the wind switched from south-southwest to northwest. As the crests of waves from the northwest met the crests of the waves from west-southwest, they produced a greater frequency of narrow, steep rogues approaching 50 feet. By the time a thoroughly exhausted Jobson was coming off his shift at 8:00 A.M., the conditions *Tenacious* was facing were different; the waves were still massive, but they were long and rolling with steadily decreasing crests. At noon, Turner announced the storm over and had the mainsail reset as *Tenacious* raced forward, crossing the finish line at 10:30 P.M.

While they had performed well and were happy to be back at harbor, the celebrations were short lived. Plymouth was abuzz. Scores of boats were missing, reporters were everywhere, and thousands of people shuffled along the docks and in the streets hoping for word of loved ones. Rescue ships and helicopters were in constant motion and a Coast Guard cutter started unloading bodies. Only now did they realize that they had been through the worst disaster in the history of yacht racing. At his hotel room, Turner was bombarded with phone calls. Overnight, *Tenacious* had been listed as missing when she couldn't be located, and no one realized she had already finished the race; Turner and his crew were presumed dead.

Finishing 40 minutes short of Turner's record time in 1971, *Tenacious* was declared the winner on corrected time. Journalists now flocked to Turner in increasing numbers, peppering him for quotes on the terror he'd been through and how he had managed to survive. They got more than they bargained for. Turner would say, "It's no use crying. The king is dead, long live the king. That ain't the ultimate storm, but I will grant you it was rough. We couldn't have taken much more wind and continued to race, but we were never in danger. If I thought we were in danger, I would have pulled out. Really, I'm amazed that more weren't lost."[23] The stunned reactions he received made him go further, and he dug his hole deeper and deeper: "The trouble with the boats sailing today is that they're designed to beat some stupid racing rule . . . The reason we got through all right was that I've got a big, strong boat. And I made sure I had one before I entered the race";[24] "The people who didn't have those went to the big regatta in the sky";[25] "Like any experience, whenever you come through it you feel better. We're not talking about the other people that died, but to be able to face it all and come through it is exhilarating. Sailing in rough weather is what the sport is all about."[26] He also made reference to the Spanish Armada, saying, "It had to happen sooner or later. You ought to be thankful there are storms like that, or you'd all be speaking Spanish."[27] When placed next to the stories of survivors who had lost shipmates, harrowing tales of sailors cleaving to lifeboats split in two and a skipper, together with his helm itself, being blown overboard, as well as reports that 15 sailors and 3 crew members of an observation boat had died, 24 yachts had been lost or abandoned, 136 sailors had been rescued from the sea, and less than 85 yachts had managed to complete the race, Turner's comments were found to be crude and insensitive.

Turner had been competing in a sport he knew could be dangerous, and despite the tragedy, he was disappointed when it was announced that a small boat named *Illusion*, which finished two days after *Tenacious*, supplanted her as winner on corrected time. After a restless night, however, it was discovered that *Illusion* had come into harbor for safety and had never rounded Fastnet Rock; *Tenacious* had won after all.

While the world protested Turner's comments, Dennis Conner, who would soon go on to his own America's Cup fame and who had also finished the race, said his biggest regret was the fact that his yacht didn't win: "It's no worse than the Indianapolis 500 race. We'll take our chances. The danger is part of it. We were racing all the time."[28] In a similar vein, Gary Jobson said, "The real mistake was that they let everybody and his brother in the race."[29] No one protested.

Back in the United States, Schonfeld and Bunky Helfrich were in Vancouver when word was relayed that Turner was missing. No one was really sure what to do, or what would happen if Turner had actually died in the storm. Helfrich, choosing to believe all was O.K., made a joke out of it, "I hope Ted is locked in his cabin. He goes crazy in a storm. We used to call him Captain Panic."[30] Schonfeld thought there was enough support at the company to keep CNN moving forward no matter what the outcome might be. Dan Schorr, who was at a cable show with Terry McGuirk when the news first came in, would later let the audience know that despite the ongoing news reports, Turner was in fact safe, something they would know if CNN were on the air.

Gary Jobson would say that Turner's demeanor and performance at the helm during the worst of the storm was his finest hour as a sailor.

NOTES

1. Roger Vaughan, *The Grand Gesture: Ted Turner, Mariner, and the America's Cup* (Boston: Little, Brown & Co., 1975), 99.

2. Although Turner has never mentioned it, the idea may well have come from Roy Mehlman's 24-hour Newstime, a slo-scan news service featuring still photos and voiceovers. Mehlman had initiated the satellite-delivered service in 1977 and charged cable systems five cents per subscriber. Mehlman was one of Turner's first hires for CNN, where he worked in the Sales department.

3. Hank Whittemore, CNN, *The Inside Story: How a Band of Mavericks Changed the Face of Television News* (Boston: Little, Brown & Co., 1990), 31.

4. Ibid., 38.

5. Ibid.

6. Ernest Holsendolph, "Adult Specials Set for Cable Systems: Atlanta Broadcaster Will Present Prime-Time Programs, News, and Shows for Children," *The New York Times*, April 24, 1979, Business & Finance, D17.

7. Ibid.

8. Ernest Holsendolph, "FCC Proposes Eased Cable Rules to Increase Television Competition," *The New York Times*, April 26, 1979, A1.

9. Reese Schonfeld, *Me and Ted against the World: The Unauthorized Story of the Founding of CNN* (New York: Cliff Street, 2001), 52.

10. Whittemore, *CNN, The Inside Story*, 43.

11. Ernest Holsendolph, "Law to Curb Cable TV Competition Urged: Sports Leaders Tell of Impact," *The New York Times*, May 15, 1979, Business & Finance, D4.

12. Ibid.

13. A video clip of Turner making this comment during his testimony, archived from Bill Tush's *17 Update Early in the Morning*, is available on Bill Tush's Web site, http://www.billtush.com/clips/ted.mov.

14. Whittemore, CNN, *The Inside Story*, 48.

15. Christian Williams, *Lead, Follow or Get Out of the Way: The Story of Ted Turner* (New York: Times Books, 1981), 181.

16. Ibid., 183.

17. Ibid., 184.

18. Ibid., 187.

19. Van Deerlin, a strong proponent of First Amendment rights, but also one of the primary advocates for this form of retransmission consent, would lose his bid for reelection the following year, and the issue, though still bandied about, would not be seriously considered for some time. It would, in a different form, finally be enacted as an either/or option pertaining to cable carriage of the broadcasters' own signals under the Cable Television Consumer Protection and Competition Act of 1992 and new FCC regulations of 1994. Though controversial, these rules are still in effect, with broadcasters able to use retransmission consent to negotiate with cable operators over the terms by which the operators would be allowed to retransmit the broadcast channel's signal or, alternately, choose to invoke a reconstituted form of the "must carry" concept.

20. Turner had signed a contract with Simon & Schuster, Inc. to do an autobiography and enlisted Williams, a friend, to write it. Simon & Schuster would reject the book, which was later published as a biography by Times Books in 1981. Simon & Schuster would win a lawsuit for breach of contract, recovering the $25,000 advance it had paid to Turner. In 1986, Simon & Schuster would sign another contract with Turner for an autobiography, paying him a $1.2 million advance. Turner would choose author and jour-

nalist Joe Klein for this attempt, but Turner, who was apparently unhappy with how the book was progressing, canceled the contract and returned the advance. An autobiography titled *Call Me Ted* would finally come to fruition in 2008. Turner again turned to a friend, Bill Burke, former president of TBS, to aid with the writing.

21. Williams, *Lead, Follow or Get Out of the Way*, 216.

22. Turner, *Call Me Ted*, 173.

23. Jack Knights, "An Awesome Warning from the Sea," *Sports Illustrated*, August 27, 1979.

24. Williams, *Lead, Follow or Get Out of the Way*, 232.

25. Robert Goldberg and Gerald Jay Goldberg, *Citizen Turner: The Wild Rise of an American Tycoon* (New York: Harcourt, Brace & Co., 1995), 245.

26. United Press International, "Turner, the Winner, Credits Crew and Jib," *The New York Times*, August 16, 1979, C21.

27. Gary Smith, "What Makes Ted Run?" *Sports Illustrated*, June 23, 1986.

28. "Fastnet Search Comes to End," *The New York Times*, August 17, 1979, A19.

29. Joanne A. Fishman, "Many Fastnet Crews Lacked Experience," *The New York Times*, August 19, 1979, Sports, S9.

30. Schonfeld, *Me and Ted against the World*, 124.

In January 1974 Ted Turner was named Yachtsman of the Year for 1973. Only Betsy (Gelenitis) Alison, five-time Yachtswoman of the Year, has equaled or exceeded Turner's four wins, for 1970, 1973, 1977, and 1979. AP Photo/David Pickoff.

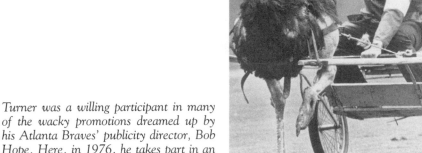

Turner was a willing participant in many of the wacky promotions dreamed up by his Atlanta Braves' publicity director, Bob Hope. Here, in 1976, he takes part in an ostrich race. AP Photo.

On May 11, 1977, in the visitors' dugout of Pittsburgh's Three Rivers Stadium, Turner awaits what would prove to be a one-game stint as manager of the Atlanta Braves. The Braves proceeded to lose their 17th straight game, and National League President Chub Feeney invoked an obscure rule to forbid Turner's assumption of the manager's role. AP Photo.

In September 1977, crew members carry Turner off from the press conference following his win of the America's Cup. Gary Jobson, Turner's tactician on Courageous, is at the extreme left. (AP Photo/J. Walter Green)

Turner shakes hands with Thomas Wyman, CEO of CBS, at a Senate committee hearing held on July 14, 1985. At the time, Turner was attempting a hostile takeover of the network, and in June Wyman had unleashed a blistering personal attack on him. AP Photo/Lana Harris.

A proud Ted Turner visits the newsroom of his Cable News Network in Atlanta, 1985. AP Photo.

Russian President Boris Yeltsin, center, exchanges laughs with Ted Turner during the Goodwill Games' Opening Ceremonies in St. Petersburg, Russia, on July 23, 1994. Turner, who created the games in 1986, believes they helped end the Cold War; Yeltsin credited CNN coverage of the 1991 Soviet coup attempt as a pivotal event in the dissolution of the Soviet Union. AP Photo/Alexander Zemlianichenko.

Turner and wife Jane Fonda arrive at the Environmental Media Awards on October 17, 1994. Turner received an award for the "Gorillas Will Be Missed" episode of Captain Planet and the Planeteers, *the animated series he created. AP Photo/Mark J. Terrill.*

Turner presents UN Secretary-General Kofi Annan with a crystal globe at a June 1997 ceremony marking reception of CNN International on UNTV. On September 18 of the same year, Turner would pledge $1 billion in support of UN projects around the globe. AP Photo/Marty Lederhandler.

Steve Case, America Online's chairman and CEO, left; Gerald Levin, Time Warner's chairman and CEO, center, and Turner at the December 10, 2000, announcement that AOL would be acquiring Time Warner. Within two years, there was nothing left to applaud and all three were effectively sidelined. AP Photo/Stuart Ramson.

At a December 11, 2002, press conference celebrating the fifth anniversary of his $1 billion pledge to the UN, Turner could still joke and feel happy that he had made his pledge when he could—despite the loss of some $6.5 billion and the turmoil at AOL Time Warner. AP Photo/ Kathy Willens.

Turner, who in 1976 named Bill Lucas the first African American General Manager in baseball, is among the select few to have their footprints added to the Civil Rights Walk of Fame at the Martin Luther King National Historic Site in Atlanta. At the induction ceremony in 2005, Turner joined fellow honorees Hank Aaron, far left; Nancy Wilson, second from left; and Valerie Jackson, wife of Atlanta Mayor Maynard Jackson. AP Photo/John Bazemore.

Chapter 11

ALMOST

By October of 1979, an old two-story wood-frame house next door to Channel 17, recently rechristened WTBS, was chosen as the planning site for the operation.[1] Previously a halfway house for troubled teens, the building shook every time a bus went by, lights flickered at the slightest wind, and rain seeped in from the roof. Lou Dobbs later remembered his first trip to Atlanta and the building that coming January, saying, "When I walked into this old ramshackle run-down Georgia Colonial I thought 'These people are nuts!' "[2] It was the general consensus.

To reinforce that consensus, one day Turner greeted some new staffers by saying, "We are going to beam this shit all over the world. And you know what? We are going to beam this shit to Russia too, because you know what? One day they are going to bomb our asses . . . but I don't know if they all speak English."[3]

On December 6, RCA launched *Satcom III* from Cape Canaveral. Four days later, engineers fired the solid fuel rocket meant to put it into geostationary orbit 22,300 feet above the equator, but when they tried to reestablish radio contact there was no response; no one would ever know exactly what happened. With just more than six months until CNN's own launch, the loss of the satellite left the network with no vehicle to distribute its signal. While the mood in Atlanta was grim, Turner, in Anaheim for the Western Cable Show, didn't seem fazed in the least. He went on to announce that CNN was on schedule and had just signed Bristol-Myers to the network's first major advertising commitment of $25 million over 10 years. At a breakfast meeting, Terry McGuirk and Turner were assured by Harold Rice, vice president at RCA Americom, that RCA would do everything necessary to get CNN some satellite space. Options were limited, however, because the next scheduled launch, *Satcom IV*, wouldn't be ready until the following December, and the use of any alternate satellite would mean cable operators would need to install a second receiving dish since each one focused on receiving signals from one satellite. Nevertheless, Jim Kitchell assured the *New York Times* that RCA was "doing a lot of wheeling and dealing to straighten this thing out. At any rate, we're proceeding with our plan."[4]

January 1980 passed with no clear resolution to the satellite issue. The sale of WRET, Turner's only source of funding, was being held up at the FCC. Work on the Techwood Drive headquarters was proceeding, but Atlanta had yet to approve a $10 million bond issue. In a 2007 interview with the Academy of Achievement, Turner said, "In my study of history, Erwin Rommel in the desert never had enough petrol for his offensives against the British to finish them. He had to depend on capturing fuel supplies from the British by attacking so quickly and catching them off guard that they would retreat and leave some petrol for him to finish. It was dicey, and it didn't always work, but I knew that was what I was going to have to do."[5] He was in a fix; if he delayed now, someone else could jump in and establish a 24-hour news service before him, but the operation was sputtering before there was any realistic hope of capturing petrol.

On January 20, Turner was named the 1979 U.S. Yachtsman of the Year, the first person to ever receive the award four times;[6] it was welcome news for a change, but it did nothing to alleviate Turner's concerns of the moment. By February, staffing for CNN was picking up steam and the management team had been rounded out. Alec Nagle, executive producer from the ABC affiliate KGO-TV in San Francisco, and Ted Kavanau, who had been executive producer and then news director for New York Channel 5's *10 O'Clock News*, were hired as senior news producers; Ed "no relation to Ted" Turner, who had started *10 O'Clock News* for WTTG in Washington and later ran *10 O'Clock News* in New York, was hired to oversee newsgathering; George Watson, recently replaced as Washington bureau chief at ABC became vice president and managing editor of the Washington bureau; Mary Alice Williams from NBC became an anchor and New York bureau chief; Lou Dobbs became the national financial anchorman. Deals were being made with United Press International (UPI) to provide wire services from their operations in major European cities, with local independents and network affiliates to provide CNN with local reports in exchange for CNN's national and international news, and with a growing list of cable operators.

In mid-February, Turner was off in the Bahamas taking part in the SORC series when RCA lawyers decided that because they would open themselves to lawsuits if they showed any preference whatsoever in assigning available space on *Satcom I*, they would hold a lottery for the available space and try to fit the losers on other satellites. When Turner was informed, he flew back to Atlanta and gathered up Schonfeld, Terry McGuirk, Ed Taylor, and lawyers Tench Coxe and Bill Henry and went to the RCA offices in New York for a meeting. Tench Coxe opened the meeting by making a case based on need and public interest. He then brought up a clause Will Sanders had added to their original 1976 contract with RCA Americom that granted Turner right of first refusal on two additional *Satcom I* transponders. Since Turner had never previously ceded that right, Turner was choosing to exercise it now, and unless that right was honored by RCA it would be a breach of contract. Andy Inglis, president of RCA Americom, and the RCA lawyers took the position that there was nothing they could do; their contracts clearly specified that all RCA obligations were contingent on a successful launch. They were quoted as saying, "Listen, Ted, we've looked at your contract with us. You've got no backup. You've got no legal ground. You'll just have to live with it."[7] Turner exploded, belittling Inglis and demanding to speak with the CEO of RCA, "because I'm gonna break this company into so many small pieces that all of you will be looking for jobs."[8] He grabbed Inglis by the shirt and advised him that if he owned any RCA stock he should sell it, yelling, "When I get done with you, it ain't gonna be worth a dollar a share!"[9] Screaming into the face of an RCA lawyer for 20 minutes, Turner said he was going to the FCC, he was going to the Justice Department, he would drag RCA through the mud in every public venue he was granted, it was his life they were talking about, every penny he had and then some. He would accuse RCA of collusion, of refusing his space on the satellite in order to protect the interests of their NBC television division. He had already spent $34.5 million in CNN startup costs and would sue them for every cent. "I'm a small company, and you guys may put me out of business, but for every drop of blood I shed, you will shed a barrel!" Turner vowed.[10]

The room was quiet. No one, not even Turner's own contingent knew what to do. Turner continued to pace around the room. The RCA group asked to be excused so they could talk it over. They still felt confident they would win a lawsuit, but there were no guarantees and they didn't doubt for a second that Turner would do everything he had just spent an hour telling them he would do. Turner attracted press and attention like no one else, and he would use it, so all in all they would be better off trying to compromise. When they returned, they said they could offer Turner a *Satcom I* transponder on a temporary basis while a court decided which interpretation of the 1976 contract was correct. If RCA won the case Turner would need to move the CNN signal from the satellite by December 1, 1980, while if Turner won CNN would stay on *Satcom I*. In either case, Turner would agree to drop all claims for damages. RCA would do nothing to hinder a quick resolution of the case. A relieved and happy Turner agreed.

On February 28, Tench Coxe filed a suit in the U.S. District Court for the Northern District of Georgia and asked for an immediate injunction granting CNN a transponder on *Satcom I*; the injunction was issued within a matter of days. The FCC would have to weigh in as well, but for the moment, Turner had a temporary reprieve.

In mid-March, Turner hired Robert J. Wussler as executive vice president of Turner Broadcasting Systems, Ted's second-in-command. Wussler was a former president of the CBS television network, and in his 21 years at the network he had also served as executive producer of CBS news and president of CBS sports. Wussler was well respected throughout the industry and had contacts at all of the networks, but though he was not officially connected to the CNN operation at all, Schonfeld was no longer the highest ranking executive of Turner Broadcasting with a news background.

By the beginning of April, just two months before launch, Turner had been able to secure a loan with First Chicago, but he had to accept terms calling for 25 percent interest. He was paying out $400,000 a month in interest alone in addition to payroll for nearly 300 CNN employees and all of the associated equipment and infrastructure costs. Vultures were circling and the FCC had not yet ruled on the satellite or on the sale of WRET, which was held up by a dispute between the station manager and a local African American group that had accused him of discrimination in hiring and failure to air minority-related programming. With time running out, Turner, accompanied by his lawyers and Hank Aaron, then on the board of Turner Broadcasting, set up a meeting with the group. When the coalition had voiced its complaints, Hank Aaron rose and pointed to Turner saying, "This guy isn't prejudiced."[11] He assured the coalition that Turner would honor whatever commitments he made, and Turner, falling to his hands and knees, begged forgiveness and pleaded, "You gotta let me sell this station or I'm a goner!"[12] With a promise of donations to the United Negro College Fund and other charities, as well as a promise that Schonfeld would meet with a prominent spokesperson in Washington to discuss minority-hiring policies at CNN, an agreement was reached.

On April 17, the FCC both approved the sale of WRET, giving Turner a badly needed cash infusion of $20 million from Westinghouse, and made a preliminary ruling agreeing with the District Court of Northern Georgia that CNN could keep its *Satcom I* transponder on a temporary basis until the case was fully resolved. By April 24, 1981, the matter was finally settled when appeals to the court and the FCC from rivals for the transponder had been exhausted. The FCC ruled unanimously that the 1976 contract was lawful under the Communications Act of 1934 despite showing Turner preferential treatment; CNN would stay on *Satcom I*.

A week before the launch, speculation was booming. Turner called the network news nothing more than a headline service that he didn't even watch. He claimed, "Newspapers have traditionally provided the depth that television hasn't, but the fact is newspapers are getting too expensive to produce and deliver. As energy resources run out, trees are becoming more precious. The Cable News Network will deliver a newspaper electronically and by the most efficient and inexpensive means available: satellite and cable."[13] But most believed CNN was vastly underestimating the costs of producing news. Roone Arledge, president of ABC News, said, "We run through the $30 million they're talking about spending for a year in two or three months,"[14] and that was just to produce one half hour of "headline news" each day. Burton Benjamin, vice president and director of news at CBS said, "On a big story, say in Cuba, or Iran, you might have to send two or three crews. One trip like that and you could feed a family of four for a year."[15] Turner himself had won grudging respect for having given free rein to Schonfeld and the news pros he'd assembled, but most figured that to last for less time than his money.

On June 1, 1980, Turner recorded the Marine Corps Band playing "Nearer My God to Thee," which legend said was the last song played on the Titanic. He sent the recording to a small studio buried in the mountains of Tennessee where, in the event of nuclear war, it would outlast the major city-based networks and be CNN's first signoff as well as the final television signal from planet earth. On a sultry afternoon, 300 guests mingled beneath two tents on the front lawn of the new TBS headquarters on Techwood Drive in a scene that could have been lifted from a Robert Altman movie. The flags of Georgia, the United States, and the United Nations arced around a podium at the head of the circular drive. Following statements from CNN and cable representatives and a benediction service given by a local Baptist minister, the CNN feed flickered to life at precisely 6:00 P.M., with Turner giving a dedication speech promising to work to bring the people of the world together "in brotherhood and kindness and friendship and in peace."[16] At the completion of Turner's speech, the CNN feed switched to a camera zooming in to the six satellite dishes behind the building as the audio played a string of what was meant to be reporters signing on from cities and countries around the world. As the camera finished zooming to a single satellite, the feed cut to a scene of the open newsroom, the titles CNN and then THE NEWS CHANNEL rolled by, and two anchors were shown at the news desk:

"Good Evening. I'm David Walker."
"And I'm Lois Hart. Now here's the news."[17]

With the entire CNN staff focused on the triumphs, trials, and tribulations of their first hours on the air, Turner found a small room where he could catch the last innings of his Atlanta Braves beating the Los Angeles Dodgers by four runs; he took it as a good omen. The next day he was off to Newport with Bunky Helfrich. The two had already spent a good part of April and May practicing for another attempt at a defense of the America's Cup, and now it was time for the June trials.

Initial reactions to CNN's first days on the air were mixed. Most agreed it showed promise and professionalism and applauded the live feeds. But despite all the pre-air talk of revolutionary coverage, critics said it was too often the same headline news Turner had deplored, "all-news radio with photographs."[18] Those early days were filled with flubs, lost feeds, unexpected switching, dead air, and anchors rambling incoherently as the producers tried to figure out what to do next. At one point, a cleaning woman walked in on Bernard Shaw while he was on the air and emptied his wastebasket. None of this bothered Schonfeld, who thought it just proved that CNN was not a pre-canned product. He was with Frank Zappa, who would come to praise the "randomonium" of it all. The networks had their own name for it, "Chicken Noodle News," and staffers were calling it "Chaos News Network." Whatever you called it, whatever its failings, Schonfeld, Helfrich, Turner, and the entire CNN team had pulled off nothing short of a miracle in getting this off the drawing board and on the air in little more than a year. As a CNN salesman in New York would tell *Newsweek*, "If Ted predicted the sun will come up in the west tomorrow morning, you'd laugh and say he's full of it. But you'd still set the alarm. You wouldn't want to miss the miracle."[19]

In Newport, Turner seemed to be running out of miracles. The seven-year-old *Courageous* was proving overmatched, not only against Dennis Conner and *Freedom*, whose team had raised over $3 million for the campaign and trained nearly non-stop throughout the year, but in a reversal of 1977, also to Russell Long and *Clipper*, a boat Turner owned and had leased to Long to serve as a trial horse. At the end of the June trials, *Courageous* had won only one of seven races. By the end of July, with Turner having a combined record of 2–19, Turner was no more than a trial horse himself. After anther dismal showing in August, again having managed just one win out of eight races, Turner's *Courageous* was the first boat eliminated. Turner had already told the

New York Times, "At the time I committed myself to the America's Cup defense, I did not anticipate starting a cable news network. If I had known what my business commitments were going to be, I might not have done it."[20] When asked when the fun had gone out of the competition, he told William N. Wallace, "It never was a blast. The computers, all the gobblydegook isn't sailing. There's too much laboratory stuff."[21] For Turner, who had helped to revolutionize ocean racing, the sport in general had passed him by. Within a few months he would have his entire 1981 racing schedule canceled, saying, "I'm through with sailing! I don't even want to talk about it. I'm sick of sailing! I'm sick of professionalism."[22] No one really believed him, thinking he was far too competitive to walk away, but by the spring of 1981, both *Courageous* and *Tenacious* had been sold. Captain Outrageous was done, at least as far as sailing was concerned.[23]

Summing up Turner's racing career, Jobson, who had been sailing with Turner since the 1977 America's Cup, said, "We probably sailed in three hundred races, and I bet we won half of them. There will never be another record like that put together."[24]

Bob Wussler would later say, "[Turner] told me 20 times that he never liked sailing. He said 'You know, Bob, I got cold and wet.'"[25]

NOTES

1. WTBS had been Turner's first choice for the station's call letters in 1970, but they were already being used by MIT's student radio station so he settled on WTCG. In 1979, Turner worked out a deal with MIT's station in which he would make a donation to the station and it would change its call letters to WMBR. On August 21, 1979, The Turner Communications Group changed its name to Turner Broadcasting Systems, Inc., and on August 27, WTCG would change its call letters to WTBS.

2. Ted Turner with Bill Burke, *Call Me Ted* (New York: Grand Central Publishing, 2008), 187.

3. Reese Schonfeld, *Me and Ted against the World: The Unauthorized Story of the Founding of CNN* (New York: Cliff Street, 2001), 138.

4. Les Brown, "Satcom III Upsetting Cable TV," *The New York Times,* December 13, 1979, The Home Section, C32.

5. Academy of Achievement, Robert Edward (Ted) Turner, http://www.achievement.org/autodoc/page/tur0int-2.

6. Betsy (Gelenitis) Alison would win the U.S. Yachtswoman of the Year award a record five times between 1981 and 1998. Turner remains the only man to have won the award four times.

7. Hank Whittemore, *CNN, The Inside Story: How a Band of Mavericks Changed the Face of Television News* (Boston: Little, Brown & Co., 1990), 91.

8. Ibid., 90.

9. Schonfeld, *Me and Ted against the World*, 116.

10. Ibid., 117.

11. Turner, *Call Me Ted*, 188.

12. Ibid., 189.

13. Tony Schwartz, "The TV News, Starring Ted Turner," *The New York Times*, May 25, 1980, Business & Finance, F1.

14. Ibid., F4.

15. Ibid.

16. Whittemore, *CNN, The Inside Story*, 143.

17. Ibid., 144.

18. John J. O'Connor, "TV: The Early Days of 24-Hour News," *The New York Times*, June 5, 1980, Home Section, C23.

19. Whittemore, *CNN, The Inside Story*, 164. Quoting the June 16, 1980 issue of *Newsweek*.

20. "America's Cup: Skippers View Race," *The New York Times*, January 13, 1980, Sports, S11.

21. William N. Wallace, "Turner's Courageous Eliminated in Trials," *The New York Times*, August 26, 1980, B14.

22. Robert Goldberg and Gerald Jay Goldberg, *Citizen Turner: The Wild Rise of an American Tycoon* (New York: Harcourt, Brace & Co., 1995), 270. Quoting the May 12, 1981 edition of *The Washington Post*.

23. Dennis Conner and *Freedom*, designed by *Courageous* designer Olin Stephens, went on to defend the 1980 America's Cup, defeating challenger *Australia* 4–1. Conner would go on to be the skipper in four additional America's Cup Challenge series, becoming the first American defender to lose the Cup in 132 years in 1983, when *Liberty* was defeated by *Australia II* by 25 seconds in the Cup's first ever seventh and deciding race of a Challenge round. Conner would regain the Cup as a challenger in 1987 in what would prove to be the end of the 12-meter era of the America's Cup. In a contentious 1988 series, challenger *KZ* of New Zealand, a swift big boat, pushed the boundaries of the prevailing rules. Conner answered in kind, easily defending the Cup with the first non-monohull boat in Cup history, the catamaran *Stars & Stripes*. He would lose the Cup again with an unsuccessful defense in 1995. Conner had also served as tactician and starter on *Courageous* in her successful 1974 defense in the Cup finals. Conner is now known as "Mr. America's Cup."

24. Porter Bibb, *It Ain't as Easy as It Looks: Ted Turner's Amazing Story* (New York: Crown Publishers, 1993), 203.

25. Priscilla Painton, "The Taming of Ted Turner," *TIME* magazine, January 6, 1992.

Chapter 12

STEPPING UP

In July of 1980, CNN had its first major defection. George Watson was never comfortable with the way news was being presented at the network, and he didn't appreciate being disrespected by some of the CNN management team. When Kissinger was set to give a speech at the Republican National Convention, Watson thought it would signal a turning point in the history of the Republican Party. In retrospect he was probably right, but Schonfeld overruled him. Kissinger was never the most dynamic of orators, but to Watson the decision signaled the triumph of style over substance. If a 24-hour schedule didn't have room for substance, the people running the schedule had a vastly different idea of news than he did. He resigned.

But if it often failed at depth and substance, if it continued to be plagued by poor writing and editing and technical snafus, CNN was redefining news. Time and immediacy provided its own form of depth, and experimentation sometimes proved compelling. CNN had a you-are-there quality akin to the early days of radio and its coverage of mining disasters, a sense of the news unfolding that brief network recaps just couldn't provide. CNN showed scenes of the Mariel boatlift, named for a harbor in Cuba from which Castro was sending his criminal and discontented to Florida beaches aboard small boats. It covered the explosion of a Titan II missile in its silo in Damascus, Arkansas, as well as the volcanic eruption of Mt. St. Helens, a fire at the MGM Grand in Las Vegas, and the scene around the Dakota in New York after the murder of John Lennon. Within hours, it aired a well-rounded and serious discussion of a Supreme Court decision limiting access to abortion, and it made a gimmicky, error-filled, but clever attempt at splicing third-party candidate John Anderson into an ongoing debate between Ronald Reagan and President Jimmy Carter from which Anderson had been excluded (later run on PBS with many of the technical problems edited out). There was precious little of Turner's "good news," but for the moment it didn't seem to bother him.

In that first year, CNN was losing $2 million a month. This was far more than projected and it overwhelmed the Superstation's record $10 million operating profit, leaving Turner Broadcasting with a loss of $3.8 million. Available in approximately 1.7 million homes at startup, the number had increased to 4.3 million by the end of 1980. However, that represented less than a quarter of homes serviced by cable systems, well below what could be expected to lure commitments from advertisers. The Superstation had significantly more viewers and it was still having trouble attracting ads, though that would be helped when a combination of pleas, reasoning, and threats saw Nielsen relent, cut their distribution requirements significantly, and begin to provide ratings for the Superstation in February of 1981, a major coup for the cable industry. By June, Turner instituted an idea to boost those ratings with the Superstation's "Turner Time" programming, which had all shows starting five minutes past the hour or half-hour. The station wound up having separate timeslot headings for its listings in *TV Guide*, and the idea worked so well it was used for years to come.

Fearing that competition could be established before CNN could become financially stable, Turner called Schonfeld into his office in late November and asked, "If we're gonna have competition, what would competition look like?"[1]

On March 30, 1981, CNN had just carried a speech by President Ronald Reagan at the Hilton Hotel in Washington and their crew was still inside the hotel when shots were fired toward the president. A major-network crew stationed outside the hotel had filmed the shooting and had pictures of a Secret Service member and Press Secretary James Brady lying wounded on the ground while the president was sped away in his limousine. The scene was chaotic. CNN's Bernard Shaw was the first to announce that shots had been fired at Reagan, the first to report the president might have been hit, the first to confirm the president had been hit, and the only network anchor to continually refer to reports that James Brady had died as "unconfirmed." CNN would also be the first network to show the president walking into the emergency room with the help of a Secret Serviceman, it would be first to report that the shooter, John Hinckley, had an infatuation with Jodie Foster and her role in the movie *Taxi Driver*, the first to provide background on Hinckley's home in Colorado and a pawnshop in Dallas believed to be where Hinckley had purchased his gun. At 10:00 P.M., CNN's *Freeman Reports*, hosted by Sandi Freeman, had interviews with two of the shooter's former schoolmates.

Being first is an important status marker in news, and "Chicken Noodle" or not, the 10-month-old CNN had an impressive amount of firsts. What it didn't have first, what it didn't have at all until Schonfeld taped its airing off ABC, were images of the shooting itself. The crew that had filmed the shooting was operating under a policy called "pool coverage," which was established during the Kennedy administration to limit the number of reporters following every move of the president. It worked by assigning a small group of rotating news organizations to cover presidential events and then provide their coverage to the larger "pool." CNN had been attempting to join the pool, but the major networks had repeatedly objected, claiming both that it was too unskilled and under-financed to be trusted and that their unions refused to handle material provided by the nonunionized CNN.

On May 11, Turner would file an antitrust suit in the Federal District Court in Atlanta, accusing the three major networks, the National Association of Broadcast Engineers and Technicians, and, audaciously, the White House, of limiting CNN's access to the news. In announcing the suit, Turner also called on Congress to investigate programming at the three networks and the motion picture industry, accusing them of "polluting the minds of our people."[2]

In August of 1981, Westinghouse Broadcasting and ABC went public with their plans to combine forces to create Satellite News Channels (SNC). Having heard of the plans as early as May, Turner had already filed a petition with the FCC to halt Westinghouse's proposed merger with Teleprompter and its 115 cable systems, again citing antitrust violations and accusing Westinghouse of engaging in a scheme to establish a monopoly in the distribution of cable news programming. The petition was denied. Now, just a little over a year since its launch, CNN was facing a major threat to its existence. Plans for the new service called for the creation of two cable news channels. The first, scheduled to launch in the spring of 1982, was to be a headline news service with the slogan, "Give us 18 minutes and we'll give you the world," and the second, scheduled to launch near the end of the same year, would offer extended coverage of breaking news and in-depth reporting on major issues, much as CNN itself. In a direct effort to undermine CNN, which was charging per-subscriber fees, both channels would be offered to cable operators free of charge.

The first of the Satellite News Channels was exactly what Schonfeld had predicted when Turner had asked him about likely competition the previous November, and within days of the ABC/Westinghouse announcement Turner pulled the schedule and budget he'd had Schonfeld prepare at the time. He'd never looked at it before and he barely looked at it now, but he called a meeting of his staff and announced that CNN would not only launch its own headline service, it would do so at midnight on December 31, 1981: "We're gonna offer everything they say they're gonna offer, except that ours will be on the air *first* and it'll be *better!*"[3]

There were plusses and minuses on both sides. CNN had been making impressive progress throughout the year, and by this time it was available in 8.5 million homes and was being added to 400,000 new homes each month. A poll found that 85 percent of viewers rated the network as excellent. It was unlikely that cable systems would carry both CNN and Satellite News Channels, so being first gave CNN advantages. As one cable operator said, "Once you give something to a subscriber, you never take it away."[4] There was also the question of satellites. Turner was working out a deal with Time Warner that would allow CNN2 to use one of their transponders on *Satcom I* in exchange for letting Time Warner sell advertising for Turner Broadcasting's stations. In contrast, Satellite News would be using a Western Union Westar satellite, meaning that cable systems would need to add a second receiving station to offer Satellite News. To most though, the war would be a financial one. As one investment banker summed it up, "It gets down to how deep everybody's pockets are, and you've got to believe ABC's are a lot deeper."[5] Despite gains at CNN and the success of the Superstation, which now reached 16.8 million homes and expected to double its 1980 operating income of $10 million, Turner Broadcasting was still going to show a substantial loss for 1981, even without CNN2, which would cost $15 million to launch and was projected to lose $1 million a month in its first year. After failing in several attempts throughout the year to secure financing, Turner had finally restructured his debt and secured a $50 million line of credit with Citibank at 3 percent over prime. With gross receipts of $54.6 million in 1980, even a healthy Turner Broadcasting was sorely overmatched against the combined ABC and Westinghouse receipts of over $11 billion.

In a war of attrition, Turner didn't stand a chance, but then Turner always relished a fight. As a grinning Schonfeld said at the original company meeting announcing CNN2, "Ted's happy—we're at war again."[6] Turner told the press, "I think we're going to beat their brains out."[7] Then, appearing on CNN's own *Take Two*, he said, "The only way they're gonna get rid of me is to put a bullet in me . . . I said it then and I say it now, that even if I knew we were going to fail when we started, I would've gone ahead and done it anyway, because even if we were only on for a short period of time we would have shown what responsible journalism on television could do . . . I don't know where we're goin', but we're goin' there in a hurry. Awwright!"[8]

The next day, Turner flew to Boston to attend a cable operators' conference and announced that, together with its plans for CNN2, Turner Broadcasting had budgeted $50 million for ad purchases to promote CNN over the coming 12 months, another $30 million to promote the Superstation, and would also launch a CNN radio network. He said the broadcast networks had "turned our people against our wonderful government, and they've turned our people against business . . . they're anti-religion, anti-family, anti-American."[9] Then he quoted a *Los Angeles Times* article from the previous weekend in which Roone Arledge, president of News and Sports at ABC, seemed to imply that ABC would withhold some news from the Satellite News Channels in order to protect ABC's own news operation, leading Turner to label them a "second-rate, horseshit operation!"[10]

Over the next months, Turner would continue his fight against the quality of the broadcast networks' programming. On October 21, he testified at a House subcommittee hearing focused on violence on television, angering Schonfeld in the process when he ordered the CNN Washington bureau to cover the hearings live, which wound up preempting coverage of a deadly Brink's armored truck robbery engineered by remnants of the radical Weather Underground and the Black Panthers. At the hearing, Turner blamed the networks for making the American public sick, saying that "the network's own television licenses should be revoked immediately and given to responsible citizens who will do good."[11] Following his testimony, right-wing Christian groups like the Coalition for Better Television (CBT) and the National Coalition on Television Violence (NCTV) echoed the same remarks. Schonfeld recalled walking in on a phone conversation between Ted and Donald Wildmon of CBT that seemed to him to have been "a conversation between conspirators"[12] Jerry Falwell, who had been buying time on CNN during this time, visited the station and Turner acted like a member of his congregation, proclaiming that television was "sex and violence . . . awful . . . shameless . . . destroying America and the family."[13] Falwell had everyone at the meeting kneel to pray that "the cloud of sex and violence on television would be lifted from the American people."[14]

Though a report by Compton Advertising, a media research agency, had predicted CNN and Turner would be run out of business by Satellite News, almost as soon as CNN2 went on the air on New Year's Eve the situation seemed to shift. A Drexel Burnham Lambert analyst said, "I think the franchise Turner has created will be very difficult to dislodge . . . I sense that ABC and Westinghouse have less enthusiasm for the services in private than they do in public. . . . the question is whether they're willing to undergo a long period of red ink in an effort to make the services work."[15]

At the beginning of 1982, CNN launched its NewsSource service. Originally the idea of Turner and a young Turner Broadcasting staffer, Tom Todd, the idea was based on the fact that smaller stations and even network affiliates often did not have access to breaking news that the networks held back for their evening newscasts. Turner decided to create a syndication service of CNN2, the first service of its kind in television news. While there was initially quite a bit of concern at CNN about what this might do to their contracts with corresponding stations that CNN depended on for local video footage, and even over how cable operators would react to selling CNN2 material to broadcast channels, it became an instant hit and has continued to be a primary source of income for the station.

On February 12, 1982, Turner would make a trip that befuddled his allies on the right and had a profound and continuing influence on both CNN and Turner himself. Cuba's Fidel Castro had been impressed with CNN's coverage of his 1981 May Day parade and speech. Castro mentioned to CNN staffers that he had been picking up the CNN signal and applauded its objective coverage. He then extended an invitation for Turner to come visit with him. Just as Turner was taking off for his visit, a young CNN correspondent, James Allen Miklaszewski, was photographing an American military adviser carrying an M-16 rifle in El Salvador. It was a direct violation of the stated Reagan administration policy, and it caused a furor in the press and within the White House itself. It was also the most important news coup yet for CNN and it came despite being outstaffed in El Salvador by as much as four or five to one by each of the broadcast networks.

Turner spent four days with Castro, talking politics, taking in a baseball game, going duck hunting, and visiting the Tropicana nightclub, and both seemed to enjoy themselves tremendously. Recounting the trip and showing pictures, Turner would later say, "I'm the only man on the planet ever to fly on Cuba's Air Force One with their president and on America's Air Force One with our president. . . . People are not all that different—all this killing and arms race is for nothing. Here's the great commie dictator we're so worried about—having a hot toddy . . . Here's us hunting. Twenty-two attempts on his life by the CIA and I'm sitting next to him with a loaded rifle! Can you believe that? . . . I could've shot him in the back! He gave me the award for shooting more [ducks] than anyone he'd ever hunted with . . . I expected Castro to be a horrible person, but he was a great guy."[16] Turner would tell Schonfeld, "Reese, Fidel ain't a communist. He's a dictator, just like me."[17] Dictator or not, Turner would be overruled when he wanted to run a promotional spot for CNN that Castro had made at his urging. After the trip, Castro had two of the ducks Turner shot on the trip stuffed and shipped to Atlanta, where Turner would display them in his office. But Ted's real gifts from the trip were in Castro's urging him to take CNN worldwide and Turner's realization that "I was just ambling through life."[18]

At the end of the same month, partly as a response to CNN's News-Source service and partly from lobbying by some staffers, the National Labor Relations Board (NLRB) and the National Association of Broadcast Electricians and Technicians (NABET) set up a vote on making CNN and Turner Broadcasting a union shop. Given Atlanta's right-to-work laws, Turner's operations had never been unionized, and that was an important consideration in having CNN based in Atlanta in the first place. Turner may have liked Fidel, but he wasn't a fan of unions. Paying union salaries and using his staff in rigidly defined job duties could deal a serious blow to CNN's ability to survive. Luckily for the station, though most of the staff were young and working long hours at low wages, the cross training and experience they were gaining at CNN couldn't be duplicated elsewhere and the vote came out 156 to 53 against unionization.

May would prove to be a busy month. SNC was originally expected to launch that month, and Turner showed up at the Cable Show in Las Vegas, Nevada with an appeal to the loyalty of the cable operators and an elaborate promotional campaign complete with buttons, stickers, and a video that featured Ted in a cowboy hat making occasional comments as a paraphrased country song, "I Was Cable When Cable Wasn't Cool," played in the background. But back in Atlanta, there was another personnel problem brewing. Reese Schonfeld and Ted Turner share November birth dates, though Schonfeld is seven years older, and while each has his own style, both are headstrong, fixed in their opinions, and most comfortable in the role of dictator. Whether any organization is better off with a dictator may be open to debate, but two dictators in the same organization is never going to work. While there is disagreement over how and why it came about, everyone, particularly Schonfeld, knew that the relationship could never survive in the long run.

Turner had originally given Schonfeld wide latitude over editorial and management decisions at CNN, but as the division began to mature and the real battle with Satellite News loomed on the horizon, friction started to develop. While Schonfeld had the allegiance of most of the news staff at CNN, he also had his detractors. Bill Bevins complained that he could never get financial reports, and others complained that the "randomonium" Reese so loved was taking a toll on the functioning of the network. No one had any idea what Schonfeld would be up to on a given day. He would substitute guests on *Freeman Reports* at the last moment with no consultation, he would assign anchors to cover stories in the field without thinking to arrange for backup at the news desk, and he would dispatch reporters to locations without any planning for how long they would be expected to stay there or any arrangements for hotel accommodations. When a popular anchor, Marcia Ladendorff, had her contract come up for renewal, Schonfeld seemed to jump at the chance to use her bargaining ploy to dump her. When talk show host Sandi Freeman had her contract renewal come up soon after, Schonfeld got into a shouting match with her agent. Having heard about the altercation, Turner had a meeting with Schonfeld and suggested he read a book Ted's father had counseled him to read, *How to Win Friends and Influence People*. Schonfeld, however, was convinced he didn't need any pointers, and soon fired Freeman as well. To make matters worse, he then hired Mike Douglas to replace her at a salary of $1 million a year without even discussing it with Turner, and he did this shortly after picking up a talk show from WRC radio in Washington, *Crossfire*, with Tom Braden and Pat Buchanan, that Turner had already expressed skepticism about.[19]

On May 16, with Schonfeld just back from his first CNN vacation, Turner informed him that he would be making changes. He had renewed the contracts of both Ladendorff and Freeman,[20] and he had decided to replace Schonfeld with Burt Reinhardt. Schonfeld has since been both bitter and defensive regarding his tenure and contribution to CNN, feeling he has too often been written out of the story. Whatever his possible failings, there would not have been a CNN without him; he was the primary organizing force for the network and without his vision and knowledge of the news business it likely would never have made it to air, never mind survive. At the same time, Schonfeld has always been a big proponent of local news, and while he didn't shun national and international stories, it is hard to conceive of a Schonfeld-run operation that would focus on an international presence to the extent that CNN would. It was probably a good time for the parting. Turner himself would say, "You can't have a twenty-four-hour news network that's totally run by one person . . . and Reese wanted to make every decision himself. It just wasn't the kind of management style that was going to make the organization strong in the long run."[21]

Several of the news staffers were upset at Schonfeld's departure and were wondering about CNN's future, and Turner would give them more reason for worry just two weeks later. Over the Memorial Day weekend, both the Superstation and CNN ran an editorial that Turner taped after seeing a news report on the trial of John Hinckley Jr. In the editorial, which ran a total of 14 times that weekend on both the Superstation and CNN, Turner stated that while he was against news censorship of any type, "I am very, very, concerned that this movie [Taxi Driver] was an inspiration to John Hinckley and was partly responsible for his attempted assassination of our president."[22] He went on to say that the executives at Columbia Pictures, which had distributed the film, "should be just as much on trial as John Hinckley himself."[23] He then cited The Deer Hunter and The Warriors as further examples of the type of movies that "must be stopped," urging concerned viewers to "write your Congressman and your Senator right away and tell him that you want something done about these destructive motion pictures."[24]

It was exactly the type of personal interference that so many at CNN had feared all along. However, armed with his protective contract, Dan Schorr would offer a rebuttal of the editorial during his primetime news-cast that Monday, saying that legislation was not the way to deal with violence in films. "The First Amendment says that Congress shall make no law abridging freedom of the press," Schorr said. "I believe that violence in media is an issue, but not an issue for Congress."[25] Unlike Ted's original editorial, Schorr's commentary would not be rebroadcast, but it served its purpose. Lou Dobbs would later caution Turner, "Ted, you simply can't do editorials. It's not appropriate. It's not what you're about."[26] Turner would never again do an on-air editorial. Off air was another story; in June, he told a Veterans of Foreign Wars convention, "American network executives should be tried as traitors. They are all traitors to this country and deserve to be tried as such."[27]

On June 21, Satellite News Channel finally launched with a poten-tial audience of 2.6 million subscriber homes. Though it was dwarfed by CNN's 13.8 million viewers, it actually surpassed CNN2, which reached less than 1.5 million cable homes—though CNN2 was also being supplied to upwards of 50 broadcast stations as well. On July 9, Pan American Flight 759 crashed on takeoff from New Orleans International Airport, killing all 145 people on board. CNN reacted like a deer in the headlights, hesitant to pick up a video feed and so concerned with cost that they even initially held off sending a film crew to the site. It was some four hours before CNN would air on-scene video and they were scooped badly by SNC. CNN was looking outclassed, just as Westinghouse and ABC said it would be.

While there was no excuse for its newsroom meltdown, CNN was in a state of financial chaos at the time. The deal they had struck with Time Warner to secure a transponder for CNN2 was proving a disaster. With Warner Amex personnel selling all CNN advertising, sales were down by an estimated million dollars a month. With the country in a deep recession, experiencing official unemployment figures of 10 percent, advertising dollars were scarce anyway, but the Warner deal made a bad situation worse. The competition from a heavily funded SNC had already made banks more reluctant than ever to provide funding for Turner Broadcasting, and losing its first head-to-head major story coverage didn't help. Turner had dismissed the new channel as "18 minutes of little tiny blurbs,"[28] but he was concerned that SNC offering their channel for free and then offering cable operators a bonus of $1.50 per subscriber could cause significant problems. He accused them of trying "to buy the market and force its competitor out of business,"[29] again raising antitrust issues. In order to counter the financial appeal of SNC's offerings, CNN first dropped the fee for CNN2 and later offered cable operators a one-dollar-per-subscriber refund for three years if they agreed to carry both CNN and CNN2, effectively cutting subscriber fees by 70 percent. Bill Bevins was raiding petty cash and receipts from Superstation sales of Ginsu knives and bamboo steamers to cover CNN payroll. By September of 1982, Turner Broadcasting came within 24 hours of having its electricity turned off for being over three months behind on payments. It was getting desperate.

In December, Turner was back in Washington to testify against the Copyright Royalty Tribunal's decision to impose increases in the royalty fees cable operators paid under the compulsory licensing scheme of the Copyright Act. In some cases, the increases could be up to six times the rate the operators were currently paying. In his testimony, Turner said the new rates would put him out of business, and, in lobbying individual senators, he was seen writhing on the floor several times with what had become his familiar "I am dead"[30] routine. In his lobbying, he convinced Georgia Republican Mack Mattingly to tack an amendment onto a spending bill in front of the Appropriations Committee that would stall the increase until a lawsuit brought by the National Cable Broadcasters Association was decided. The NCBA would lose that lawsuit by the following December, but Turner had bought himself some time.

At the beginning of 1983, CNN2 was rechristened with the name it still holds today, CNN Headline News. SNC and CNN were still locked in a battle, each spying on the other. SNC raided CNN staffers who had been in favor of unionizing, and at one point TBS headquarters was burglarized and staffers thought it appeared as if NewsSource syndication contracts had been photographed. With little else to hang onto, Turner Broadcasting launched an antitrust lawsuit against Westinghouse and ABC based on statements from an ABC executive and an allegation that Westinghouse was actively preventing cable systems it owned from signing any of CNN's services.

With all of their finances, SNC was still having difficulties. With the advertising market in a general squeeze, and made even more difficult by the unexpected glut of news provided by the Headline News Service and its syndicated services for local broadcasters, advertising revenue was well below forecasts. SNC had a peak of 7.5 million subscribers and was not Nielsen rated, so the advertising it was getting was sold at lower price points than anticipated. The structure of the operation was also awkward, with ABC providing a minimum of news to the operation and holding back big stories for its own broadcasts and most of SNC's contributing local stations being CBS affiliates. There was no compelling reason to choose it over CNN. With losses mounting and ABC taking a hit in the value of its shares, the launch of their planned second channel was delayed. SNC admitted to a loss of $60 million in the venture, but others estimated it was probably closer to $100 million. If they lost an antitrust suit to Turner at treble damages, they could be looking at another $300 million. In an effort to revive the service, ABC approached Reese Schonfeld about coming in to get the service on track, but Schonfeld had already said it was a service for people who don't like news, and, given its structure and business model, he thought the cause was hopeless. By September of 1983, SNC called Bill Daniels, revered as "The Father of Cable Television,"[31] to approach Turner about a deal. By October, Turner agreed to pay $12.5 million each to ABC and Westinghouse in return for their shutting the venture down, with its 7.5 million subscribers switched to either CNN or Headline News, and agreeing that neither would launch another competing venture for at least three years. The battle with SNC had been severely costly, and though the agreement left Turner Broadcasting with debt of over $100 million, most at the company didn't think they would have survived another month. On October 27, SNC went off the air with a party at their studio and the words, "That's it for now. In fact, that's it, period. And now, Ted buddy, it's in your hands."[32] Turner had won, and CNN would not face another direct competitor in the cable space for over a dozen years.

While the effects of the battle with SNC would continue to impact CNN profits for several years due to the three-year deals it had signed with cable operators, by 1985 CNN had its first pre-tax profit, $12.5 million. It was also well on its way to becoming the global network that Castro had suggested it could be, available in Europe, Japan, Australia, and China. It had won plaudits from all corners, even, reluctantly, the major networks' news services, for its coverage of the 1985 hijacking of TWA Flight 847, a 17-day ordeal in Beirut, Lebanon, and its exclusive footage and ongoing coverage of the Space Shuttle Challenger exploding 73 seconds into its flight on January 28, 1986.

Manifestations of the new global-citizen Ted Turner first started appearing not on CNN but on the Superstation, first in a 1983 deal with famed oceanographer and environmentalist Jacques Cousteau and the Cousteau Society, signed to an initial $6.5 million contract to produce documentaries of his expeditions, and soon after with deals to air documentaries by the National Audubon Society and National Geographic. A documentary series, *Portraits of America*, also began a six-year, 60-episode run the same year. By March of 1984, CNN launched *International Hour*, the first U.S. television news program dedicated to global news

In 1985, Turner put up $500,000 to initiate a foundation named The Better World Society. The non-profit society was formed to fund documentaries on nuclear arms control, overpopulation, global warming, global poverty, disease, and malnutrition. Its board would include Russell Peterson from the Audubon Society, Lester Brown of Worldwatch, former president Jimmy Carter, and representatives from India, Pakistan, Japan, China, the Soviet Union, Nigeria, Norway, and Costa Rica. While always short of funding, and often most reliant on Turner himself, the foundation produced 48 documentaries before it folded in 1991. Most of these ran on WTBS, CNN, or other cable channels, while several were provided to China and the Soviet Union at no charge.

It was also in 1985 that Turner, who had always wanted to carry the Olympics on WTBS, negotiated with the Soviet Union, which had withdrawn from the 1984 Olympics in Los Angeles in response to the U.S. boycott of the 1980 Olympics in Moscow, to initiate a new off-year Olympics meant to bring the two sides together. Dubbed the Goodwill Games, the inaugural games were held in Moscow in 1986. TBS helped fund them, helped persuade the American federation to attend, and broadcast the games on WTBS. While generally poorly received and sparsely watched, the games would continue in Seattle in 1986, St. Petersburg in 1984, New York City in 1998, Lake Placid, New York in winter of 2000, and Brisbane, Australia in 2001. Turner lost $26 million on the inaugural games and over $100 million throughout their tenure, but the games attracted over 20,000 athletes from over 100 countries and Turner saw them as forging the friendships he had hoped to foster from the beginning. He also pointed out that millions of dollars were raised for several charities, including UNICEF. In later years, Turner has claimed that the Goodwill Games deserve partial credit for ending the Cold War.

In 1986, Ed "no relation to Ted" Turner would pioneer the use of "flyaway" transmitters, portable satellite uplink dishes contained in suitcases, allowing CNN contributors to file stories from anywhere in the world. In 1987, CNN would take a more radical and controversial step, beginning *World Report*, a weekly two-hour series airing unedited documentaries and other programming submitted by contributing countries around the globe. Frequently cited as propaganda rather than having any merit as news, it nevertheless provided a platform from which countries could speak to one another and provide their unmediated viewpoints. While it would be moved from CNN to CNN International in the early 1990s, it is still produced today with over 145 contributing countries. Through *World Report* and its contributor conferences, CNN would develop a trust on the global stage that was unmatched by any other news service.

NOTES

1. Reese Schonfeld, *Me and Ted against the World: The Unauthorized Story of the Founding of CNN* (New York: Cliff Street, 2001), 226.

2. United Press International, "Ted Turner Files a Suit against 3 TV Networks," *The New York Times*, May 12, 1981.

3. Hank Whittemore, *CNN, The Inside Story: How a Band of Mavericks Changed the Face of Television News* (Boston: Little, Brown & Co., 1990), 203.

4. William A. Henry III, "Shaking up the Networks," *TIME*, August 9, 1982.

5. Reginald Stuart, "He's Getting Interference 1970–1981," *The New York Times*, September 13, 1981.

6. Whittemore, *CNN, The Inside Story*, 203.

7. Stuart, "He's Getting Interference."

8. Whittemore, *CNN, The Inside Story*, 206–207.

9. Ibid., 209.

10. Ibid., 210. Italics omitted.

11. Porter Bibb, *It Ain't as Easy as it Looks: Ted Turner's Amazing Story* (New York: Crown Publishers, 1993), 222.

12. Schonfeld, *Me and Ted against the World*, 241.

13. Ibid.

14. Ibid.

15. Tony Schwartz, "Turner Opens 2D Network in Cable-News War," *The New York Times*, January 4, 1982.

16. Gary Smith, "What Makes Ted Run?" *Sports Illustrated*, June 23, 1986.

17. Schonfeld, *Me and Ted against the World*, 237.

18. Smith, "What Makes Ted Run?"

19. *Crossfire* would of course go on to a long life with CNN. Airing from 1982–2005 with a succession of hosts, *Crossfire* became one of CNN's most recognized, if frequently controversial and criticized, talk shows. It would also go on to become the format of a yearly debate sponsored by the National Forensic League, which for a time in 2003 was named the Ted Turner debate.

20. Freeman would remain at CNN until 1985, when she was replaced by Larry King, who shares a birth date with Ted Turner, though he is five years Turner's senior. Larry King has been the biggest star of CNN programming ever since.

21. Whittemore, CNN, The Inside Story, 241.

22. Bibb, It Ain't as Easy as it Looks, 230.

23. Sally Bedell, "Editorial on CNN Stirs Dispute," The New York Times, June 4, 1982.

24. Ibid.

25. Ibid.

26. Whittemore, CNN, The Inside Story, 245.

27. Bibb, It Ain't as Easy as It Looks, 222.

28. Sally Bedell, "2D All-News Service to Emphasize Brevity," The New York Times, June 21, 1982.

29. Ibid.

30. "Turner Wins Cable Skirmish," The New York Times, December 18, 1982.

31. In the early 1950s, Daniels had set up the country's first cable system using antennas and microwave relays in Casper, Wyoming. In 1956, he had been elected as the president of the then one-year-old National Community Television Association (NCTA), where he quickly set up a lobbying group in Washington to represent the interests of the nascent industry. Following his term as president of NCTA, he set up his own company, RBC Daniels, to serve as something of an investment bank for people interested in getting involved in cable, and he was really a central figure in the development of the industry.

32. Richard Hack, Clash of the Titans: How the Unbridled Ambition of Ted Turner and Rupert Murdoch Has Created Global Empires That Control What We Read and Watch (Beverly Hills, CA: New Millennium Press, 2003), 198.

Chapter 13

REACHING OUT

Following the launch of CNN, Turner increased his attacks on the immorality and general quality of broadcast network programming. In part, this was a strategy to increase support for cable and his own channels as a diversification of media voices in the country, but it wasn't all or even primarily cynical; Turner really did believe what he preached, and by this time it was a personal mission he felt was within reach.

Throughout the early 1980s, Turner explored all sorts of opportunities to merge with or take control of one of the major networks. There were talks with CBS, meetings with oilman T. Boone Pickens about a joint takeover of RCA and its NBC division, even meetings with ultraconservative Jesse Helms, the senator from North Carolina, who had founded a group called Fairness in Media with the specific intent of acquiring enough stock in CBS to force a change in what he perceived as a distinct liberal bias in the network's news division and anchor Dan Rather. For one reason or another, often because of Turner's flamboyant and unconventional personality and the unmistakable impression that Turner always saw himself as the principal partner and de facto leader of any joint venture, none worked out.

By 1985, Turner had seen the CBS Cable venture of cultural programming of 1981–82 fail, he had vanquished the ABC/Westinghouse partnership of Satellite News, and both the Superstation and CNN were gaining penetration in a cable universe that had doubled in the past five years. While CNN was still losing money, the Superstation had become the most profitable television station in the country, and Turner Broadcasting had shown a modest but significant after-tax profit of just over $10 million in 1984. All speculation of imminent demise was in the past, its shares were trading at ever higher multiples, and financing was readily available. Turner had started the year by spending $64 million for a 70 percent share in the Omni complex in downtown Atlanta, with plans to make it the new home of CNN. On April 18, despite rumors that had been swirling for months and despite Capital Cities' Warren Buffet-supported takeover of the four-times-larger ABC in March, Turner shocked everyone with his announcement of a hostile takeover attempt of CBS.

Given the rumors, and the fact that Wall Street considered a then-beleaguered CBS to be ripe for a takeover, it was not a surprise that Turner Broadcasting, with revenues of $282 million in 1984, was trying to acquire a corporation with $4.9 billion in revenues for the same year. The big surprise was the structure of the deal. E. F. Hutton, one of the only investment banks willing to work with Turner on the deal, had constructed a package valued at $5.41 million, but with no upfront money at all, instead offering stockholders an exchange of CBS stock for Turner-issued "junk bonds." In defending the offer, Turner said, "I've never called them junk bonds. That's what the doomsayers call them. CBS pays a dividend of two to three dollars, but I'll pay twenty-one dollars in interest. Call them anything you want to. I like to call them *high-yield*."[1] Essentially, he was seeking to acquire CBS with its own future profits while selling off its radio stations, one of its television stations, and its non-broadcast holdings in everything from music and publishing to musical instruments and toys.

Even for Turner, the move was audacious. Lee Wilder, from Robinson Humphrey in Atlanta, who had worked with Turner in his purchase of WTCG and WRET in 1970, said, "The only thing Turner didn't throw into the deal were the bamboo steamers and Ginsu knives,"[2] the now-famous advertising staples of the Superstation. Edward Attorino, media analyst at Smith Barney, summed it up more explicitly, saying the offer "borders on the ludicrous . . . asking CBS's public shareholders, over 70 percent of which are institutions with presumably some fiduciary responsibility toward their holdings, to become his creditors. He expects them to swap highly liquid equity in a profitable business to become lenders to an overwhelmingly leveraged company."[3]

At a stockholders' meeting just days after the announcement, Thomas Wyman, the Chairman of CBS, began what would be a full-frontal assault on Turner, saying, "Those who seek to gain control of CBS in order to gain control of CBS News threaten its independence, its integrity—and this country,"[4] an apparent attempt to link Turner more directly with Jesse Helms and Fairness in Media. Mike Wallace, a correspondent on 60 Minutes was quoted as saying, "I have yet to run across anybody at CBS News who has the slightest desire to work for Turner. No one takes him seriously."[5] Walter Cronkite chimed in that he "would be devastated. CBS News has achieved the greatest credibility. It would be terrible to change all that."[6] In a letter to shareholders, CBS cited several "pejorative statements" attributed to Turner in various publications: a 1977 statement, "I'll tell you the way Kapstein [a baseball players' agent] conducts his business and the reason I don't like him—after all, you should have some reason to dislike a guy besides the fact that he wears a full-length fur coat and is a Jew";[7] a 1982 statement on solving problems of African American unemployment and the underground rail system then proposed for shifting locations of MX missiles, "blacks should carry missiles from silo to silo just as the Egyptians carried rocks during the building of the pyramids";[8] and a 1984 statement, "Before 1990 there'll be more Mexicans in Texas, California, and Arizona than there are Americans. What we should do is build an iron curtain down there, or they'll be taking back the border states."[9] The letter went on to cite an incident arising from a meeting between Turner and Jesse Jackson in 1982, and a letter later sent to Turner by Jackson, in which Turner was criticized for drinking too much, being racist, and showing contempt "for me, the black community in general and black leadership in particular."[10] As a CBS lawyer told BusinessWeek, "We intend to challenge his fitness not just to operate a network, but to be a broadcast licensee at all."[11]

Filing a petition with the FCC in early June, CBS asked that Turner's bid be stopped. Supported by 100 CBS affiliates and 97 groups, from the National Organization of Women to the Hispanic National Bar Association, which accused Turner of demonstrating "insensitivity for blacks, Hispanics, women, and Jews,"[12] it said that control by Turner would begin a "death spiral"[13] beneath $4.5 billion in debt. The petition included a statement Turner made during an appearance before Congress that "I'm eventually going to go broke, but so is our federal government. That's why I love it up here in Washington so much. You operate at massive deficits every year and keep smiling, and so do I."[14] It also included a quote from a *Los Angeles Times* article written by Daniel Schorr—who had recently left CNN when the unique addendum to his original contract wasn't offered at renewal—that claimed Turner "encouraged companies to sponsor features associated with their products"[15] and that "business leaders are subjects of flattering interviews and their companies [are] sometimes solicited afterwards for commercials."[16]

Turner was keeping his mouth shut. Some, including Jesse Jackson, who said, "The way to tell about him is not just to take statements he has made here or there. Insensitivity is his flaw, but anyone who knows Ted knows he has a basic streak of fairness."[17] Others questioned the use of ad hominem attacks and whether anyone wanted to see government agencies judging qualifications based on their assessment of someone's personal views. A true turnaround came, though, when the SEC approved Turner's registration statement in late June and the financial community had a chance to examine Turner's filing in detail. Bill Bevins had been excruciatingly detailed in his preparation of the filing, and the numbers worked. Despite the massive debt Turner Broadcasting would assume, it could still show a profit within the year. While still unconventional, the takeover attempt was no longer roundly ridiculed; Turner could well pull it off. A flood of people suddenly wanted in on the deal, strengthening Turner's hand and for the first time really tilting the fight in his favor.

But CBS had an answer of its own. Just before Independence Day, CBS announced that it would be repurchasing 21 percent of its own stock at $150 per share, a figure well above its current trading price. CBS would pay $40 in cash along with a 10-year note that paid just under 11 percent interest. The notes themselves would carry a provision that the corporation could not sell off any major assets or exceed a debt-to-equity far lower than what Turner would be assuming with his package. Purchase of the stock would be partly financed by selling preferred stock to a group of institutional investors, and CBS would retain right of first refusal on any purchase of these preferred shares. If that wasn't enough, the right to waive any of these rules, already stringent, would disappear entirely if the corporation changed hands.

Turner went through the motions of trying to fight the cleverly calculated structuring of the CBS proposal, but it was clear he was beaten, and he'd lost $18.5–$23 million dollars in the trying. One of Turner's stated reasons for attempting the takeover was that "size matters," and he had been schooled on just how right he was. CBS had done a masterful job in deploying its financial clout and political influence, limiting Turner's options at every turn.

Marshaling his forces for the defense against Turner may well have been Wyman's finest hour as chairman of CBS, but it wasn't without its consequences. On the heels of the takeover attempt, Laurence Tisch was urged to invest in CBS in order to protect it from continuing takeover attempts. By 1986, Tisch held a 24.9 percent stake in CBS, and in September, he and William Paley demoted Wyman for his unilateral intention to sell the company to the Coca-Cola Company, as well as a tenure marred by poor purchasing decisions. Wyman would be out of the company by 1987. Tisch would be chairman of CBS from 1986–1995, during which time he would sell off several of the assets that Turner had intended to sell. He was generally thought to be degrading the quality of the network, and specifically its News division, with cutbacks and layoffs. In 1995, Tisch would engineer the sale of CBS to Westinghouse Electric for $5.4 billion, making a windfall for shareholders, himself included, though the price was $100,000 less than the accepted valuations of Turner's bid 10 years earlier.

On July 31, 1985, both the FCC and the courts approved the CBS stock repurchase scheme, making it clear to everyone that Turner had lost. However, Turner had already shifted gears weeks before and was in talks with Kirk Kerkorian to purchase Metro-Goldwyn-Mayer (MGM), the fabled but fallen Hollywood movie studio. For years, the Turner spin maintained that he had still been in the hunt for CBS when a call from Kerkorian came in and Turner decided that MGM, a company he had been inquiring about off and on for at least five years, was more important to his future than CBS. In *Call Me Ted*, Turner admits that "everyone now knew that we no longer had a reasonable shot at getting CBS."[18]

Kerkorian had purchased MGM in 1969, but he had always been focused on his Las Vegas hotel properties and never seemed very interested in the studio, though he did add United Artists (UA) to his holdings in 1981. For Turner, always a movie lover, the idea of owning the historic studio and breaking into the film business held its own allure, as did the chance to assure his stations would have access to a continuing line of programming. The real attraction, though, was the film libraries. MGM/UA libraries included not only MGM releases, but United Artists, RKO, and pre-1948 Warner Brothers releases. In addition to the films, they also held over 1,000 cartoons, including MGM titles and 335 of Warner Brothers' pre-1948 *Looney Tunes*. All in all, it was a treasure trove of Americana, and an unrivaled collection of the best of Hollywood's Golden Era.

Having already turned down an offer to sell MGM/UA for $22 per share, Kerkorian, claiming to have an interested buyer in the wings, offered a non-negotiable price of $29 per share. Altogether, he was asking for a full purchase price of $1.6 billion, and that didn't include United Artists, the old RKO library, or the 1,457-title, pre-1948 Warner Brothers library. It was an absurd price, multiples above value, but Turner saw something he wanted and almost immediately agreed to the price if the withheld libraries were included in the deal.

Kerkorian was pressing Turner to complete the deal within two weeks, and Bill Bevins started to negotiate the details while a swarm of lawyers was sent to Los Angeles to do what they could of due diligence. Turner flew back to Atlanta where he encountered more than the usual amount of resistance from his board, but Turner insisted it was a question of survival. Programming was increasing in price and some studios were refusing to sign a contract with Turner at any price. If they couldn't control more programming, they would be dead in the water. The board finally acquiesced, and on August 6, Turner signed a purchase agreement and the deal was announced.

Having hooked his eager fish, Kerkorian now insisted that the entire deal be done in cash, and to help Turner raise the cash he brought him to Drexel Burnham Lambert's Michael Milken. Known as the king of junk (high-yield) bonds, Milken had already been handling Kerkorian's side of the deal. Though it was a bit peculiar to have him handle both sides of the deal, Turner had previously worked with Michael in securing financing for CNN; his familiarity with MGM was beneficial, and there was little question that Milken was probably the most adept person available to raise the substantial amount of money needed to close the deal. Whatever questions it brought up, it certainly assured that he would have an interest in seeing the deal through to a successful conclusion.[19] As Milken readied his offering, the already weak underpinnings of MGM continued to sag as the studio took major losses on nearly every one of its new releases. With Milken apparently having an unusually difficult time finding buyers, a series of other problems arose, not least of which was the revelation that many of the films Turner would be buying were already licensed out to other companies, many under long-term deals. In October, both sides agreed to a restructuring, reducing the upfront cash and thus the cost of the bonds by $6 per share, but the difference was made up by a grant to Kerkorian of 53.3 million preferred shares in Turner Broadcasting, and an agreement that Turner would assume $578 million of MGM's debt. Still stalled in trying to sell the bonds, Milken then had Turner agree to pay off $600 million of the bond issue within six months. As finally structured, if Turner did not pay off the specified debt in time, Kerkorian's dividends for his preferred shares would, by June of 1987, be paid in common voting shares of Turner Broadcasting; even then, if TBS shares dropped below a certain level, Kerkorian would receive additional shares of preferred stock, a potentially endless dilution of Turner's control. If that wasn't enough, as the deal closed, Milken upped the fee he was charging Turner from $80 million to $140 million.

On March 25, 1986, the MGM deal was completed and Turner became the proud if ridiculed owner of MGM. By general consensus, Turner had been hoodwinked: "Turner got the worst screwing in the history of American business";[20] "Ted Turner came to town fully clothed and left in a barrel";[21] "Drexel has put a gun to his head."[22] Regardless, Turner was happy; he'd bought the "Rembrandts"[23] of Hollywood, and now held "35% of the great films of all time! We've got Spencer Tracy and Jimmy Cagney working for us from the grave!"[24] "We're protecting WTBS. It's an extremely valuable asset, but its future was clouded," he said. "I'd rather have good old programming than bad new programming."[25] Of his detractors he said, "It's easy to be a Monday morning quarterback, but we won the game!"[26] He even made light of the debt. While driving in a car with his mother and a *Sports Illustrated* columnist, he said, "Two billion dollars I owe! Actually, it's closer to one point nine, but I like the sound of two billion better. *Two billion.* No individual in history has ever owed more. That's a million dollars a day in interest, Mother. Here, look at my picture in today's newspaper. Do I look worried?"[27]

Immediately after closing on the deal, Turner sold a now debt-free United Artists back to Kerkorian as agreed. By July, he had sold off the Culver City lot and film lab to Lorimar Telepictures for $190 million, and the MGM logo, together with the movie, television, and videocassette production operations, were sold back to Kerkorian himself for $300 million, leaving Turner with some 3,560 films and 1,000 cartoons for a purchase price of $1.1 billion. There were certainly some good Ted Turner jokes making the rounds of cocktail parties that year, but as it turned out, Turner was right all along. By 1990, the consensus had changed; Turner hadn't overpaid for the film library at all, and in fact, he got a bargain. With the growth of the Internet and digitization, the consensus was even more favorable; Turner was a seer, and the value of "content" (a term Turner never used) was virtually limitless. Jimmy Cagney and Spencer Tracy, as well as Humphrey Bogart and Clark Gable and Vivien Leigh and Bette Davis and Orson Welles and Judy Garland, not to mention Tom and Jerry, Bugs Bunny, and countless others, worked very, very well for him from beyond the grave; but not without some consequences.

Despite his sunny veneer, Turner was in fact worried. Throughout the second half of 1986, Turner was in a frantic search for a merger or sale that could save him from his tremendous debt before he would really face ridicule by ceding control of Turner Broadcasting and its hardworking stable of nitrate and acetate movie stars to Kirk Kerkorian. He had talks with Rupert Murdoch, Time-Life, Gannett Newspapers, and a host of others on cooperating ventures of all sorts, but none worked out and Turner still couldn't imagine losing control. As the clock ticked, though, there was only one way out.

According to Porter Bibb, Turner first approached Bill Daniels at the beginning of 1987 to voice his concerns, and it was Bill Daniels who set up a "cable summit"[28] in Las Vegas to discuss how to deal with the situation Turner was in. In other accounts, Daniels seems to be stricken from any record of involvement. In *Call Me Ted*, Turner says he called

John Malone of TCI directly, and Malone recounts receiving such a call in the middle of the night as a desperate Turner pleaded, "You've got to do something or else CNN will become KNN. The KERKORIAN NEWS NETWORK!"[29] In any case, Turner knew his best hope for sufficient help to save and maintain control of his company was the cable industry itself, and the cable industry knew that Turner's programming was too important to them to let it fall into the wrong hands. As Bill Daniels noted, "The only thing worse than having Ted Turner as the most important person in cable is not having Ted Turner as the most important person in cable."[30]

Variations of the deal were reported as early as late January, but it wasn't really finalized until the first days of June, precipitously close to Kerkorian's deadline. At least 26 cable operators pooled a total of $562.5 million, purchasing 37 percent of Turner Broadcasting. Turner, who had previously held over 80 percent of the company, would still be in control with 51 percent, but 7 of the 15 board seats would go to the largest cable operator investors, including TCI, Time Inc., Continental Cablevision, and United Cable Television. Turner also had to accept a covenant that the board had to approve any expenditure over $2 million, a severe restriction on Turner's style of doing business, and even worse, both TCI and Time Inc., the largest investors, would hold veto power over any deal the board might approve.

John Malone, who played a lead role in getting the deal structured, had at first wanted to keep Time Inc. out of the mix of saviors, but Viacom was sold to Sumner Redstone and Redstone wasn't interested, so there was no other choice. TCI and Time Inc. had competing interests and neither really trusted the other. Malone, in particular, was sure that Time had a very strong desire to control or acquire CNN, so the two having veto power meant there would be little chance of first getting board approval and then escaping a veto on any truly significant expenditure. And while independent programming was important to all of the contributing cable operators, their interests would be directly contradictory to Turner's when it came to terms and fees for that programming. Turner put, and still puts, a positive spin on the deal, refusing to call it a rescue or a bailout, but there's little else to call it. In *Call Me Ted*, he goes so far as to say, "Handing out veto power to Time and TCI would ultimately become one of my greatest regrets."[31] Bill Bevins, who would have a mild heart attack and soon after leave the company, put it most succinctly when he told the *Wall Street Journal* on June 5, 1987, "It's clear from the transaction as it's structured, and I think it's an economic fact of life, that Ted no longer runs the company."[32]

NOTES

1. Hank Whittemore, *CNN, The Inside Story: How a Band of Mavericks Changed the Face of Television News* (Boston: Little, Brown & Co., 1990), 264.

2. Stephen Koepp, "Captain Outrageous Opens Fire," *TIME*, April 29, 1985.

3. Porter Bibb, *It Ain't as Easy as it Looks: Ted Turner's Amazing Story* (New York: Crown Publishers, 1993), 275.

4. Koepp, "Captain Outrageous."

5. Ibid.

6. Ibid.

7. Sally Bedell Smith, "CBS Criticizes Turner Views," *The New York Times*, May 3, 1985.

8. Ibid.

9. Ibid.

10. Ibid.

11. "How CBS Plans to Keep Raiders at Bay," *BusinessWeek*, April 15, 1985, 144.

12. "CBS Attacks," *TIME*, June 17, 1985.

13. Ibid.

14. Whittemore, *CNN, The Inside Story*, 265.

15. "CBS Attacks," *TIME*.

16. Ibid.

17. Smith, "CBS Criticizes Turner Views."

18. Ted Turner with Bill Burke, *Call Me Ted* (New York: Grand Central Publishing, 2008), 235.

19. Milken would later be accused by Ivan Boesky, an arbitrageur who would be investigated and jailed for insider trading, of having Boesky buy up MGM stock in an effort to keep the share price up and help Milken in his bid to find buyers for the bonds he was offering on Turner's behalf. Boesky allegedly made $3 million on the shares, and split this profit with Milken. Boesky would be sentenced to 3.5 years in jail and a fine of $100 million in a plea bargain based partly on information concerning Milken. Milken escaped any charges for his role in the MGM sale, but was tried in 1989 on a litany of racketeering and securities fraud charges. Milken would plead guilty in his own plea bargain and be sentenced to 10 years in prison, though he was released after serving less than 2 of those years. Turner has always defended Milken and

still counts him as a friend, but though Ted was as anxious as anyone to make the MGM purchase, it certainly appears that Milken was always working for Kerkorian in creating a package that would in the end be injurious to Turner. Just how hard had he actually tried to sell those bonds?

20. Straford P. Sherman, "Ted Turner: Back from the Brink," *Fortune*, July 7, 1986, http://money.cnn.com/magazines/fortune/fortune_archive/1986/07/07/67824/index.htm.

21. Robert Goldberg and Gerald Jay Goldberg, *Citizen Turner: The Wild Rise of an American Tycoon* (New York: Harcourt, Brace & Co., 1995), 360.

22. Ibid.

23. Geraldine Fabrikant, "Some Promising Signs Foe Turner's Empire," *The New York Times*, January 23, 1989.

24. Sherman, "Back from the Brink."

25. Ibid.

26. Ibid.

27. Gary Smith, "What Makes Ted Run?" *Sports Illustrated*, June 23, 1986.

28. Bibb, *Citizen Turner*, 316.

29. Ibid., 319.

30. Quoted by John Malone in a sidebar to Turner's *Call Me Ted*, 250.

31. Turner, *Call Me Ted*, 252.

32. Goldberg and Goldberg, *Citizen Turner*, 380.

Chapter 14

GETTING PERSONAL

For those driven to succeed in their given profession, marital success frequently takes a backseat, and in this Turner was no exception. Between running a business at 24 years old and chasing his personal ambitions as a yachtsman, there was little time left for his family. Turner set a frenetic pace in his sailing life, away for weeks and months at a time as he hopped from one race to another, and his business life was just as full; as soon as he attained one goal, he was planning a next step, he was off selling advertising, promoting his stations to cable operators, negotiating for programming, securing financing, and lobbying for cable television. By the 1980s, he had adopted environmentalism and internationalism as causes, and he was traveling the world to promote both in conjunction with CNN.

Janie Smith Turner and their five children were largely left to fend for themselves, with the help of Jimmy Brown, who had served a similar role in Ted's early life. When Turner was home he was determined to make up for lost time, instilling the discipline he felt was so important in his own life, organizing schedules and activities, jumping on every imperfection, and setting goals and agendas for Janie and his children to meet while he was next away. Crying was forbidden. Emotions were kept in check. In essence, he ran his family as if he were the headmaster of a military school rather than a husband or father.

As Turner reveals in his autobiography, his elder children suffered even more. Laura Lee and Teddy, children of his first marriage, suffered not only the absence of their father, but also the emotional neglect of their stepmother. Whether unconsciously or out of resentment of Turner's absences and emotional distance, Janie doted over her own children, while Laura Lee and Teddy were frequently left to the care and attention of Jimmy Brown. Whether neglected by his stepmother or not, however, Teddy told *Atlanta* magazine in 1993, "Dad was often away in those days. When he was home, there was a lot of yelling and tension and getting smacked around. I never could decide which was worse—having him away or having him home."[1]

Throughout their marriage, Turner made it clear to Janie that his priorities were sailing, business, and family, with the first two sometimes being switched in rank but family always taking up the rear. Roger Vaughan described a dinner he and his wife Possum attended at Turner's house as early as 1968, "While Ted regaled Possum with romantic descriptions of world ocean racing courses, across the table Janie talked to me about the problems of an absentee husband and father: he's just off sailing all the time . . . the kids don't even know him . . . I don't quite know what to do. . . . Every so often the two conversations would come together, two cars careening down the straightaway of a demolition derby."[2] Somehow that derby continued for another 18 years, with Turner doing his best "Take my wife, please" Henny Youngman routines in public and being more cuttingly rude and dismissive at home. Janie, for her own part, continued to play the role of good Southern wife, defending Ted and their life together for years and convinced that at heart Turner really loved and needed her. If difficult for outsiders to see, from those who know Turner best it's clear that this was true on some level. The vulnerable core that makes Turner so appealing beneath his oversized personality needs stability and reassurance, and given their time together, Janie certainly saw more of that well-guarded core than anyone else.

But after years of fading into the background, submerging her own needs, and being humiliated while Turner pursued his ever-more-public dalliances, Janie finally stood up and demanded that she and Ted see a marriage counselor in the early 1980s. If there had been any hope that Turner would change after his sailing career was over, those hopes were short lived. Rather than settle down to any semblance of a home life, Turner was practically living at his TBS office in the early years of CNN while maintaining two serious extramarital affairs. Janie had been reduced to a shell of herself, drinking heavily, wandering aimlessly through the woods on the Hope plantation, and ruminating on her plight to nearly everyone she came into contact with.[3]

Janie's ability to finally stand up for herself was certainly due to interventions by friends who had become increasingly concerned for her wellbeing, but it also coincided with the appearance of the first undeniable threat to her marriage. Turner had met Jeanette H. (J. J.) Ebaugh while sailing in the 1980 America's Cup. A pert and attractive blonde, J. J. was a commercial pilot, a racecar driver, and a sailor, and Turner was smitten on sight. By 1983, she was living in Atlanta and Turner had hired her as his private pilot. She would regularly fly Turner, Janie, and the Turner children to one of their South Carolina plantations on weekends. As time went on, Turner became ever more enamored by Ebaugh, who was as active and energetic as Turner and shared his interests in internationalism and the environment. She was instrumental in Turner's founding of The Better World Society in 1985, and Turner's autobiography credits Ebaugh as being an influence on his life. A business associate called her "sort of a cheerleader with a social conscience. She does a good imitation of a bimbo, but she's really very bright."[4] By this time, Janie was adept at picking out Turner's paramours. They'd been paraded before her for years, sitting close by the family at Atlanta Braves games, working on Turner's boats, accompanying him to Cuba, kissing him at Hawks games, but here she had to interact with one on a weekly basis, and if that wasn't bad enough, Turner soon set J. J. up in a small mansion just a short distance from the Hope plantation. Janie herself was still the mostly conservative Southern woman she had always been, with little real interest in saving the world or being in the spotlight, but she was determined to try to save her marriage.

Turner was open to counseling and, perhaps because Ebaugh herself was a strong proponent of therapy, seems to have been a willing participant. The effort, at least in terms of the marriage, would prove fruitless. What would come of the effort was a diagnosis by the doctor, Frank Pittman, that Turner suffered from cyclothymia, a mild form of bipolar disorder characterized by less drastic, shorter term, and more intermittent mood swings. He prescribed a treatment of lithium, which Turner would continue to take for several years in the mid-1980s. Friends thought it had a markedly positive affect on him, generally agreeing with Ebaugh's evaluation that "before, it was pretty scary to be around the guy sometimes because you never knew what in the world would happen next . . . That's why the whole world was on pins and needles around him. But with lithium he became very even tempered. Ted's just one of those miracle cases. I mean, lithium is great stuff, but in Ted's particular case, lithium is a miracle."[5]

In 1986, Turner took Janie and his children to Moscow for the inaugural Goodwill Games. Ebaugh would be there too, together with Liz Wickersham, who had had her own close, long-time involvement with Turner that had overlapped his relationship with Ebaugh. Following the games, Turner took his family to Africa on a safari where he learned that Ebaugh, apparently upset with the amount of attention he had lavished on Janie during and after the games, had taken up with someone else. Following the trip to Africa, Turner tried everything he could to make Ebaugh return. As she told *TIME*, "He put up the most aggressive campaign to get me back that I have ever heard about or read about in my entire life."[6] Janie, finally having had enough, decided in late August that it was time to separate. Their divorce was made official by the summer of 1988, with Janie receiving $40 million and the Kinloch plantation in South Carolina. Friends described her condition at the time as "like someone coming out of a prison camp in North Vietnam."[7] For years, Janie would make a conscious effort to avoid speaking Turner's name. In a 1992 interview with David Frost, Turner would say, "I caused a lot of pain to my second wife, and if I could set anything right, I would have liked that marriage not to have occurred or to have made her happier. That's probably been my greatest regret.[8] In *Call Me Ted*, Turner says, "Our marriage was never easy, but Janie and I had a lot of good times together and when we officially went our separate ways, our children were fine young adults. I'll always be grateful to her."[9]

Turner officially moved in to Ebaugh's house in Roswell, just outside of Atlanta, in September of 1986, the same month CNN moved its headquarters to the Omni Hotel, which would soon be renamed the CNN Center. Early in 1987, Turner received news that Teddy, working in Moscow as a CNN cameraman and editor, had been in a serious accident. He had gone out drinking after work and hitched a ride home with a colleague from CBS who wound up losing control on the icy streets and slamming head-on into a streetlamp. Teddy broke all the bones in his face, lost all of his lower teeth, had his jaw wired shut, and had glass in his eye and internal bleeding. Six days later, when he had been stabilized, a distraught Turner had an air ambulance take him to Atlanta's Emory University Hospital for facial reconstruction. The entire family was shaken, and as had happened with the death of Bill Lucas in 1979, Turner was reminded of his own mortality. Teddy would say, "That was a turning point in my relationship with Dad. . . . he wasn't going to live forever and we really didn't know each other that well."[10]

If there was a bright side to Turner's life at the time, it was Ebaugh. She had made him promise to stop drinking, he changed his diet, and he actually tried to be monogamous. J. J. wanted him to slow down a bit; she introduced him to fly-fishing, aided in reestablishing communication with his children, cooked most of their meals, and accompanied him on all of his business trips. Most of all, she stood up to him, demanding his respect and attention, teaching him about women's rights, and working toward making him more aware of her own and other people's feelings and perspectives. Under her influence, Turner said, "I started to listen, and not be judgmental, and wait until someone was through rather than interrupting them, and then think about what they said before I prepared an answer. I learned to give and take better than I had previously."[11] Friends could see the change; Turner seemed to be in love for the first time in his life and everyone expected the pair to be married. But not long after his divorce from Janie was official, Ted and J. J. appeared on the cover of the November 1988 issue of *Atlanta* magazine and inside was an article titled, "The Woman Who Tamed Ted Turner." Ebaugh was quoted saying that Turner would do anything she wanted him to do: "He gave up $40 million and a whole harem. That's a hell of a lot."[12] Soon after, Turner would break up with her, reportedly by telephone. The feeling was that Turner didn't appreciate the article, which was probably true, but in addition to her other interests, J. J. was also a devotee of occult spirituality—pyramids, crystals, and tarot—that was definitely out of Turner's element, and her thrill seeking was just too dangerous and draining. In his autobiography, Turner says that Ebaugh had some psychological problems of her own at the time.

In 1987, with changes in his personal and professional life wearing him down, Turner visited the Wyoming ranch of an old friend and neighbor, Peter Manigault. Turner, who can never sit completely still, had always relished the natural world, escaping for long walks on his grandparents' farm in the Mississippi delta during his early summers, and taking in stray animals at McCallie. While he had the pristine beauty of his Avalon and Hope plantations, the big skies and expansively majestic beauty of Wyoming's Western landscape left him awestruck. By the second day of his visit, he knew he needed a place like this, and within days of that he agreed to buy a Montana property halfway between Helena and Bozeman. Of modest size as ranches go, it was about 4,000 acres, but he would quickly add adjoining properties and rename it the Bar None.

In early 1989, Turner saw a newspaper report that Jane Fonda was separating from Tom Hayden and Turner immediately thought, "Jane Fonda is someone I'd like to go out with."[13] To Turner, bygones are bygones and thoughts mean actions, so Fonda received her first phone call from Ted the day after her divorce was announced. Rather than bother with prologue, Turner opened the conversation with, "Is it true?"[14] After establishing what "it" was, and Jane making it clear that it would be at least three months before she would be able to consider dating again, Turner added, "Hey, I know just how you feel. I just broke up with my own mistress. I wrecked my whole family and my marriage two years ago to go and live with her, so now I'm having a hard time myself."[15] It was a typical, intriguingly dissonant introduction to Ted Turner.

Three months later, to the day, Turner called back. Most of what Fonda knew about Turner wasn't nearly as intriguing, but she had to admire his persistence and agreed to a date. Once she had agreed to the date, she discovered that Turner was one of her brother Peter's heroes, and he filled her in on Turner's recent activities, making her realize that there just might be more to the man than she had thought. From Jane's retelling, Turner's charismatic sexuality was apparent at first sight, made all the more appealing by the vulnerable nervousness he was obviously feeling. When they had climbed into his car his first words were, "I have friends who are Communists. . . . Gorbachev is my buddy and so is Castro."[16] He then went on in a stream-of-consciousness monologue that included the fact that he had had CNN do a printout on her so he would know a little more about her and that her printout was a foot tall while his own was three feet tall.

Throughout their dinner, Turner kept up the running dialogue, going through his entire life story, including what many would say was a sign of his recent growth; calling himself a sexist by rearing and crediting J. J. with making him aware of the fact, saying, "I was actually . . . ahhh . . . magn . . . ahhh . . . mong . . . ahhh . . . magnanimous with her,"[17] unable to even say the word "monogamous." Fonda's retelling of the date makes it clear just how authentically and endearingly cute Turner can be. Overlooked, though, is that except for the words "sexist" and "feminist," and a much briefer life story, it could have been a retelling of his first date with Judy Nye over 28 years earlier. Turner never hid the fact that he "played the field," that he struggled against his libidinous instincts; it was part of his arsenal when he really wanted to make an impression.

By the end of the evening, they were mutually smitten.

With help from the fact that Peter Fonda lived in Montana, Turner convinced her to visit his Bar None ranch for a weekend in June.[18] The monologue continued as he showed her around the property, complete with quotes from the classics that he had committed to memory and a recitation of his early life at boarding schools, the latter of which brought Fonda to tears. He did finally elicit some words from Jane as well. They quickly realized that they actually had a lot in common; both had had domineering fathers and both had had a parent commit suicide (Jane's mother, Frances, committed suicide when Jane was 12). Turner was a gentleman throughout, and he impressed Jane with his knowledge of animals and his ability to quickly identify birds on the wing. For their last night together, Turner took her to another ranch he was thinking of buying. It was a few hours south of the Bar None, bordering Yellowstone National Park, and it was closer to the airport. It was also a much bigger property, over 113,000 acres, and though Fonda couldn't understand why anyone would need two ranches, he was obviously excited. He had plans to bring it back to the way it had been before "the

white man" showed up and to establish a herd of bison (American buffalo). To show the depth of his commitment, he soon pulled out his
"Ten Voluntary Initiatives," the update of the Ten Commandments that
he carried, and still carries, in his pocket. "'The problem with the Ten
Commandments,' he explained, 'is that nowadays people don't like to
be commanded, so I've rewritten them as initiatives.'"[19]

1. I promise to care for planet earth and all living things thereon,
   especially my fellow human beings.
2. I promise to treat all persons everywhere with dignity, respect,
   and friendliness.
3. I promise to have no more than one or two children.
4. I promise to use my best efforts to save what is left of our natural
   world in its undisturbed state, and to restore degraded areas.
5. I promise to use as little of our non-renewable resources as possible.
6. I promise to minimize my use of toxic chemicals, pesticides and
   other poisons, and to encourage others to do the same.
7. I promise to contribute to those less fortunate, to help them
   become self-sufficient and enjoy the benefits of a decent life including clean air and water, adequate food, health care, hous-
   ing, education, and individual rights.
8. I reject the use of force, in particular military force, and I support United Nations arbitration of international disputes.
9. I support the total elimination of all nuclear, chemical and biological weapons and ultimately the elimination of all weapons
   of mass destruction.
10. I support the United Nations and its efforts to improve the
    conditions of the planet.[20]

As far as Turner was concerned, the deal was done, with only the details to be worked out. He let her know that she was perfect for him
other than some concern for her age (Fonda is slightly older than
Turner) and her career, which he thought she might not want to give
up until she had won an Oscar, not realizing that she'd already won
two. He penciled her in for a series of dates over the coming months.
But Fonda, smitten though she was with the depths of Turner and their
common interests, wasn't quite ready. Soon after, she would fall for

someone else. When that was over, Turner was immediately on the phone again, but after another try with Turner, Fonda noted, "During dinner I again noticed that my words lay like droplets on an oil slick, never penetrating his surface. This vague indifference to what was not himself left me feeling unseen."[21]

Despite her reticence, it was Fonda who would really get their relationship started when she called Turner in January of 1990. Sightings of the incongruous power couple started showing up in the gossip columns. Both were supra famous, transcending their careers, controversial in one way or another, and somewhat mysterious because of it. No one really knew what to make of either one, and in some ways, both were seen as naïfs, not to be taken completely seriously. Despite the changes Turner had exhibited over the past years, he was still in a gray area in most people's minds, a bit liberal, a bit conservative, a bit principled, a tad psychotic, gung-ho capitalist, and commie apologist. Despite the workout videos that Fonda was currently famous for, a good portion of the population still saw her as treasonous "Hanoi Jane" for her trip to North Vietnam during the war and her marriage to Hayden, one of the founders of the 1960s' Students for a Democratic Society (SDS), the author of their Port Huron statement, and a defendant in the wild and widely publicized Chicago Seven trial that resulted from the demonstrations and chaos at the 1968 Democratic convention. To the confirmed right, Turner taking up with Fonda was final proof that he was indeed now a Commie loony. To the confirmed left, Fonda being with Turner was proof that she had always been a shallow poseur. But no one could stop talking.

Turner continued his often awkward rapprochement with his children, and Fonda proved a willing and active contributor to the cause. In late 1990, Ted established the Turner Foundation, a philanthropic trust to fund conservation efforts around the world, naming himself and all five of his children as trustees.[22]

Turner nearly derailed the relationship after again having problems with being "magnanimous," but his self-flagellations and prostrated promises managed to patch it up. In April of 1991, Fonda announced that she was retiring from her film career. It was something she said she was considering doing in any case, but Turner had made it clear that it was a non-debatable prerequisite of any commitment. On May 4, Fonda accompanied Turner to the wedding of his eldest daughter, Laura

Lee. This was an elaborate affair with over 800 guests, including Ted's mother, Florence, and his first wife, Judy Nye, the mother of the bride, who had not seen either of her two children or Ted for nearly two decades. Turner beamed with pride, and no doubt thought back to his own wedding to Judy, a night he would tell an interviewer in 2008 was the happiest of his life,[23] when he and his father shared a similar pride. In November, Turner celebrated his 53rd birthday, reaching a psychological milestone as he attained the same age at which his father had committed suicide. On December 21, Jane Fonda's 54th birthday, Jane and Ted were married at a small ceremony on Turner's Avalon plantation in Tallahassee, Florida, with Jimmy Brown serving as Turner's best man. On the way to their honeymoon, Ted and Jane stopped off in Cincinnati to visit his mother, the rock of his life, who had been too sick to attend their wedding; she passed away in mid-January.

It was immediately apparent to Turner's children and friends that Ted and Jane shared a special relationship built on respect, support, understanding, and mutual interests. Turner seemed lighter, softer, less rushed. The man who would wait for nothing and no one could even sometimes wait for Jane without any apparent agitation. His often voluble temper remained largely in check, even without the lithium, which he had stopped taking when he thought it had made no difference anyway and another psychiatrist said he suffered only from anxiety, not any form of bipolar disorder. He not only learned to say the word monogamy, he actually began to embrace it. Jane, the workout guru, got Turner to exercise, drink less, and pay attention to his wardrobe, finally getting past the disheveled suits he had been wearing since his days at Brown. She got him to celebrate Christmas and organize family reunions at least twice a year.

Having sold off her old properties after the wedding, Jane and Ted built a beautiful log house on the 113,000-acre Montana ranch on which they had spent the last night of their first weekend together in June of 1989. Turner had bought the property, the Flying D, shortly afterward. It was the closest thing to a home they had, though with a growing list of ranches they had more homes than they could count. Ted had started building his bison herd by now, but his acreage was increasing faster than his herd. In 1992, he bought the 156,000-acre Ladder Ranch in south central New Mexico; in 1994, he purchased the 358,000-acre Armendaris Ranch, with its fully contained San Cristobal Mountain range, just a bit northeast of the Ladder; in 1995, he bought the 126,000-acre Spike-box Ranch in Nebraska; in 1996, he bought the 590,000-acre Vermejo Park, the largest contiguous property in the United States, stretching from northeastern New Mexico into south-central Colorado; and he purchased numerous others that were smaller, though still substantial. Ted and Jane spent some amount of time at them all, as well as at Big Sur, his southeastern plantations, and the 700-square-foot penthouse apartment Turner had had built atop the CNN Center in Atlanta in 1987. Jane started learning about plants to complement Ted's knowledge of birds and animals. She documented all of their properties with photographs that she collected under the title Home Sweet Homes. They went fly fishing as often as possible and hunting when feasible.

They were together all the time, meeting world leaders, organizing meetings with community and environmental groups, and supporting their causes. Turner did admit that he felt a little odd when they visited Mikhail Gorbachev, who spent the entire meeting speaking to Jane with his back to Ted. Ken Auletta tells of a 1994 Asian trip on which Jane had dominated attention in Hong Kong and China and Turner started getting annoyed when the pattern repeated itself in Japan. With their flight home diverted to a small airport in Canton in the middle of the night for emergency repairs, Turner, who had been feeling ill, went into the terminal to sleep. In the morning, Turner started recounting a nightmare he had had to a colleague, saying despite assurance that all was well, the plane would crash. When the colleague reassured him that they wouldn't crash, Turner interjected, "I haven't gotten to my nightmare yet. The nightmare is that the headline will be: 'Jane Fonda and others die in plane crash!'"[24] It was a joke, sort of. Still, for the most part, Turner was more than happy to occasionally yield the spotlight to Fonda, and often jokingly called himself "Mr. Fonda." As long as Jane's attention was focused on him, all else could be forgiven.

NOTES

1. Robert Goldberg and Gerald Jay Goldberg, Citizen Turner: The Wild Rise of an American Tycoon (New York: Harcourt, Brace & Co., 1995), 297. Quoting James Dodson, "Teddy Comes About," Atlanta, May 1993, 108.

2. Roger Vaughan, The Grand Gesture: Ted Turner, Mariner, and the America's Cup (Boston: Little, Brown & Co., 1975), 31.

3. I find further elucidation unnecessary, but if more detail is important, see Porter Bibb, It Ain't as Easy as it Looks: Ted Turner's Amazing Story (New

York: Crown Publishers, 1993), 237, 249–51 and Goldberg and Goldberg, *Citizen Turner*, 298, 304–7.

4. Michael Mason, "When Ted Met Jane," *People*, March 29, 1991, http://www.mikemason.net/work/magazines.php?cat=people&id=3.

5. Priscilla Painton, "The Taming of Ted Turner," *TIME*, January 6, 1992.

6. Painton, "The Taming of Ted Turner."

7. Goldberg and Goldberg, *Citizen Turner*, 387.

8. Porter Bibb, *It Ain't as Easy as It Looks: Ted Turner's Amazing Story* (New York: Crown Publishers, 1993), 403. Quoting the January 6, 1992 broadcast of "Talking with David Frost."

9. Ted Turner with Bill Burke, *Call Me Ted* (New York: Grand Central Publishing, 2008), 263.

10. Goldberg and Goldberg, *Citizen Turner*, 374–5. Quoting Dobson, *Atlanta* magazine, 112.

11. Painton, "The Taming of Ted Turner."

12. Mason, "When Ted Met Jane."

13. Turner, *Call Me Ted*, 264.

14. Jane Fonda, *My Life So Far* (New York: Random House, 2005), 468.

15. Ibid., 469.

16. Ibid., 471–2.

17. Ibid., 473.

18. Craig Sager, a sports reporter for TNT, tells an amusing story of flying with Turner to Seattle to attend a one-year countdown to the 1990 Goodwill Games when Ted unexpectedly broke off from their connecting flight in Denver in order to be with Fonda for the weekend. The next week, Sager reports, was Jane Fonda week on the Superstation. Turner has since denied the story. A link to the video is provided under Further Resources.

19. Fonda, *My Life So Far*, 481.

20. Several versions of this list appear on the Internet. The version referenced here is found as a PDF available through the Turner Enterprises Web site: http://www.tedturner.com/enterprises/pages/5AZ_Ten_Voluntary_Initiatives_PDF.pdf. A slightly reworded list, with a since-added eleventh initiative—"I support renewable energy and feel we should move rapidly to contain greenhouse gases"—together with further elucidation that he can't consistently live up to the entire list, appears as an appendix to *Call Me Ted*, 415–16.

21. Fonda, *My Life So Far*, 489.

22. To date, the Turner Foundation has made grants totaling nearly $300 million.

23. In a later interview, he would change this to all three of his wedding nights.

24. Ken Auletta, *Media Man: Ted Turner's Improbable Empire* (New York: Norton, 2004), 61.

Chapter 15

COLOR MY WORLD

One of Turner's key arguments for the MGM film library purchase centered on a technology Turner had heard about a few years earlier, colorization. Turner's contention was that while the library in its original form held several programming and revenue advantages for Turner Broadcasting, that value would significantly increase if the black and white versions could be transformed into true-life color, which would increase their audience potential and revive interest in the gems these old movies truly were. Turner's name would in fact become synonymous with the process, but he didn't invent it. Colorization, in Toronto, and Color Systems Technology, in Los Angeles, had pioneered it and been in business for several years. Hal Roach Studios[1] started colorizing *It's a Wonderful Life* in 1983[2] and had several more titles out by the spring of 1986. Viacom was already distributing some colorized versions of older episodes of the *Twilight Zone* in 1984, and Color Systems Technology was planning a color version of *Casablanca* in that same year. In fact, MGM itself was in the process of having *Yankee Doodle Dandy* and the 1941 version of *Dr. Jekyll and Mr. Hyde* colorized. Turner, high profile as he was and always a magnet for attention, became a leading and often rather lonely defender of the process, but even his often repeated dictum that if you don't like the color you can always turn it off predates his involvement with the technology.

In 1986, Turner announced that he would be colorizing some 100 of the films from his new MGM library. A spokesman for WTBS said, "We're not trying to make bad films great, we're trying to make great films better."[3] Woody Allen would respond, "If a movie director wishes his film to be colorized, then I say, by all means, let him color it. . . . The presumption that the colorizers are doing him a favor and bettering his movie is a transparent attempt to justify the mutilation of art for a few extra dollars."[4] Turner was fond of comparing the process to women wearing makeup, but given that the technique was still in its infancy, Richard Corliss would say that makeup "looks like an Earl Scheib paint job left too long in the sun."[5] Russell Baker said the films "made funeral cosmeticians around the world proud of their profession."[6] George Romero, co-writer and director of *Night of the Living Dead* said, "I think the actors in all of these movies look like the walking dead."[7] Colors were often poor, and halos of color could be seen following characters across the screen. Busy backgrounds could be rendered in flat sepia tints, backgrounds of similar objects would lose depth and realism when rendered with a single tint of color, and parts of a scene might appear as if they were still black and white. Color could alternately be washed out and garishly overdone. Ginger Rogers bemoaned, "All those lovely girls in '42nd Street' suddenly had the same orange face, the same orange legs, the same green costume and the same blank look."[8] Comparing the colorized version of *King Kong* to its original, an online reviewer noted, "In black and white, fleeing New Yorkers fit right in at Kong's feet. In color, they fade away transparently like ghosts and then re-appear just a few seconds later."[9]

The quality of the colorized versions varied, even in the earliest attempts, but the cost, complexity, and refinement of the technique had much to do with those types of problems. As the state of the art matured, most of these objections would no longer be valid, but questions of art direction wouldn't. Bette Davis, after seeing a colorized version of *Dark Victory* said, "All those beautiful clothes—everything is now pink. And blue. It saddens me."[10] In a written statement for a Congressional hearing on the subject, Jimmy Stewart said that the colorized *It's a Wonderful Life* was "a bath of Easter egg dye. Gloria Graham played a character named Violet, so someone thought it would be cute to have all her costumes in violet. That is the kind of obvious visual pun that Frank Capra never would have considered."[11]

Those against the process frequently argued that it would destroy the greatest treasures of our film history, but in fact the colorized versions didn't harm the originals any more than normal viewings would. Colorizing was done on a TV-quality video transfer and the original film print was usually restored in whole or in part in preparation for the transfer. For the defenders, the often repeated argument cited above, that if you didn't like the color you could just turn it off, was at best misleading, since the contrast of color images is generally lower than that of black and white and notably lower than black and white when used artistically, as it tended to be in most of the classics being considered for the process. In time, the argument devolved into Turner representatives' populism against purists' elitism. As Roger Ebert said, "to put it bluntly, anyone who can accept the idea of the colorization of black and white films has bad taste. . . . If you "like" colorized movies, it is doubtful that you know why movies are made, or why you watch them."[12]

The fact remained that many people did like and even preferred the colorized versions of many of the old black and white movies, for whatever reason. As Turner points out, airings of colorized versions of movies on the Superstation regularly outrated the black and white originals, sometimes drawing nearly six times the number of viewers. He would say, "Colorizing was not inexpensive—it cost about $2,000 per minute or about $200,000 for the average length film. But updating these classics helped us earn new syndication revenues, especially overseas, where many television stations had stopped buying black and white product."[13] Turner would go on to sell videotapes and DVDs as well as syndication rights to both color and black and white versions and has claimed that his right to colorize the movies he owned has always won in the courts. In the United States, that's true, because the owner of copyright has always held sway in American law. In a reasonable, if still unsatisfactory, compromise Congress would create a National Film Registry, a growing list of films that if colorized, need to carry a disclaimer. In France, however, where ownership can be viewed more critically, the heirs of John Huston were successful in having a colorized version of the director's *The Asphalt Jungle* banned when an appeals court ruled that artistic rights belonged to MGM and Huston, not Turner.

As time went on, Turner Broadcasting would actually become a major player in film preservation, preserving and restoring many films that were deteriorating and in danger of being lost forever. In 1989, on its 50th anniversary, Turner would premiere a restored version of *Gone With the Wind* at an elaborate costume party meant to recreate the fancy-dress ball that was held with the original premiere in 1939. Turner opened his comments with, "All I can say is, thank God they shot *Gone With the Wind* in color."[14] By 1987, "'Gone With the Wind' looked more like 'Confederates from Mars.' Scarlett and Rhett had grown green and blue, a result of unstable film stocks and generations of badly duplicated prints. Hair styles and costumes, once marvels of spectral subtlety, looked as though captured in Crayola, not Technicolor."[15] The restoration was brilliant for the time and widely applauded, but there were still some critics. Martin Scorsese, who had been a vocal opponent of colorization but a long time proponent of preservation, commented that the color in the new print was colder than the original Technicolor version. The Technicolor process used a prism behind the lens to capture three separate negatives that were then combined in a dye transfer process to a single master negative. The process had its own distinct tonality and tended to be warm, almost yellowish in character; to Scorsese that yellowish warmth was missed in the new print. Similar issues of original color and intent came up with restoration of the Sistine Chapel in Rome, where many felt that Michelangelo's bright original colors were intentionally muted by overlying resins and not intended to be viewed in the rawer state that the restoration revealed. The intentional altering of the original in a colorization process is a different case, but restoration of any kind calls for artistic judgments not altogether different from those so derided by the opponents of colorizing.

MGM had already started film preservation and restoration of its film libraries more than a decade before Turner purchased them, but Turner vowed to continue the process and as time went on his company's accomplishments in restoring our great films have far surpassed any bitterness engendered by his colorization efforts. While Turner Broadcasting continued to show and sell colorized versions of many films, by the mid-1990s they were virtually out of the colorizing business. A much more refined process is starting to be seen now, however, and in *The Aviator*, Martin Scorsese would actually colorize some of the black and white sequences of Howard Hughes's *Hell's Angels* and *The Outlaw*; the original footage was provided by Turner Broadcasting.

NOTES

1. Named for the Hal Roach film library that the company purchased; it is not owned by Hal Roach or his family. Colorization, the company in Toronto that actually performed the colorization process, was a subsidiary of Hal Roach Studios.

2. A DVD of this version is available at Amazon.com.

3. Richard Corliss, "Raiders of the Lost Art," *TIME*, October 20, 1986.

4. Maureen Dowd, "Film Stars Protest Coloring," *The New York Times*, May 13, 1987.

5. Corliss, "Raiders of the Lost Art."

6. Russell Baker, "OBSERVER; And the Winner Is . . . " *The New York Times*, March 31, 1987.

7. Corliss, "Raiders of the Lost Art."

8. Dowd, "Film Stars Protest Coloring."

9. Matt Paprocki, Movie Review: King Kong (1933) Colorized, posted December 27, 2005, http://blogcritics.org/archives/2005/12/27/012348.php.

10. Glenn Collins, "Tribute for a Dauntless Bette Davis. Yes," *The New York Times*, April 20, 1989.

11. Dowd, "Film Stars Protest Coloring."

12. Roger Ebert, "Casablanca gets colorized, but don't play it again, Ted," *Chicago Sun Times*, October 3, 1988, http://rogerebert.suntimes.com/apps/pbcs.dll/article?AID=/19881030/PEOPLE/10010305&template=printart.

13. Ted Turner with Bill Burke, *Call Me Ted* (New York: Grand Central Publishing, 2008), 254.

14. Robert Goldberg and Gerald Jay Goldberg, *Citizen Turner: The Wild Rise of an American Tycoon* (New York: Harcourt, Brace & Co., 1995), 391.

15. Max Alexander, "FILM; Once More, the Old South in All Its Glory," *The New York Times*, January 29, 1989.

Chapter 16

REMOTE CONTROL

Turner did in fact continue to run the company, though between his frequent trips overseas seeking access to international markets for both his entertainment and news programming, and changes in his personal life, he would spend less and less time at TBS offices. Throughout 1987 and 1988, Turner would complain of being exhausted, and he initially was diagnosed with the trendy chronic fatigue syndrome or Epstein-Barr virus and then with a virus associated with his frequent jetting around the world. Despite the new board, and with a good amount of credit going to the 1984 Cable Communication and Competition Act that deregulated cable and resulted in significant upgrading of cable services and further expansion into urban areas, the following years would see significant growth at Turner Broadcasting.

CNN continued its global expansion, opening a Beijing bureau in 1987, starting a Spanish newscast, Noticiero CNN, for U.S. and Latin American markets in 1988, opening a Manila bureau and being beamed by a Soviet satellite to Africa, the Middle East, India, and Southeast Asia in 1989, making it a true worldwide news service. CNN would again garner acclaim for its unique coverage of student protests and the amassing military presence in China's Tiananmen Square, continuing to tape as the crew, including anchor Bernard Shaw, negotiated with Chinese officials and were told to end their coverage, only to ask for it in writing before the signal finally went dark.[1] Rupert Murdoch would say, "Watching the events in China on CNN was the most amazing experience. It was an extraordinary moment in history, to know that what was happening in China was happening in part because we were all watching it."[2] Later in the year, Turner would become the first entrepreneur in history to win the prestigious Paul White award from the Radio and News Directors Association. When the United States invaded Panama in December of 1989, the Soviet Union's first call to denounce the move was not to the U.S. Embassy but to CNN.

By the time it celebrated its 10th anniversary in June of 1990, CNN had a staff of over 2,100, was available in over 89 countries to seven million homes internationally and 54 million homes in the United States, and its operating profits for 1989 were $134 million. Its purposely unscrambled signal was pirated even more widely. It was seen in more than 200,000 hotel rooms outside the United States, and had become a staple of world leaders in Beijing and Moscow, as well as King Fahd in Saudi Arabia, Muammar Khadafi in Libya, Yasir Arafat, Margaret Thatcher, Kim Il Sung, and, of course, Fidel Castro. Diplomats used it to find out their governments' positions on unfolding events before being wired. Intelligence services watched to gain better and more current information than their own networks could deliver, President George H. W. Bush told other world leaders, "I learn more from CNN than I do from the CIA."[3] From Poland, to Kenya, to Buenos Aires, to Tunisia, CNN, the "Chicken Noodle News," had become the world's synonym for news.

At TBS, Turner was able convince his board to let him start another network. Turner Network Television (TNT) was launched on October 3, 1988 as a venue for high-profile sporting events, original movies, and an outlet for Turner's MGM library. When it debuted with a showing of Gone With the Wind, it had 17 million subscribers, making it the most successful launch in cable history; within a year, it had 50 million subscribers and generated nearly $100 million in subscription revenues. Though it took a long time to make good on its promise to air high-profile events, it ranked among the top six highest rated basic cable offerings from its inception. Late in 1988 and early in 1989, Turner also wanted to purchase an initial 45 percent interest in the Financial News Network (FNN), which was then near bankruptcy. Aware that NBC was preparing for an April launch of a business news service named

CNBC, Turner wanted to quickly bulk up FNN and fight off the new venture, which he saw as the first wave of a new threat against CNN, but TCI's John Malone vetoed the idea. Turner would, however, launch Turner Pictures in 1989, a production company that would create films for TNT and eventually make some attempts at theatrical releases. He also launched Turner Publishing to produce books related to TBS enterprises in documentaries, entertainment, and news.

By July of 1989, though Turner had not in any way changed his views on morality and violence in films and television, he would anger his former allies on that issue by airing a decidedly pro-choice documentary on the Superstation, *Abortion for Survival*. Turner announced that the documentary would be followed by a discussion of abortion that would include the views of those who opposed abortion, whom he referred to as "bozos [who] look like idiots anyway."[4] By 1990, Turner would outlaw use of the word "foreign" at TBS, assessing a $100 fine for each use of the word or failure to use "international" in its stead, and he would be quoted in Colorado saying, "It was a terrible realization for me to come to, because no one loves our country more than I. But I have come to the conclusion from studying it, from a global circumstance, that *we* are the greatest problem in the world."[5]

He had already begun production of an original animation of his own creation, *Captain Planet and the Planeteers*, in which defenders of Gaia (Earth), the title characters, battle the forces of environmental degradation embodied in villains with names like Sly Sludge, Hoggish Greedly, Looten Plunder, Verminous Skumm, and, most famously, Duke Nukem. It would begin airing in September of 1990 on TBS, and despite its rather overt message orientation, it would become quite popular.[6] Offshoots of the series included a line of toys that was produced for several years and five video games.

On August 1, 1990, Turner would replace the 70-year-old Burt Reinhardt, president and CEO of CNN, with an outsider to TBS and television when he hired W. Thomas (Tom) Johnson Jr., former publisher of the *Los Angeles Times*. He offered the job to Johnson after a three-minute conversation. On August 2, 1990, Johnson's second day on the job, Iraq invaded Kuwait. CNN's *World Report*, to which Iraq was a contributing member, would earn untold dividends during the conflict based on the trust and personal relationships it had formed with Tariq Aziz and other high-ranking members of the Iraqi government and communications infrastructure. CNN would have access denied to other news operations. As the year progressed and it became obvious that President Bush would launch retaliatory action, CNN would bolster their offices throughout the region. Tom Johnson would ask Turner how much he should budget for the operation, and Turner's response was, "You spend whatever you think it takes, pal."[7] In October, CNN would air a Bernard Shaw interview with Saddam Hussein, who was still ignoring deadlines for withdrawal from Kuwait. The interview would draw wide criticism from public officials and political commentators and be followed shortly by strong recommendations from Johnson's high-placed sources in Washington that CNN personnel be pulled from Iraq. While Johnson initially favored heeding the warnings, Turner would say that those who wanted to leave could do so, but those who wanted to stay would not be forced out.

Operation Desert Storm, or the Persian Gulf War, was launched on January 16, 1991 and lasted through February 28. CNN reporters Peter Arnett, Bernard Shaw, and John Holliman remained in Iraq throughout and brought the world a whole new experience of war, with bombs raining on Baghdad and Scud missiles launched against Saudi Arabia and Jerusalem. When CIA Director William Webster received satellite notification of the launch of a Scud, he would tell Brent Scowcroft, "Turn on CNN and see where it lands."[8] The network would continue to receive widespread criticism from competing news services and commentators, and CNN headquarters would be evacuated when it received two bomb threats in early February, but coverage would prove to be the defining moment for CNN, as the major networks were forced to watch CNN along with everyone else and CNN scored its highest ratings ever.

In August of 1991, reactionaries in the Soviet Union, unhappy with the policies of Mikhail Gorbachev, staged a coup attempt, seizing Gorbachev while he was on vacation in the Crimea and cutting his communications to Moscow. Russian president Boris Yeltsin would issue a declaration, distributed around Moscow on flyers, calling the coup unconstitutional, urging the military not to take part, and calling for a general strike while demanding that Gorbachev be allowed to communicate with the people. On August 19, Yeltsin would mount a tank outside the parliament building and make a speech to the people. Though state TV had been blocked by the coup organizers, CNN continued airing throughout, and Yeltsin's speech from atop the tank reached Soviet satellite states and a lower but significant number of Soviet citizens, who flocked to the capital to protect the sitting government. When Gorbachev was finally released, he thanked his friends and CNN for being instrumental to his release. Boris Yeltsin would cite CNN and its coverage of the coup attempt as being one of the most significant contributions to the dissolution of the Soviet Union. On Christmas day, CNN would cover that final dissolution, and Mikhail Gorbachev would borrow a pen from Tom Johnson to sign the official papers.

By December of 1991, CNN had opened new bureaus in Amman, New Delhi, Rio de Janeiro, and Bangkok, and it had started its first regular live programming of CNN International from its London bureau. Turner had also prevailed upon his board to allow the purchase of Hanna-Barbera Productions, Inc., an animation studio that had created *The Flintstones*, *the Jetsons*, *Huckleberry Hound*, *Yogi Bear*, *Top Cat*, *Scooby Doo*, and *Tom and Jerry*. Costing $320 million, it provided Turner with one of the most significant holdings of animations in the world when combined with the older cartoons he had received with the purchase of MGM; it would prove to be one of Turner's best acquisitions. On October 1, 1992, he would launch a new service, the Cartoon Network, with which he would briefly flirt with using the new must-carry/retransmission consent rules to gain carriage by cable networks. The new network would air a revamped sequel to *Captain Planet*, which had aired on TBS through December of 1992. *The New Adventures of Captain Planet* would air from 1993 through 1996, and new animated series like *Johnny Bravo*, *The Real Adventures of Jonny Quest*, and *Powerpuff Girls* were introduced.

In 1992, former Carter aide Hamilton Jordan and other southern power brokers, unhappy with the choice between President Bush and Bill Clinton in the upcoming presidential elections, were casting around for a third-party candidate. Ted Turner was second on their list to Ross Perot. Turner's previous use of lithium was a drawback, and Jane Fonda, who had had her fill of political campaigning with Tom Hayden, did not want any part of it. According to Turner, she threatened to leave him if he chose to run, but when Ross Perot accepted the challenge the idea became moot anyway.

Throughout 1992, Turner Broadcasting would expand TNT and the Cartoon Network into Europe, Latin America, and Asia. CNN would gain 10 million new homes in Europe, enter a partnership with n-tv in Germany, and add 88 new U.S. affiliates. By the end of the year, TBS profits surpassed any of the major networks'. Turner had been thwarted in his efforts to buy or merge with a major network or a major film studio, but in 1993 Turner would receive approval from his board for a new acquisition—this time the more modest, though significant, purchase of New Line Cinema and Castle Rock Entertainment for a combined $600 million and the assumption of $250 million in debt. Though Castle Rock had no film library of its own, it produced the *Seinfeld* television series and movies such as *Misery, When Harry Met Sally, City Slickers,* and *A Few Good Men.* New Line, while heavy in gothic horror like *Nightmare on Elm Street* and *Friday the 13th,* had also produced *Glengarry Glen Ross, Teenage Mutant Ninja Turtles,* and *My Own Private Idaho.* As owner of New Line, Turner would give the approval for *The Lord of the Rings* cycle, the most ambitious and expensive production ever attempted by the studio and a major critical and box office success.

With TNT now featuring more contemporary material and major sporting events, on April 14, 1994, Turner would start still another network, Turner Classic Movies, devoted to the classic gems of Hollywood that Turner had purchased from MGM. Like TNT, its inaugural program would be Turner's favorite, *Gone With the Wind,* and while it, like the Cartoon Network, would take a bit of time to develop a wide audience, it now has a highly loyal viewership that considers it alone worth subscribing to cable. By the end of 1994, CNN itself would show more profit than any of the major networks.

NOTES

1. A year later, at a Better World Society conference in Beijing, Turner would tell Beijing's Foreign Press Association, "Students were breaking the law. We bleed in our hearts for the students. We also bleed in our hearts for the government and the soldiers who felt like they were forced to take that action. The students should have known better, don't you think? They had been warned." Quoted in Porter Bibb, *It Ain't as Easy as it Looks: Ted Turner's Amazing Story* (New York: Crown Publishers, 1993), 349.

2. Richard Hack, *Clash of the Titans: How the Unbridled Ambition of Ted Turner and Rupert Murdoch Has Created Global Empires That Control What We Read and Watch* (Beverly Hills, CA: New Millennium Press, 2003), 277.

3. William A. Henry, III, "History as It Happens," *TIME*, January 6, 1982.

4. Damian Whitworth, "Ted Turner's next big thing," *Times* Online, Times Newspapers Ltd., November 22, 2008.

5. Bibb, *It Ain't as Easy as it Looks*, 348.

6. Regularly scheduled viewings of the series appear on Boomerang. The Mother Nature Network, MNN.com, started running episodes of the series on its site in February 2009 with plans to continue through February 2010.

7. Robert Goldberg and Gerald Jay Goldberg, *Citizen Turner: The Wild Rise of an American Tycoon* (New York: Harcourt, Brace & Co., 1995), 440.

8. Henry, III, "History as It Happens."

Chapter 17

TIME WORN

While Turner Broadcasting had obviously continued to prosper and had grown to operate six cable channels, Ted still felt boxed in and unable to escape the restrictions he had accepted in order to escape losing the company in the wake of the MGM deal. With FCC regulatory changes in the early 1990s, made partly in response to the unfettered growth of cable that resulted from the 1984 Cable Act, the box seemed even smaller. Relaxing of the "Fin-Syn" rules of the 1970s—limiting network involvement in producing and owning content, particularly primetime content—began in 1991, and the Cable Television Consumer Protection and Competition Act of 1992 finally instituted the must-carry/retransmission consent rules that Turner and the cable industry had previously fought off.[1] Under these rules, all cable operators whose systems carried 12 or more channels would have to make up to one-third of their channel capacity available for local broadcast stations, and broadcast channels could either elect that their signal must be carried by cable systems or that the cable systems had to negotiate with them to receive their consent for the cable systems' carriage of their signals. Without these provisions being enacted, Turner may have been content to continue within the strictures placed on him by his high-powered board of cable operators, avoiding big gambles and serving as a cautious overlord, but the new regulations made it clear that a series of media acquisitions and mergers was on the horizon and

Turner was afraid of being marginalized, unable to acquire programming, and ultimately being faced with erosion that would force him to sell from weakness. If he were going to survive, he would have to purchase or align himself with major studios or broadcast networks while Turner Broadcasting was riding high and still dealing from a position of strength.

The problem was that his board partners, particularly TCI and what was now Time Warner, which both held veto powers, had conflicts with many of Turner's best options for a merger and weren't willing to risk their investments on one of Turner's ambitious and risk-filled attempts to make purchases that were beyond his ability to pay. Time Warner, the more corporate of his two biggest investors, was suffering its own financial travails and reasoned that any risk Turner assumed would hurt not only the worth of Turner Broadcasting shares but its own flailing shares as well. Throughout this period, Turner tried everything to free himself from his veto-wielding partners, but while Time Warner's own debt was deep enough to consider being bought out of its Turner position, it insisted on a cash settlement so large that Turner would be left incapable of any independent takeovers.

In May of 1993, Turner went public with his frustrations over "the limitations and conflicts of interest"[2] inherent in the structure of his board, and he talked about having initiated plans to break up the company in order to escape the veto powers of TCI and Time. While he didn't give specifics, he envisioned "'a change in roles,' with him getting stock in the other two companies and sitting on their boards while still retaining an active role managing some or all of Turner Broadcasting's channels."[3] In late September of 1994, Turner again spoke of his frustrations during a speech at the National Press Club in Washington D.C.: "This could mean that I have to sell out, that's what it could mean. I'd put my company up for sale. That's the only way to resolve this thing."[4] Claiming that he had been close to acquiring NBC the year before only to have the deal scuttled by Time Warner, he referred to a CNN report on clitorectomies, the practice in some societies of mutilating women's genital organs, and said, "You talk about barbaric mutilation. Well, I'm in an angry mood. I'm angry at that too. I'm being clitorized by Time Warner!"[5]

In 2001, Turner told Paul Maxwell at The Cable Center that he had had a handshake on the deal to acquire NBC, citing $5 billion as the price in what he called a "100% financed . . . turnkey deal"[6] that TCI had approved but that Gerry Levin vetoed. Turner was certainly active in seeking mergers and acquisitions between 1992 and 1995, and many of Turner's comments from that time period and later spoke of deals that were all but done if not for opposition from one or more of his veto partners. But how close Turner really came to acquiring a network or a major studio in the 1990s is an open question. Jack Welch claimed that GE had never really been that close to a deal with Turner, and in *Call Me Ted*, Turner indicates that mergers and deals with ABC and NBC at the time were lost more by his own reluctance or actions, never explicitly citing an intervention by his board. The threat of a veto, however, and the knowledge by those he negotiated with that his board held veto power, definitely weighed on Turner and impacted his negotiations. Martin Davis, CEO of Paramount, one of those with whom Turner had spoke about a merger, said, "Ted has no authority. Any expenditure over $2 million he has to go to the board for. He's a minor player. He's got no control over his destiny."[7]

Perhaps one of the more intriguing discussions Turner had at the time was with Bill Gates at Microsoft, who was looking to acquire news content for MSN.com, Microsoft's new Internet service. Microsoft was willing to invest $1 billion in Turner Broadcasting in order to establish a 50/50 joint venture in CNN.com. The investment, while not enough to buy out either TCI or Time Warner, could possibly have gone a long way in diluting them enough to escape their veto, allowing Turner to make another serious run at CBS. It's unlikely that either partner would have accepted the dilution, but it does still look to have been Turner's best bet at the time. Microsoft, though, already had a reputation for ruthless business practices and that, together with Turner's worries about what his board might think of the move (for all the restrictions his board arrangement imposed on him, there were distinct advantages to having your distributors invested in your business), made Turner uneasy. Microsoft would later partner with NBC in creating both a cable news channel and a website for the channel.

On July 31, 1995, Disney announced a $19 billion buyout of Cap Cities/ABC. On August 1, Westinghouse Electric announced a deal to purchase CBS for $5.4 billion.[8] On August 19, at Turner's Flying D ranch in Montana, Turner interrupted his weekend with guests and agreed to Jerry Levin's proposal that Time Warner purchase Turner Broadcasting in a deal originally estimated at $8.5 billion. Of all the deals that came so rapidly one after the other, this was the most surprising.

Levin himself hadn't been sure how Turner would react to his proposal, but Turner knew from the moment he'd received a call from Levin the previous day that the offer would be made, and he had all but made up his mind to accept. When Levin assured him that he would be a partner rather than an employee and that Turner Broadcasting would be "the pivot point in the center of the company,"[9] his remaining concerns were alleviated. Turner was tired, the deals involving ABC and CBS confirmed his sense of how the media world was conglomerating, and he was fenced in by a board that he had to fight in order to make any move, large or small. At one moment, John Malone was helping Turner try to buy Time Warner out of its Turner stake so that he could pursue a network, and the next Malone was meeting with Rupert Murdoch, who wanted to discuss his own strategy for taking control of Turner Broadcasting. After agreeing to the deal, Turner called Malone, who has always referred to himself as a libertarian, to ask for his blessing and offer the following explanation: "You know we love you guys but you're too far right-wing for me."[10]

Holding the TCI veto, Malone still had to agree to the plan, but as he worked to gain all the advantage he could from that fact, the intended sale was made public. No one could quite comprehend how the hard-driving, irascible Turner could even contemplate the move. As one division president of a talent agency said, "I think the question is 'Why?' As soon as you figure out the why, everything else falls into place."[11] Robert Goldberg, coauthor of *Citizen Turner*, speculated, "The hard part for him won't be being No. 2, but being part of a corporate culture like Time Warner's. He's always been a quintessential outsider; when he was a kid he named his boat *Pariah*. The question is, will Ted Turner be able to bend Time Warner to his will, or will Time Warner bend Turner? At some point, something will have to give."[12]

By the end of September, the deal was finally worked out. Turner would be named a vice chairman of Time Warner, signing a five-year contract to head the Turner Broadcasting services together with supervisory responsibilities for HBO. He would receive stock that would amount to 10 percent of Time Warner's shares, making him the biggest stockholder in the company, and he would receive two seats on the Time Warner board while drawing a salary equal to Levin's (about $1.05 million) plus an amount equal to 90 percent of Levin's annual bonus. In all of Turner's talks on mergers, no one had ever offered a similar role or compensation package. Malone, who traded his shares at a higher rate than other TBS stock holders would acquire between 8–9 percent of Time Warner shares and receive very favorable terms for TCI's licensing of Turner's channels through 2015; he would not, however, sit on Time Warner's board, and due to FCC restrictions, his shares would be non-voting. In public he said that both he and Turner were supporting Levin and would not attempt a palace coup, but privately he told Turner, "As a practical matter, Ted, you're taking over Time Warner if you play your cards right. . . . I see this as him [Levin] working for you—not you working for him."

At the press conference announcing the deal, Turner admitted, "We haven't sorted out what my priorities and responsibilities are exactly [but] I'm looking forward to having some muscle on my bones for a change."[13] "I don't feel like I sold the company. I'm going from like a 23 percent owner of Turner Broadcasting to a 10 percent owner in a lot bigger, more powerful, stronger company."[14] "I've been a C.E.O. for 33 years, and that's a long time for anyone. I'm married to Jane Fonda so I know what it's like to be No. 2."[15] "You fight the establishment for so long, and one day, you wake up and you're part of it."[16] He reasoned as well that Time Warner stock had been underperforming and that he could help focus the company, which had never entirely meshed the Time Inc. and Warner Communications entities since their merger in 1989.

For Time Warner, the merger vaulted them back in front of newly combined Disney/Capital Cities/ABC as the world's largest media company. While it increased Time Warner's debt somewhat from $15 million to roughly $17 million, the infusion of Turner Broadcasting's at least $2.8 billion in annual revenues and $650 million in operating cash flow would improve the company's ratio of debt to cash flow. The move would reunite Turner's old Warner Brothers cartoons with Time Warner's own considerable cartoon library, and the Cartoon Network would help it to leverage those holdings. There were synergies between Time Warner's magazines and CNN, and the ad-based TBS and TNT joining the HBO subscriber channel helped to round out the company's cable programming. Levin called the merger "a sublime combination"[17] that made the company "complete."[18]

Turner worked to protect his interests at Time Warner, stopping a sale of Warner Brothers movies to CBS by arguing that they should be offered to the company's own cable interests first, winning control of all new international channels, blocking a withdrawal from its share of Court TV to prevent GE from buying it and competing with CNN. But his interests were also now in the company as a whole, and he argued for cost cutting at the Hollywood studio and throughout the company, getting rid of corporate jets and company perks. Levin would recall that when meeting with employees, "Ted would get up and say 'I've got one suit. I don't spend money on suits. I own ten percent of this company and each dollar you waste, ten cents comes from me.'"[19] Even Turner's son Teddy, a promotions manager at the now redundant TBS home-video unit, became a victim. As overheard by a reporter while the merger awaited FCC approval, Turner was dining with his family at an Atlanta restaurant when Teddy asked whether his job would be safe. Turner replied, "You're toast."[20]

It's at this time as well that Turner reignited a personal war with Rupert Murdoch. The genesis of their conflict had begun in one of Turner's rare post-1980 yachting races, the 1983 Sydney-Hobart. Turner's *Condor* would win after a Murdoch-sponsored boat, *Nirvana*, ran him aground just as Condor was overtaking her six miles from the finish. As Turner's views became ever more progressive and Murdoch's media empire became ever more powerful, the feud continued to simmer. When in April of 1996 Murdoch announced that he would be launching a Fox News Channel on cable, Turner said he was "looking forward to squishing him like a bug."[21] But the real eruption followed when Time Warner, which had already met its FCC obligation to carry one competing news channel when it agreed to carry MSNBC, the co-venture of Microsoft and NBC that had launched that July, announced in late September that they would not be carrying Murdoch's Fox News Channel, being promoted as a conservative answer to CNN. An incensed Murdoch blamed Turner and launched a blistering attack against him and Time Warner while enlisting New York Mayor Rudolph Giuliani to his cause. On October 6, the same day that Fox News launched, New York City's Franchise and Concession Review Committee opened hearings to review Time Warner's cable franchise agreement. Roger Ailes, president of Fox, testified, "New York City now has a cable-system czar who can control access and tell New Yorkers what they can and cannot see. Unfortunately, the New York City cable czar lives in Atlanta. His name is Ted Turner."[22] Ted Turner said he had nothing to do with the decision. In a later deposition, he said he had suggested that MSNBC and Fox each be carried on half of Time Warner's franchises, but he had been overruled by Levin. "I don't really favor one over the other. . . . It would be like, would you rather be defeated by the Nazis or Japanese in World War II? Neither one of them is going to give you much of a break. You die in one concentration camp as fast as another."[23] Time Warner pointed out that there were more than 30 channels they had not picked up without anyone ever objecting and wondered why Giuliani was so interested in this one. At a press briefing, Turner said Murdoch "used his publications to settle scores 'like the late Fuhrer,'"[24] while Murdoch's New York Post briefly dropped CNN listings from its TV programming grid, canvassed Jewish leaders about Turner's references to the Fuhrer, and added a straitjacket to a picture of Turner under the headline "Is Ted Turner Crazy?"[25] By July of 1997, an agreement between Time Warner and Fox News was worked out and the feud returned to a low simmer, though neither Murdoch's news operation nor Turner ever let an opportunity for a dig go by.

Since the MGM deal, the bailout by his cable partners, the dissolution of his second marriage, and the 1987 purchase of his first ranch, Montana's Bar None, Ted had been increasingly stepping back from Turner Broadcasting, and at this point was spending no more than two to three days at its offices. He had reshuffled his priorities, and land, fly-fishing, philanthropic support of the causes he felt strongly about, and his life with Jane Fonda all trumped the importance of the empire he had worked so long and tirelessly to build. When he had realized that he could never independently grow his company to a point where it would be stable in the long run, he aligned with a company that gave it that stability and essentially cashed out in a way that would give him some control of just how much cash he would be getting. More than at any earlier time in his career, his attention would focus on stock price.

When the stock price finally did start improving, the worth of his holdings increased from $2.2 billion to $3.2 billion. When he was scheduled to receive a Global Leadership Award from the United Nations Association of the United States of America on September 18, 1997, Turner astounded his audience, including Secretary General Kofi Anan, by making a $1 billion contribution to the United Nations, nearly a third of his net worth. The man who had previously said that money was how you kept score in the game of life and who had just been ranked #25 on the Forbes 400 list of the richest men in the country had hinted about his views toward his new scorecard the year before, saying, "That list is destroying our country! These new super-rich won't loosen up their wads because they're afraid they'll reduce their net worth and go down on the list. That's their Super Bowl."[26] During the speech in which he announced the pledge, Turner again chided the wealthy on increasing their charitable contributions as well as the United States for being $1.5 billion in arrears on its UN dues. Despite being conservative in his early life and having been friends with many members of the John Birch Society—always virulently anti-UN—Turner had always been drawn to the organization; as he became more involved with world affairs after starting CNN, he had increasingly seen it as the best hope we had for global understanding and peace.

The contribution involved a mixed grant of cash and stock that would be paid over 10 years. Since the UN could not accept grants from individuals, Turner set up The United Nations Foundation and appointed former Colorado congressman and senator Tim Wirth, who himself had long been a supporter of the cable industry as well as environmental and population issues, as president of the organization, with a board comprising luminaries from around the globe. Rather than just give the money to the UN, the idea was to form a discussion with the UN on projects it was pursuing and then to support those projects the foundation felt would have the best impact on issues like children's health, global warming and sustainable energy, and the empowerment of women, as well as disaster relief and lobbying for a stronger United Nations. Wirth and the foundation would seek additional donations while reaching out to other foundations, organizations, and businesses that would be interested in supporting similar causes. The foundation has worked on eradicating obstetric fistula, malaria, polio, measles, and AIDS, combated violence against women, and promoted environmental awareness among children, while serving as a vital resource for the Bill and Melinda Gates Foundation and Save the Children.

NOTES

1. Turner Broadcasting, joined by others in the cable industry, sued to stop the Cable Act in District Court in Washington D.C. The District Court weighed retransmission consent under *Daniels Cablevision v. FCC*, 835 F. Supp. 1, and must-carry under *Turner Broadcasting Inc. v. FCC*, upholding the Act in both cases. In an appeal to the Supreme Court decided in 1994, *Turner Broadcasting Inc. v. FCC*, 512 U.S. 622, the Court upheld the constitutionality of the must-carry provisions, citing them as content neutral. However, it remanded the case back to the District Court for review on whether indirect burdens on the cable industry resulting from the must-carry provisions were acceptable when weighed against the government interests in the case. The District Court found that the indirect burdens were minimal and that the must-carry provisions were the best way to advance the government's goal of preserving broadcast television. In a return to the Supreme Court, *Turner Broadcasting Inc. v. FCC*, 520 U.S. 180, decided in 1997, the District Court's ruling was again upheld.

2. Bill Carter, "Ted Turner's Time of Discontent," *The New York Times*, June 6, 1993.

3. Ibid.

4. "Turner Lashes out at Time Warner," *Cable Regulation Digest*, October 3, 1994, http://bubl.ac.uk/ARCHIVE/journals/crd/941003.htm.

5. Ken Auletta, *Media Man: Ted Turner's Improbable Empire* (New York: Norton, 2004), 66. Gerry Levin, who had originally dismissed Turner's comment as Ted being Ted, would tell Kara Swisher years later that this was the one remark of Turner's that he could never forgive: "To compare a brutal practice like that to his business life was just beyond the pale of even Ted." Kara Swisher with Lisa Dickey, *There Must Be a Pony in Here Somewhere: The AOL Time Warner Debacle and the Quest for a Digital Future* (New York: Crown Business, 2003), 87.

6. The Cable Center, Oral History Collection, Paul Maxwell interview with R. "Ted" E. Turner, November 2001. Transcript and video available at http://www.cablecenter.org/education/library/oralHistoryDetails.cfm?id=179.

7. Bryan Burrough, "The Siege of Paramount," *Vanity Fair*, February 1994, 132.

8. In his unsuccessful attempt to take over CBS in 1985, Turner offered what was generally accepted to be a $5.41 billion purchase price for the network, which would be approximately $7.63 billion in 1995 dollars. Additionally, despite CBS's posturing over its vaunted news division at the time, by 1995 CNN was a more successful and arguably more trusted news operation.

9. Auletta, *Media Man*, 76.

10. John Malone sidebar in Ted Turner with Bill Burke, *Call Me Ted* (New York: Grand Central Publishing, 2008), 318.

11. James Sterngold, "The Media Business: The Industry; Hollywood the Blasé Is Impressed," *The New York Times*, August 31, 1995.

12. Rebecca Ascher-Walsh, "Executive Suite: Can Ted Be Led?" *Entertainment Weekly*, September 15, 1995, 22.

13. Lawrie Mifflin, "Ted Turner Nonchalant about Not Being the Chief," *The New York Times*, September 23, 1995.

14. Richard Hack, *Clash of the Titans: How the Unbridled Ambition of Ted Turner and Rupert Murdoch Has Created Global Empires That Control What We Read and Watch* (Beverly Hills, CA: New Millennium Press, 2003), 340.

15. Mifflin, "Ted Turner Nonchalant."

16. "Ted Turner: The Titan Once Known as Captain Outrageous Pulls off His Most Surprising Year," *People*, December 25, 1995, http://www.people.com/people/archive/article/0,,20102448,00.html.

17. Mark Landler, "Turner to Merge into Time Warner," *The New York Times*, September 23, 1995.

18. Mark Landler and Geraldine Fabrikant, "Turner Deal a Chance for Time Warner to Fulfill Promises," *The New York Times*, September 23, 1996.

19. Auletta, *Media Man*, 78.

20. Hack, *Clash of the Titans*, 362.

21. Guardian.co.uk, "Turner: Murdoch is a 'warmonger,'" April 25, 2003, http://www.guardian.co.uk/media/2003/apr/25/newscorporation.pressandpublishing.

22. Hack, *Clash of the Titans*, 12.

23. Ibid., 15.

24. Mark Landler, "Cable News Feud Has Personal and Political Roots," *The New York Times*, October 5, 1996.

25. *The Economist*, "Mouth of the South v the Dirty Digger," December 11, 2008, http://www.economist.com/books/displaystory.cfm?story_id=12758308. In November 1996, when the Friars Club honored Turner at a black-tie dinner and a comedic roast, Ted accepted the award and gave a short speech. He then promptly grabbed Jane Fonda's arm to leave as Alan King, preparing to initiate the roast, screamed after him, "Rupert Murdoch was right—you are nuts!" Quoted in Ken Auletta, "The Lost Tycoon," *The New Yorker*, April 23, 2001, http://www.kenauletta.com/2001_04_23_thelosttycoon.html.

26. Maureen Dowd, "Ted's Excellent Idea," *The New York Times*, August 22, 1996. After reading Turner's remarks in this article, Michael Kinsley, founding editor of the online magazine *Slate*, was inspired to begin *Slate* 60, an annual listing of the top 60 philanthropists. The first *Slate* 60 was published on December 3, 1996, but was revised in early 1997 to include December contributions. While Kinsley is no longer with *Slate*, the list is still published annually. The most recent list can be found at http://www.slate.com/id/2589/landing/1.

Chapter 18

SYNERGY CRISIS

On January 3, 2000, Ted Turner and Jane Fonda separated. Most often attributed to Fonda's having become a born-again Christian, a fact she had kept from Ted for some time, this was just symptomatic of a relationship that had run its course. Communication in general had grown strained while Fonda yearned for meaning and connections in her life that Turner just couldn't understand. Despite seeking counseling, Turner could not change and Fonda felt she needed to. In her autobiography, Fonda says, "Out of love and respect for Ted and his children, I will not go into specifics about what was not working in our relationship. Quite honestly, it is not necessary, and I have already given you a sense of the issues."[1] This has generally been taken to mean that Turner was again having trouble with monogamy, and given Fonda's account of their relationship it seems fairly certain that this was at least part of the problems with the relationship.

Six days later, Turner received a call from Jerry Levin that Time Warner was moving forward in a deal with America Online (AOL). AOL, co-founded by Steve Case as Quantum Link in 1985 as a service for dealers and users of Commodore 64 computers, was the easy-access service provider/portal for dial-up connections to the World Wide Web. By organizing and filtering Web content and creating a community atmosphere, it made the Web less cumbersome, "safer," and friendly as it introduced the country to the new medium. It was soon the largest ISP

(Internet Service Provider) in the marketplace, five times as large as the next largest provider, with significant advertising revenue. While still the reigning king of dial-up, however, it had not had much luck in transferring its success to the burgeoning broadband access market, particularly cable, and it owned no real content, so its future was clouded. By 1999, Levin was convinced that the Internet was the future of communications and that Time Warner, which had failed in several past attempts at "new media," needed a strong presence in the arena or risk obsolescence. Just five years after being "complete" with the purchase of Turner Broadcasting, Time Warner was so incomplete that a deal with a company having less than one-fifth its revenues but nearly two times its market capitalization was not only expedient, but also necessary. In the stock deal, AOL shareholders would receive one share of the combined company for each share of AOL, and Time Warner shareholders would receive 1.5 shares for each share of Time Warner, a 70 percent premium for Warner shareholders and a "purchase price" of $160 billion. Levin would become CEO of the new company and Case would become chairman of the board, which would consist of eight members each from the two companies, Turner would become vice chairman and sit on the board.

Levin told Turner to be in New York for a board meeting and a vote on the merger that Sunday, January 9. Turner was certainly aware of the Internet and the buzz it had been generating, but he had never been a computer user of any kind and had never really given the Internet much serious thought. Despite what else he may have thought of Jerry Levin, though, he did see him as forward-looking, and according to *Call Me Ted*, Turner trusted Levin's judgment that the Internet was important to the future of media. Turner claims to have checked with four of his closest confidants before that Sunday meeting, but the majority of those confidants claim his recollections are either wrong or overstated.[2] At the meeting that Sunday, supporters of the deal were gushing over every aspect of the combined company and its position and potential in the media industry. Turner, convinced, signed his shares over in an irrevocable commitment. His approximate 10 percent ownership of Time Warner would be diluted to 4 percent of AOL Time Warner, but he would still be the largest shareholder in the combined company.

The press conference announcing the deal the next day was a virtual love-in. Steve Case and Jerry Levin hugged and slapped high-fives as Mike Kelly and Bob Pittman from AOL and Dick Parsons and Ted Turner from Time Warner looked on with broad smiles. Turner would say that the deal would "create the most exciting and socially conscious company the world has ever seen,"[3] and speaking of having been first to vote his shares in favor of the merger, he said, "I did it with as much or more excitement and enthusiasm as I did when I first made love some forty-two years ago."[4] He told *TIME* magazine, "'We had a big uphill job as a corporation to catch up to the established Internet players."[5]

Turner was apparently as happy and positive as everyone else on the inside of the deal. Everyone was talking of the synergies and brave new world of "clicks and mortar," dominance in the convergence of telephones, television, music, and the Internet, and growth rates never seen before outside of dotcoms. With some dissenters, the media and financial communities were just as ecstatic, calling the merger "transformational," and the stock price of Time Warner shares shot up to new highs on the day of the announcement, giving Ted Turner a net worth of $10 billion. Curiously, Turner's reference to his first sexual experience echoed a comment he made before the first meeting of Turner Broadcasting's new bail-out board back in 1987, when he said, "This is our first meeting, I've waited all these years for it. It's sort of like the first time I had sex. I waited eighteen years. I waited fifteen minutes for the second."[6]

By mid-March of 2000, the U.S. economy started to show signs of weakening, and as results from online retailers covering the 1999 Christmas season showed lackluster e-commerce numbers, the dotcom bubble just seemed to burst. After hitting a high of 5,048 on March 10, 2000, the tech-heavy NASDAQ began plummeting after enormous sell orders of several major tech company stocks were processed the same day. By March of 2001 it had fallen as far as 1,794, and by October 2002 it went as low as 1,108. No one really knows why tech stocks fell so rapidly at this time, but many of the dotcoms that had fueled the rise in the NASDAQ had little else but perceived potential; revenues and profits were often non-existent, and as their stock price fell many of these companies went bust, becoming "dotcompost" or "dotgones" in the parlance of the times. AOL shares also suffered losses, and the company saw steep declines in advertising revenues.

In May, Turner, at his Vermejo Park ranch in New Mexico, received a call from Levin in which he was told that while he would retain his title as vice chairman and his seat on the board, he had effectively been removed from any operational responsibility in AOL Time Warner. Robert Pittman, who had been president at AOL, would oversee business development, AOL, cable, magazine, and television properties, including the WB network, all of Turner Broadcasting, and HBO, while Dick Parsons, who had been president of Time Warner, would become an apparently junior co-COO overseeing the film studios, music, books, and Human Resources. Turner, not believing what he was hearing, said, "Jerry, I've got a contract that still has a year and a half to run and it stipulates that I'll be in charge of the networks,"[7] but Levin's response was that the contract didn't really matter. If needed, he would continue to be paid as if the contract were still in effect. Ted Turner had been fired.

From the day Turner had decided to sell Turner Broadcasting to Time Warner, he knew this day could come, he had even prepared for it, but he never fully expected it. While he had never grown close to Levin and never fully respected him, he had trusted him. For Turner, who prided himself on being a good judge of character and who valued professional loyalty above nearly all else, it was a blow to his very core. Turner tried to protest, calling Steve Case and others, but it did no good. By the time he received a fax of the press release outlining the structure of the company, John Malone was visiting him at his ranch, and Ted, described as "ashen-faced," said, "How could Jerry Levin do this to me? He was supposed to be my best friend in the world."[8]

At the 20th anniversary party for CNN the following month, Turner would be lauded with faint praise. Steve Case said, "Ted Turner has been a hero of mine for 25 years and he and I are basically going to be joined at the hip."[9] Levin said Turner would have "a much larger canvas"[10] and would be "a transcendent figure" in guiding the company forward. Turner himself was cordoned off from the media, but did manage to be quoted afterward saying simply, "I'm happy."[11] But as he told Ken Auletta, "'Vice chairman' is usually a title you give to somebody you can't figure out what else to do with."[12] For Turner, the year grew worse when the one-year-old daughter of his youngest daughter Jennie was diagnosed with Hurler's syndrome, a rare genetic disorder that inevitably leads to death. In December 2000, Turner invited Ken Auletta to a meeting of the CNN Executive Committee only to have the invitation rescinded by an executive of AOL Time Warner who told Auletta, "He invited you to a meeting that is not his meeting."[13] Through it all though, Turner continued to be Turner. In December of 2000, he brokered a deal between the United States and the UN over the United States' unpaid dues, putting up $35 million to make up for the shortfall on what Congress was willing to pay and reducing the United States' share of future UN operating costs from 25 percent to 22 percent and its share of the UN peacekeeping budget from 31 percent to less than 27 percent. In January of 2001, inspired in part by a visit to a Russian nuclear command center earlier in the year, he announced the formation of the Nuclear Threat Initiative. Pledging $50 million per year for the following five years, he tapped Sam Nunn, who had served as senator from Georgia for 24 years and chairman of the Senate Armed Services Committee, to be co-chairman and CEO of the foundation. Its goal was, and is, to reduce the threat of nuclear weapons and all weapons of mass destruction.

By the time the FCC approved the merger and AOL Time Warner was officially born on January 12, 2001, the landscape of the merger had changed considerably. The deal that had originally been estimated at $160 billion had dropped to $106 billion due to AOL's falling share price, and many wondered if the deal would have been structured the same way if negotiated at this time rather than a year earlier. Given the drop in the dotcom valuations that Levin had placed great faith in when the deal was announced, it's likely there would have been no deal at all.

On February 28, 2001, Turner was at CNN's Washington studios to attend a farewell party for Bernard Shaw, CNN's original co-anchor. As he looked out on the gathered staff members, he told them he had first thought the "grime" on their foreheads was from covering an earthquake in Seattle, but remembering it was Ash Wednesday, said, "I realize you're just Jesus freaks . . . Shouldn't you guys be working for Fox?"[14] It was typical Turner, a poorly considered comment, even more poorly considered phrasing, and an ill-timed joke. On March 7, Brit

Hume of Fox News reported the comments, slightly out of context—though context wouldn't help much—and *The New York Post* made them front page fodder as a firestorm of protest ensued. The remarks were conflated with previous Turner comments on religion reaching back to 1989 when he had said, "Christianity is a religion for losers,"[15] and referred to his 1999 Polish joke directed at Pope John Paul II when Turner picked up his foot and said, "Ever seen a Polish mine detector?" While there were no official comments from AOL Time Warner, he certainly was not making any new friends on the board. Never mentioned, however, were some of his official remarks. They were more about Ted than Bernard Shaw, of course, but they give some insight into his mental state in this period. After noting that CNN no longer reported to him and he was just a figurehead, he went on, "We did a movie about Crazy Horse. And whenever he was threatened, they told him he was going to—if he went into battle, he might die. He said, 'Only the rocks live forever.' Nothing lasts forever. We've got—change is part of life."[16] Death and dying and suicide have always been a ready topic for Turner, but those closest to him say they had never seen him as depressed, and feared that he might in fact commit suicide, and though Turner himself has said he never thought of it, there is a forlorn element to his statement that stands out.

When relating this period to Charlie Rose in 2004, Turner said the loss of his job and his wife "really humbled me . . . knocked me down off my high horse." When Rose asked, incredulously, "*Humbled* you?" Turner smiled and said, "Oh . . . I really used to think a lot of myself."[17]

As the country officially settled into a recession in March of 2001, Terry McGuirk, who had assumed the CEO position at Turner Broadcasting with its 1996 merger with Time Warner and who had tried to placate the new hierarchy with his own reorganization and recitation of its Internet and convergence mantras in late 2000, was replaced by Jamie Kellner from ABC. Turner was not even consulted. CNN had been losing market share to both MSNBC and Fox News since 1997, and it was a major concern, but the first thing Kellner did was to cancel all professional wrestling from both WTBS and TNT. Wrestling had been a fixture of Turner programming since 1972, and Turner had owned the World Championship Wrestling league since 1989. However, of late it had been trounced by its rival, World Wrestling Federation, and it was said to be losing some $10 million per year.

With the recession affecting advertising sales in both old media and new, all divisions of AOL Time Warner fared poorly, and none of the glorious synergies spoken of the year before showed any signs of coming to any real fruition. Executives from the two companies never meshed. Case kept making public pronouncements on the glories of technology and the convergence of media, but for the most part Levin ignored him. When the company switched to AOL e-mail to save an estimated $30 million a year, it proved to be a disaster, with lost messages, users being bumped, and larger attachments being blocked. AOL was making absolutely no headway with extending their dial-up dominance into broadband, and their dial-up subscriber base had plateaued. Market watchers noted that many of the company's top executives had sold huge chunks if not most of their stock in the company that spring, when FCC rules allowed it, and wondered if it wasn't a signal that the executives themselves had questions about the company's valuation. With the attacks of September 11, the economy received more shocks and AOL Time Warner was nowhere near meeting its projected growth estimates. Its share price had dropped to $30 and Turner's stake had dropped to about $3.2 billion. As Turner admits in *Call Me Ted*, if the stock price had performed near expectations, his demeanor may have been different, but that wasn't the case.

The always imperious and distant Jerry Levin had grown ever more so after his son, a schoolteacher in New York, was brutally murdered in 1997. He had started professing a greater purpose in life ever since, and in many ways that sense of a greater purpose led to his decision to merge with AOL. At a board meeting in November of 2001, Turner had had enough and lashed out at Levin, quoting from an interview Levin had had with Ken Auletta in which he said he had always been satisfied to live through his son but had been on a mission after his son's death. Levin had gone on, "I'm not a big consultant with boards . . . .There's nothing anyone can say to me, write about me, that can affect me. I used to care somewhat because it affected the stock price. Now it's his view I care about."[18] Turner then used his own words, saying, "How dare you insult directors when you have led this company to ruin. . . . We have overpromised. We have oversold AOL as the engine for the company's resurgence. We need a new CEO."[19] No one else in the room spoke up, either in agreement or disagreement. Following the meeting, Steve Case started calling board members on his own to lobby for removal of Levin, though Turner wasn't even aware of these calls. Dick Parsons and other directors stood up for Levin and made Case back down. *BusinessWeek* quoted one as saying, "A number of us were absolutely opposed to the idea that the CEO could be fired on the telephone."[20] By the time he attended a cable conference late in the month, Turner was again ruefully recalling when Jerry Levin had called him his best friend. His response at the time had been, "I'm your best friend? Jerry, I've never even been to your home. If I'm your best friend, who's your second-best friend? Nick Nicholas?"[21] On December 5, Levin resigned on his own, saying, "I want the poetry back in my life."[22] He announced that he would step down in May of 2002; Dick Parsons was named the heir-apparent. It was also in December that AOL Time Warner completed a deal with Bertelsmann AG to purchase its nearly 50 percent stake in AOL Europe. The deal, originally negotiated and signed by AOL in 2000, was for $8 billion in stock or cash, but that total would be reduced to $6.7 billion if Bertelsmann asked to be paid early. After renegotiations in March, and then in December, AOL Time Warner agreed to pay Bertelsmann $6.7 billion in cash, but as part of the deal, Bertelsmann agreed to purchase $400 million in advertising on AOL over the next two years. Most analysts thought the sale price vastly overvalued the 50 percent stake of AOL Europe, but that, as it turned out, was just the tip of the iceberg. The purchase in cash had to have had Levin's approval at some stage, but it just failed to make sense. At least some of the company's woes were attributable to its already steep debt, yet it was choosing to bump that debt up to $28 billion rather than base the purchase in stock that was in the middle of a free fall.

On February 11, 2002, Turner again made comments that were widely found to be offensive. In what was reported as a rambling speech titled, "Our Common Future," at Brown University, he said the September 11 terrorists were "a little nuts [but] brave at the very least,"[23] and went on to say, "The reason the World Trade Center got hit is there's a lot of people living in abject poverty out there who don't have any hope for a better life."[24] Much of the coverage of the remark headlined Turner saying the terrorists were brave, and by the next evening Turner put out a press release saying the remarks had been taken out of context. But while the standalone quote did lose some context, again, context was not entirely exculpatory. As the *Brown Alumni Magazine* said, "Given the loose structure of the speech, however, it was difficult to find any context at all."[25] This time, even AOL Time Warner was quick to disown and condemn the comment. Turner would later tell Mike Wallace, "Brave was a bad . . . word. But I do not think . . . for instance, my father committed suicide and he was not a coward. He was very brave when he shot himself in my opinion . . . that's why to a degree, I said that."[26] It did not help, though, that in June he was back in the headlines for saying that Israelis were terrorists too.

As it turned out, Bertelsmann's $400 million advertising agreement was booked as advertising revenue for AOL in 2002, accounting for 20 percent of the unit's advertising and commerce sales for the year, but Bertelsmann itself had booked the $400 million as a reduction to the sale price. By July of 2002, the *Washington Post* would run a series of articles looking into a number of questionable marketing arrangements with other companies, reporting that AOL essentially paid the companies to buy online advertising on AOL, increasing both advertising and overall revenues of the company while presumably increasing the stock price and market capitalization of the company. The articles prompted the Securities and Exchange Commission (SEC) to announce an investigation of these practices later in the same month, and the $400 million advertising deal with Bertelsmann, which had not been cited in the *Post's* series, was added to the mix. Bob Pittman, who Parsons had reassigned to try to fix the online division, resigned under pressure on July 18, the day the first *Washington Post* story was run. Though never directly implicated in any of the practices the SEC would be investigating, outsiders would nevertheless link his resignation to it. Parsons announced a restructuring and named two Time Warner veterans, Dan Logan and Jeff Bewkes, both of whom had been critical of the merger from the beginning, to top positions. The stock price, down to $13 per share earlier in July, dropped to $8.70 when the SEC investigation was announced.

Turner, who had earlier supported his fellow entrepreneur Steve Case and respected Dick Parsons, was supremely disenchanted by this time.

Long mostly ignored on the board, he had watched helplessly as his beloved Goodwill Games had been canceled, Turner Broadcasting properties had been saddled with wildly unrealistic growth targets, and CNN's
international news gathering bureaus had been gutted while its programming was increasingly turned to talk shows and personalities in an effort to reverse its sagging ratings. When he counseled against Parsons's
decision to sell off some of the company's old-line media holdings, like
the book publishing group, no one paid any attention. By late 2002, he
had pretty much decided to resign as vice chairman when Gordy Crawford, his close friend and another significant shareholder in AOL Time
Warner as a result of the Turner Broadcasting merger with Time Warner,
decided that it was time for Steve Case to go. Since both Turner and
John Malone had been thinking the same thing, Ted decided to stay on
to give Crawford more support. When Crawford first approached Case
about resigning, Steve refused, but, like Levin before him, he knew he
had no real support at the company. Case would finally step down in
mid-January of 2003, the last of the AOL management team to leave.
Turner's own resignation as vice chairman—he would remain on the
board—would be announced just two weeks later on January 30, 2003.
On the same day, AOL Time Warner reported a net loss of $98.7 billion
for 2002, an ignominious record at the time, after a fourth-quarter write
down of $45.5 billion in the value of the America Online unit. Parsons
was named to replace Steve Case, making him chairman and CEO. As of
October 16, 2003, the company officially dropped AOL from its name.

Following the announcement of his resignation as vice chairman,
Turner, who had continued to hold onto most of his shares in the company, increased his divestiture. By May of 2003, he was down to about
seven million shares and the market capitalization of the company, valued at $350 billion at the announcement of the merger, was down to
near $61 billion. In December, as if an exclamation point was being
placed on the changes in Turner's life, Jimmy Brown, who had provided
Turner with the closest thing to stability for most of his life, who had
taught him to sail and served as a caregiver to Ted and all of his children, passed away.

While still a member of the board, Turner wrote an often cited piece
published in the July/August 2004 issue of *Washington Monthly*, "My
Beef With Big Media: How Government Protects Big Media—And

Shuts out Upstarts Like Me." Decrying the relaxing of regulations in media ownership rules and the consequent media conglomerates—like Time Warner—he wrote:

"In the current climate of consolidation, independent broadcasters simply don't survive for long. That's why we haven't seen a new generation of people like me or even Rupert Murdoch—independent television upstarts who challenge the big boys and force the whole industry to change. . . . In this environment, most independent media firms either get gobbled up by one of the big companies or driven out of business altogether. . . . As a business proposition, consolidation makes sense. The moguls behind the mergers are acting in their corporate interests and playing by the rules. We just shouldn't have those rules . . . Big media today wants to own the faucet, pipeline, water, and the reservoir. The rain clouds come next. . . . When that happens, quality suffers, localism suffers, and democracy itself suffers. . . . When all companies are quarterly earnings obsessed, the market starts punishing companies that aren't yielding an instant return. This not only creates a big incentive for bogus accounting, but also it inhibits the kind of investment that builds economic value. . . . Had Turner Communications been required to show earnings growth every quarter, we never would have purchased those first two TV stations. . . . I freely admit: When I was in the media business, especially after the federal government changed the rules to favor large companies, I tried to sweep the board. . . . Yet I felt then, as I do now, that the government was not doing their job."

By May of 2006, he stepped away from the company completely. At his last board meeting, held in Atlanta, there was a video tribute to his career, after which Turner took the stage and said simply, "I just wish the last five years I could have made a bigger contribution. I hung in there as long as I could. I've done my best."[27] In his own following remarks, Tom Johnson, who had resigned as head of CNN in June of 2001 said, "How lucky we are to have known and still know one of the most remarkable men in world history,"[28] but Turner had already left the building.

NOTES

1. Jane Fonda, *My Life So Far* (New York: Random House, 2005), 545.

2. In separate sidebars in Ted Turner with Bill Burke, *Call Me Ted* (New York: Grand Central Publishing, 2008), 368–71, Taylor Glover, Gordy Crawford, Michael Milken, and John Malone tell their own recollections. Both Crawford and Malone said that by the time they either heard of the deal or had a conversation with Ted he had already agreed to the sale. Glover, who was away in Europe, tells of a phone conversation with a poor connection and filled with rhetorical questions. Milken reports that whereas he did advise Ted that the deal would be financially beneficial, future performance of the company was an unknown.

3. Salon.com, "AOL and Time Warner's Marriage of Insecurity," January 10, 2000, http://archive.salon.com/tech/col/rose/2000/01/10/aol_time/index1.html.

4. Nina Munk, *Fools Rush In: Steve Case, Jerry Levin, and the Unmaking of AOL Time Warner* (New York: HarperBusiness, 2004), 179.

5. Daniel Okrent, "Happily Ever After?" *TIME*, January 24, 2000.

6. Robert Goldberg and Gerald Jay Goldberg, *Citizen Turner: The Wild Rise of an American Tycoon* (New York: Harcourt, Brace & Co., 1995), 382.

7. Turner, *Call Me Ted*, 374.

8. John Malone sidebar in Turner, *Call Me Ted*, 377.

9. Munk, *Fools Rush In*, 193.

10. Jim Ruttenberg and Alessandra Stanley, "At 63, Ted Turner May Yet Roar Again," *The New York Times*, December 16, 2001.

11. Johnnie L. Roberts, "As Ted's World Turns," *Newsweek*, June 12, 2000, http://www.newsweek.com/id/85082.

12. Ken Auletta, "The Lost Tycoon," *The New Yorker*, April 23, 2001, http://www.kenauletta.com/2001_04_23_thelosttycoon.html.

13. Ken Auletta, *Media Man: Ted Turner's Improbable Empire* (New York: Norton, 2004), 109.

14. Jim Ruttenberg, "MediaTalk; AOL Sees a Different Side of Time Warner," *The New York Times*, March 19, 2001.

15. Ibid.

16. CNN.com. Transcripts, "Special Event: A Farewell Tribute to Bernard Shaw," aired March 2, 2001, http://transcripts.cnn.com/TRANSCRIPTS/0103/02/se.07.html.

17. Charlie Rose, "An hour with CNN founder Ted Turner," © Charlie Rose LLC, July 24, 2004, http://www.charlierose.com/view/interview/1337.

18. Auletta, *Media Man*, 152.

19. Ibid.

20. *BusinessWeek*, "Can Dick Parsons Rescue AOL Time Warner?" May 19, 2003, http://www.businessweek.com/print/magazine/content/03_20/b3833001_mz001.htm?chan=gl.

21. Munk, *Fools Rush In*, 193. Nicholas had been co-CEO of Time Warner and Levin had essentially been his protégé, but Levin engineered Nicolas's firing in 1992 and his own ascension to the position. Levin would tell Nina Munk, "I don't have justifications for it other than that I'm a strange person." Quoted in Munk, *Fools Rush In*, 43.

22. Auletta, *Media Man*, 154.

23. Emily Gold Boutilier, "Captain Outrageous," *Brown Alumni Magazine*, March/April 2002, http://www.brownalumnimagazine.com/march/april-2002/captain-outrageous.html.

24. Ibid.

25. Ibid.

26. David Kohn, "Ted Turner: Career at a Crossroads," cbsnews.com, February 5, 2003, http://www.cbsnews.com/stories/2003/06/11/60II/main558076.shtml.

27. Harry R. Weber, Associated Press, "Turner Steps Down Quietly," *The Boston Globe*, May 20, 2006, http://www.boston.com/business/technology/articles/2006/05/20/turner_steps_down_quietly/?rss_id=Boston+Globe+—+Business+News.

28. Ibid.

Chapter 19

CLEAR CUT REMINDER

With his media career behind him, Turner's business career would increasingly center on his ranchlands and bison herd, and his public appearances would continue to center around building the global understanding that he sees as crucial to facing the problems of the modern world.

By 2008, Turner's landholdings would reach over two million acres in the United States, comprising some 20 properties in 12 states—an area exceeding the size of Delaware and Rhode Island combined,— as well as approximately 130,000 acres in Argentina. The acreage includes personal homes in Atlanta and Big Sur, plus some 1,300 acres in Arkansas, 29,000 acres in Florida, and nearly 11,000 acres in South Carolina. Most of his land, however, is ranchland in Western states, with over a million acres in New Mexico alone. Nearly all of his properties have conservation easements that severely restrict development of any kind, and through the Turner Foundation and the Turner Endangered Species Fund, he has worked toward restoring the land to its native state. In collaboration with several state offices, universities, and environmental groups, he has worked to restore the Longleaf Pine and red-cockaded woodpecker on the Avalon plantation in Florida and preserve or reintroduce species such as cutthroat trout, Desert bighorn sheep, Mexican spotted owls, black footed ferrets, prairie dogs, Aplomado falcons, and Bolson tortoises on his ranchlands

Primarily, though, the ranches are meant to show that environment can be sustained and restored while still providing income. The primary business centers on Turner's private herd of bison, the largest in the world at over 50,000 head, that is spread out over most of the ranches but concentrated primarily in Nebraska, Kansas, and South Dakota. The ranches are also used for limited commercial big game hunts—some costing as much as $12,000 per week—commercial fishing, corporate retreats, limited wildlife excursions, farming, and sustainable timber harvesting. Turner, who made a substantial investment in solar energy in 2007, is now even considering building wind turbines on some of the properties.

In 2000, Turner agreed to a partnership with George McKerrow Jr., founder of Longhorn Steakhouses, on a new restaurant chain, Ted's Montana Grill. While bison burgers are far from the only thing on the menu, the ideas of promoting bison as a healthier, more environmentally friendly alternative to beef and making bison an economically viable industry were central to the formation of the chain. Since opening their original restaurant in Columbus, Ohio at the beginning of 2002, Ted's now has over 54 locations in 19 states. Most of the bison comes indirectly from Turner's own herd through the North American Bison Cooperative (NABC). The chain itself, like the ranches, is also meant to serve as an example of how economically run restaurants can be as environmentally friendly as possible. Turner and McKerrow have started The Green Restaurant Revolution to provide guidelines for the industry. The goal at Ted's Montana Grills is to be 99 percent free of plastics, and the chain utilizes paper straws, to-go cups made from corn starch, to-go cutlery made from potato starch, low flow toilets, waterless urinals, biodegradable Boraxo powdered hand soaps, low wattage compact-fluorescent bulbs, and menus printed on recycled paper.

While Turner's environmental stewardship of his ranchlands has won him numerous awards and acclaim from environmental groups, it has also sparked a good amount of controversy, something Turner seems unable to escape no matter what his endeavor. When he first bought his Montana ranches and started divesting their cattle operations in favor of bison, he angered many of his cattle rearing neighbors by decrying the negative effects of cattle on the environment. His neighbors have also resented that the ranches are off-limits to private hunting, and have complained about fencing meant to contain the bison. Native Americans have criticized the bison operations themselves, with the InterTribal Bison Cooperative (ITBC) pointing out that Turner's bison are finished with a minimum of 100 days of grain feeding, a NABC requirement, but one that artificially fattens up the animals. Turner hopes to be able to escape grain feeding in the near future, but others have pointed out that NABC slaughtering techniques are also less than humane.

Turner has even been criticized by some environmentalists for allowing the extraction of coal bed methane gas on the largest of his properties, Vermejo Park in New Mexico, despite the fact that the mineral rights had been bought prior to his purchase of the land and he negotiated strict covenants on how the gas could be extracted.

Sport-fishing enthusiasts were originally outraged when in 2003 Turner provided $500,000 to help fund a project by the Montana Department of Fish, Wildlife, and Parks that involved poisoning Cherry Lake in the Gallatin National Forest and Cherry Creek that runs from the lake through Turner's Flying D ranch. The idea of the ongoing project is to kill off the non-native rainbow and brook trout in order to reintroduce the endangered indigenous westslope cutthroat trout. Turner himself originally had reservations, but a broader effort to protect and reintroduce the species has since won wide support from government, conservation groups, Native Americans, and sport-fishing organizations. Turner is now involved in a similar effort being undertaken in New Mexico to reintroduce the Rio Grande cutthroat trout.

In 2007, as Turner became the largest landowner in Nebraska, residents wondered whether his goal was to put other ranchers and farmers out of business, corner all the land over the Ogallala Aquifer to gain some sort of control over the water-starved West, or create a vast park of free roaming bison. Turner would say, "I acquired more land because I required more land. I wanted it. I never like to buy anything but land. It's the only thing that lasts."[1] By 2008, Turner would add, "I'm almost done. I've got enough. You know what 2 million acres is? If my land was all connected, in one long straight line, a mile deep, it would stretch from New York to San Francisco. I've been thinking of doing some swaps. I'd be able to cut the United States in half and charge people going from North to South."[2]

While his losses with AOL Time Warner and subsequent losses in the economic downturn of 2008 have reduced Turner's net worth to what Forbes estimated to be $1.9 billion in March of 2009, including the value of his land, Turner has continued supporting a variety of causes both financially and as a spokesperson. The $1 billion dollar pledge to the UN has been extended over a longer than anticipated timeframe and both the UN Foundation and the Nuclear Threat Initiative now depend on ever wider contributions and support from Warren Buffett and the Gates Foundation, but both still serve unique and critical roles.

In April of 2005, Ted Turner was presented with the Alan Cranston Peace Award by Mikhail Gorbachev at the UN, the former Soviet leader's first visit to the institution since 1998. In his remarks, Gorbachev said that Turner was one of his heroes for his efforts on behalf of the environment and global security and noted that Turner not only knew how to make money but also, in reference to his philanthropy, knew how to spend it. Later in 2005, Turner took a trip to North Korea in order to promote the idea of turning the Demilitarized Zone (DMZ) between North and South Korea into a "peace park" and UN World Heritage Site to honor those who died during the Korean War. In the 50 years since the conflict ended in a cease-fire, the swath of land approximately 2.5 miles wide and 155 miles long has become a virtual wildlife preserve, despite containing an estimated one million land mines. Extremely rare species like the Amur goral—a type of goat-antelope—Amur leopard, black vulture, Asiatic black bear, and black-faced spoonbill have been identified, and it is the only place in the world where two species of cranes, white-naped and red-crowned, winter together, and that in numbers estimated as high as 4,000. The idea has continued to be widely considered, but the trip itself was marred by comments Turner made to Wolf Blitzer on CNN after his return, when he mentioned that the North Koreans looked healthy and thin, that he had not personally witnessed any ill treatment, and that he was convinced that North Korea was serious in seeking peace. The comments were and continue to be trumpeted by right-leaning news organizations and bloggers as a prime example of Turner's naiveté.

In September of 2006, Turner made a speech at the World Trade Organization (WTO) in Geneva, Switzerland, where he said that the results of global trade were uneven and needed to be rewritten, "It's one of the biggest moral failures in the history of humanity that we allow half the world's people to live in intolerable conditions, on less than 2 dollars a day. A billion live on less than a *single* dollar a day. A billion have no drinking water. Poverty is cruelty. And poverty persists in part because the trade that has created so much prosperity for the world's wealthy countries is bypassing the poor countries. . . . Of the 20 poorest nations on earth, 16 have suffered civil war over the last two decades. If we can't reverse it, poverty is going to crack the world apart."[3] He went on to criticize the agricultural subsidies and tariffs of developed countries and urged them to end these practices and promote a changeover in their domestic agricultural land to production of crops for biofuels.

In 2007, Turner, who had been an outspoken critic of the Iraq War and President Bush, made a keynote speech at the Solar Power 2007 conference in Long Beach, California in which he said that the United Sates should drop solar panels on other countries rather than bombs. "I can't say U.S. President George W. Bush gets it very well, but hopefully we'll get someone a little smarter next time," Turner said.[4] Saying that the world had never faced a more complex problem than global warming, he went on to call solar power the "greatest opportunity in the history of humanity . . . I've already made one fortune and lost it and I'm ready to make another. So let's get rich together and do some good."[5]

In April of 2008, Turner announced another in a broad array of efforts to curtail malaria in Africa. This effort would partner the UN Foundation with the Lutheran and Methodist churches, the Gates Foundation, and others, all of whom have also been involved with the Nothing But Nets[6] campaign originally organized by Rick Reilly, a *Sports Illustrated* contributor, that is run through the UN Foundation. That night, in a wide-ranging interview with Charlie Rose, he noted that global warming, its consequent effects on agriculture, and overpopulation would inevitably lead to wars and even cannibalism. Again, right-wing bloggers and news organizations jumped on his cannibalism comments and equated his call for worldwide restrictions on child bearing with an embracing of eugenics. During the same interview, Turner mentioned that he had finally made peace with Rupert Murdoch, spurred on by Murdoch's embracing of green technologies, though he added, "I'm not sure I want to be chummy with him."[7]

In October of 2008, Turner announced the Global Sustainable Tourism Criteria (GSTC), a set of standards to help assure that ecotourism really is following best practices to protect local communities and the environment. The standards are meant to provide certification that will allow the tourist industry and consumers to know that packages billed as ecological are in fact not doing more harm than good in some of the world's most precious environments. That same month, while having no overt connection to Turner, a lawsuit was brought by David McDavid, who was seeking $450 million in damages from Turner Broadcasting. It was McDavid's contention that he had had a deal with Time Warner on purchasing the Atlanta Hawks basketball team and the Atlanta Thrashers hockey team—an expansion team in the NHL that had started in 1999 and been owned by Turner—only to have the deal scuttled when the teams were instead sold to a consortium named the Atlanta Spirit, with principals including Turner's son-in-law, Rutherford Seydel, Turner's friend, former Turner Broadcasting board member and Hawks executive, Michael Gearon Jr., and Turner's youngest son, Beau. According to McDavid's lawyers, the Spirit's offer was lower than McDavid's and only an inside job could have swept the deal out from under his client. In early December, after a trial in which Turner's name came up daily but he was never called as a witness, Turner Broadcasting/Time Warner was ordered to pay McDavid $281 million in compensation. Turner Broadcasting's request for a new trial was turned down on April 22, 2009, but the company is seeking to take the issue to the Court of Appeals.

Curiously, in 2007 Turner's old friend, John Malone, and his company, Liberty Media, made a deal with Time Warner in which Malone acquired the Atlanta Braves baseball team, cash, and "other assets," in exchange for 60 million of Liberty's 170 million shares of Time Warner. Terry McGuirk, who had been president of the Braves since being supplanted as the CEO of Turner Broadcasting, became CEO of the Braves. Though during the same period, Malone was buying three regional sports networks, the Braves is the only sports franchise he has ever owned.

On November 10, 2008, Turner released the autobiography, *Call Me Ted*, written with his friend and former colleague, Bill Burke. The book is honest and written in a warm and unencumbered conversational tone that provides a good sense of Turner as a speaker, and Turner himself reads the audio-book version. It is a wonderful introduction to Turner the man and entrepreneur, but Turner himself says he always looks to the future and doesn't like to reflect on the past, and you sometimes get the sense that he relied on previous biographies in coming to some of his own recollections. New and deeper insights into his early family life and even his career are few and far between, and some of the most compelling revelations are offered by family, friends, and colleagues, who provide a generous number of sidebar commentaries. The fact that they seem largely uncensored and sometimes contradictory to Turner's own monologue is in itself revealing.

Critics and journalists who have looked with skepticism on Turner's repeated citing of his father as his best friend and a positive influence on his life were disappointed that Turner provided no new insights into their relationship. Most mentions of his father in previous biographies and magazine pieces highlight his domineering presence and mental and physical abuse of the young Turner. They use the best available insight into their relationship, the letter from Ed to Ted while the latter attended Brown University, to underscore the point while going on to reduce Turner's drive to an Oedipal struggle to both win approval from and outdo Ed. But though there are no doubt elements of this in Turner's makeup, it seems both overly simplistic and unfair to both men. While the stories of the many beatings Turner received from Ed have primarily come from Turner himself, he has tended to call them "spankings" rather than beatings, and some degree of physical discipline in child rearing was far more common in the 1940s. The accounts of Ed Turner provided by Turner, Judy Nye, Peter Dames, Irwin Mazo, and Jimmy Brown seem to paint a more nuanced picture of a deeply troubled, hard-driving, and volatile man that was also warm, amiable, and deeply involved in his children's upbringing, if afflicted with some very odd ideas of best practices in doing so. Even the Brown letter, which out of context seems to clearly show Ed's instability, shows no sign of a physical threat or alienation of affection, but a remarkable blend of righteousness, ignorance, intelligence, love, a reliance on reasoning, and even acceptance. Turner was certainly scarred by his repeated abandonment during his formative years, but the beatings and Oedipal struggle seem overstated in explaining Turner's makeup, though that is precisely why further probing of his youth would have been helpful.

Besides the relationship with his father, the autobiography has also been cited for its broader lack of personal detail in exploration of his sister's illness and death, his marriages, his relationship with his own children, and his sexual dalliances. To be fair though, Turner does come off as generally honest about his human failings in marriage and as a father, and seems to show an understanding of the injury his sexual proclivities have caused. While there seems to be an abundance of prurient interest in his extramarital affairs, in a life so full there is little reason to dwell on these except in how they affected his family, which he also skirts over. As many have pointed out, there seems a huge disconnect between Turner's public condemnations of sex in media and his own personal addiction, with Turner often being accused of being a hypocrite. But unlike those who rail against personal behaviors that they practice themselves, Turner has kept his criticism to media displays and has never tried venturing into people's private bedrooms and behaviors.

The truly fertile ground in understanding both Turner and his father seems to hover around Mary Jean, especially given the odd coincidence that every woman either Ed or Ted married following Mary Jean's diagnosis had a name that began with "J," and three of the four have been named Jane, which seems to have been her nickname. Here too, there is very little depth provided in the autobiography.

In *Call Me Ted*, Jane Fonda wrote, " . . . he can't go back to the past and heal himself. He can't because he's too afraid that it will all come in and drown him."[8] She made a similar comment in her own autobiography concerning their breakup, saying, "If he'd bothered to look closely, Ted could have seen the silent me, like a trout swimming out from beneath a rock and coming closer to the surface. But Ted is not a close looker, especially if what he might find would risk muddying his waters."[9] In November of 2008, Turner himself told the *San Francisco Chronicle*, "I don't examine my conscience much, but my conscience is clear. A conscience is to help you deal with guilt about anything. I don't want to live with guilt, so I've avoided things I'd feel guilty about."[10]

The surprisingly brittle Turner has never been self-reflective, but that in part is what gives Turner the childlike innocence that is so often used to describe him. His loose "Kids Say the Darnedest Things" lips, his dogged creativity in business, and his wide-eyed wonder at the world are what make Ted, Ted, for better and worse. During the 1980s, Turner pictured himself as Charlemagne, saving Christendom from the infidels, or Jiminy Cricket, and there was this marvelous and unintentionally heartbreaking response from Turner when a Russian once asked who Jiminy Cricket was. "A conscience of a little wooden boy . . . ,"[11] Turner replied. He no doubt went on to describe the Disney movie, but the abstracted phrase is so apropos. Turner is always relating life to the movies, always on a stage set. When he told the *Chronicle*, "Life is like a grade B movie. You don't want to walk out in the middle, but you don't want to sit through it again,"[12] it ran deeper than it would for most of us.

Yes, Turner has human failings. He can be rude, biting, and obnoxious, overawed by his own intelligence and grandiosity, but it is all part of the package that has produced one of the most remarkable public lives of the past 50 years. Apple Computer got it right when they included him on a stage with his latter day heroes, Martin Luther King Jr. and Mahatma Gandhi, in their 1997 Think Different campaign, and even more right when his visage appeared toward the end of the voiceover phrase "glorified or vilified." If truth be told, we probably all harbor some degree of both when we consider Turner. But the accomplishments, the charisma, the sheer bombastic verbosity of the man, have been, and continue to be, a wonder to behold.

If we were to judge Turner's life according to the goals he described to Irwin Mazo—making Channel 17 the fourth national network, going into the production business, becoming the world's wealthiest man, and being president of the United States—he would seem to have not fared very well. Turner did go into the production business and produced good movies on the Civil War, including *Gettysburg* and *Gods and Generals* (he also played bit parts in both), Native American history, and even Bible stories that have been well accepted for authenticity, but his overall film production career has to be termed lackluster at best. Unless we were being very generous in saying that satellite distribution of Channel 17 made it the fourth national network, it would mean Turner has batted around .200. Personal dreams, however, are not what fill out our scorecards.

Like the businesses he created, the whole is greater than the sum of his parts. Who has had a broader series of accomplishments? From sailing, to baseball, to media, to culture wars, to internationalism, to philanthropy, his name is writ large.

Yes, Turner benefited from being in the right place at the right time, from his relatively privileged upbringing, from luck, from regulatory policies and the contributions of others, but he was the one that put it all together, having a drive to try to win at all times while tempting utter failure in the process. While he certainly wasn't alone in defining and expanding cable television, the economic and legal risk he assumed when he launched his ad-based Superstation and created basic cable was the lynchpin of its expansion. His charismatic lobbying and wiring of congressional offices, while self-serving, proved invaluable to everyone to the industry. His bet on 24-hour cable news was both inspired and revolutionary. His purchase of the MGM library predefined the "content" revolution. His fight against sex and violence in media and for a return to American values wrote the playbook for the religious right before he stunned everyone with a nuanced perspective that put black and white in their proper places on a spectrum of grays.

Yes, you can footnote the Superstation to HBO's being first on the satellite, you can argue that Reese Schonfeld was ultimately more integral to the realization of CNN, you can point out the tepid analyses that have been a failing of the news venture since the beginning. You can examine the multidimensional effects of 24-hour news and how its very presence can become the primary motivator of both action and inaction or how it ultimately over-covers the tawdry and trivial, giving it undue significance. You can question whether CNN's internationalism is ultimately elitist and marred by a decidedly American worldview. You can argue that CNN's NewsSource has ultimately done more harm than good for the local news services that Turner bemoans the loss of. You can debate the naïveté and unintended consequences of Turner's personal crusades. All of that is beside the point.

Turner is fond of comparing his career to Columbus, saying, "He didn't know where he was going, didn't know where he was when he got there, and didn't know where he had been when he got back."[13] That's an exaggeration of course, but mixed in with the inspired brilliance there is in Turner part accidental tourist and part tragic hero.

In an April 7, 2009 interview with Ned Lamont at the World Affairs Council in Connecticut, he said that he was the only person at AOL

Time Warner ever to have received the *TIME* Man of the Year award, but they still fired him, noted that he had been "irrelevant"[14] for 10 years, and that while he once traveled the world meeting with foreign leaders, he can now barely rouse a bellboy.

In 2001, Christiane Amanpour said of Turner, "He's the last of the revolutionary and creative minds in our business, [yet] he's been shunted aside."[15] Turner, who has often seemed arrogant himself, was too early, easily, and rudely dismissed in the merger of AOL Time Warner, a merger that remains one of the most disastrous in the history of American business and a study of overreaching and arrogance. In the final analysis, Rupert Murdoch may have put it best when he said, "They gave away their company for a mess of porridge, and they've got to live with that forever."[16]

In a merger all about transformation, synergy, and social consciousness, Ted Turner, who better exemplified all three than anyone else at either AOL or Time Warner, had been shunted aside, ignored, and disrespected by the executives of both companies, none of whom was ever able to effect any of their grand vision. If Fonda had been Turner's trophy wife, as she was often called in the press, Turner was AOL Time Warner's trophy executive. He was cable, and cable was no longer cool.

In an interview that was part of the promotional tour for *Call Me Ted*, Turner commented, "I led the technical revolution. Led the way to satellite TV, and cable. And then I went back to study history. There's never been anyone who led two revolutions. Not George Washington, not anybody."[17] Let's hope he's wrong.

NOTES

1. The Land Report, January 10, 2009, "Ted Turner—2 million acres," http://www.landreport.com/category/land-report-100/acreage/2000000.

2. Paul Hamel, "Turner 'Almost Done' Buying up Ranchland," *Omaha World-Herald*, February 7, 2008.

3. Ted Turner, text of speech at the World Trade Organization Public Forum, Geneva, Switzerland, September 25, 2006.

4. Jennifer Kho, "Turner: Drop Solar Panels, Not Bombs," greentechmedia. com, http://www.greentechmedia.com/articles/turner-drop-solar-panels-not-bombs-108-.html.

5. Ibid.

6. In April of 2009 the Nothing But Nets campaign received a boost when Ashton Kutcher issued a challenge to CNN over whether he or the network would be first to reach one million followers on Twitter. He later made a video saying that if Ted Turner were to help him win the challenge he would donate 1,000 nets to the charity. Turner endorsed Kutcher's win and Nothing But Nets received both 1,000 nets and significant publicity.

7. Charlie Rose, "A Conversation with Ted Turner," April 2, 2008, © Charlie Rose LLC, http://video.google.com/videoplay?docid=3235659543898 921467.

8. Jane Fonda sidebar in Ted Turner with Bill Burke, *Call Me Ted* (New York: Grand Central Publishing, 2008), 363.

9. Jane Fonda, *My Life So Far* (New York: Random House, 2005), 545.

10. Leah Garchik, "Fasten Your Seat Belt, It's Ted Turner," *San Francisco Chronicle*, November 27, 2008, E-1.

11. Tom Callahan, "Less Than Goodwill Games," *TIME*, July 21, 1986.

12. Garchik, "Fasten Your Seat Belt."

13. "Ted Turner Looks at the World, an interview with Ted Turner," World Affairs Council of Connecticut, April 7, 2009, http://fora.tv/2009/04/07/Ted_ Turner_Looks_at_the_World#chapter_07.

14. Ibid.

15. Ken Auletta, *Media Man: Ted Turner's Improbable Empire* (New York: Norton, 2004), 143.

16. *BusinessWeek*, "Can Dick Parsons Rescue AOL Time Warner?" May 19, 2003, http://www.businessweek.com/print/magazine/content/03_20/b3833001_ mz001.htm?chan=gl.

17. Garchik, "Fasten Your Seat Belt."

SELECTED BIBLIOGRAPHY
AND FURTHER RESOURCES

Alexander, Max. "FILM; Once More, the Old South in All Its Glory." *The New York Times*, January 29, 1989. http://www.nytimes.com/1989/01/29/movies/film-once-more-the-old-south-in-all-its-glory.html?scp=2&sq=Once%20More,%20the%20Old%20South%20in%20all%20It's%20Glory&st=cse.

Alter, Jonathan. "Ted's Global Village." *Newsweek*, June 11, 1990. http://www.newsweek.com/id/127550.

Associated Press. "Yachtsman Turner Purchases Braves." *The New York Times*, January 6, 1976, Sports, 59.

Auletta, Ken. "The Lost Tycoon." *The New Yorker*, April 23, 2001. http://www.kenauletta.com/2001_04_23_thelosttycoon.html.

Auletta, Ken. Media Man: Ted Turner's Improbable Empire. New York: Norton, 2004.

Bart, Peter. "Ted Turner's Deals Tend to Look Better with Age." *Variety*, November 15, 1993. http://www.variety.com/article/VR1117859436.html?categoryid=1&cs=1.

Bart, Peter. "Ted Turner Turns out to Be a Time 'Family' Man." *Variety*, September 22, 1995. http://www.variety.com/article/VR1117859519.html?categoryid=1&cs=1.

Bedell, Sally. "Editorial on CNN Stirs Dispute." *The New York Times*, June 4, 1982. http://www.nytimes.com/1982/06/04/movies/editorial-on-cnn-stirs-dispute.html.

Bedell, Sally. "2D All-News Service To Emphasize Brevity." *The New York Times*, June 21, 1982. http://www.nytimes.com/1982/06/21/arts/2d-all-news-

service-to-emphasize-brevity.html?scp=1&sq=2d%20All%20News%20
Service%20To%20Emphasize%20Brevity&st=cse.

Bibb, Porter. *It Ain't as Easy as It Looks: Ted Turner's Amazing Story.* New York: Crown Publishers, 1993.

Boutilier, Emily Gold. "Captain Outrageous." *Brown Alumni Magazine,* March/April 2002. http://www.brownalumnimagazine.com/march/april-2002/captain-outrageous.html.

Brewer, Ted. *Understanding Boat Design.* Camden, ME: International Marine, 1994.

Cable Regulations Digest. "Turner Lashes out at Time Warner." October 3, 1994. http://bubl.ac.uk/ARCHIVE/journals/crd/941003.htm.

Cady, Steve. "A Brash Captain Courageous: Robert Edward Turner 3d." *The New York Times,* September 18, 1977, Sports, 60.

Carter, Bill. "Ted Turner's Time of Discontent." *The New York Times,* June 6, 1993. http://www.nytimes.com/1993/06/06/business/ted-turner-s-time-of-discontent.html.

The Chronicle of Philanthropy. "Ten Years Later, Turner's U.N. Fund Continues to Evolve." 20(17): June 12, 2008. http://www.globalproblems-global-solutions-files.org/pdf/articles/cp_6122008.pdf.

CNN.com. Transcripts. "Special Event: A Farewell to Bernard Shaw." March 2, 2001. http://transcripts.cnn.com/TRANSCRIPTS/0103/02/se.07.html.

CNN.com. Transcripts. "Special Event: Ted Turner Introduces Former Senator Sam Nunn to Head Nuclear Threat Initiative." January 8, 2001. http://transcripts.cnn.com/TRANSCRIPTS/0101/08/se.01.html.

Cohen, Elliot D. News Incorporated: Corporate Media Ownership and its Threat to Democracy. Amherst, NY: Prometheus Books, 2005.

Collins, Joseph. "Toll in Yacht Race Reaches 17, One Boat Still Missing." *The New York Times,* August 16, 1979, A1.

Corliss, Richard. "Raiders of the Lost Art." *TIME,* October 20, 1986. http://www.time.com/time/magazine/article/0,9171,1075237,00.html.

Corliss, Richard. "Time Warner's Head Turner." *TIME,* September 11, 1995. http://www.time.com/time/magazine/article/0,9171,983403,00.html

Crandall, Robert W., and Harold W. Furchtgott-Roth. *Cable TV.* Washington, DC: Brookings Institution Press, 1996.

Creech, Kenneth. *Electronic Media Law and Regulation.* Burlington, MA: Focal Point, Elsevier, 2007.

Denisoff, R. Serge. "Ted Turner's Crusade: Economics v. Morals." *The Journal of Popular Culture* 21(2004): 27–42.

Dowd, Maureen. "Ted's Excellent Idea." *The New York Times,* August 22, 1996. http://www.nytimes.com/1996/08/22/opinion/ted-s-excellent-idea.html.

Ebert, Roger. "'Casablanca' Gets Colorized, but Don't Play It Again, Ted." *Chicago Sun-Times*, October 30, 1988. http://rogerebert.suntimes.com/apps/pbcs.dll/article?AID=/19881030/PEOPLE/10010305.

Einstein, Mara. *Media Diversity*. Mahwah, NJ: Lawrence Erlbaum Associates, 2004.

Elmer-DeWitt, Philip. "Play It Again, This Time in Color." *TIME*, October 8, 1984. http://www.time.com/time/printout/0,8816,955342,00.html.

Elmer-DeWitt, Philip. "Sailing Close to the Wind." *TIME*, August 25, 1986. http://www.time.com/time/magazine/article/0,9171,962141,00.html.

Fabrikant, Geraldine. "Is Cable Cornering the Market?" *The New York Times*, April 17, 1988. http://www.nytimes.com/1988/04/17/business/is-cable-cornering-the-market.html?scp=1&sq=Is%20Cable%20Cornering%20the%20Market?&st=cse.

Fabrikant, Geraldine. "Ted (Don't Fence Me In) Turner." *The New York Times*, November 24, 1996. http://www.nytimes.com/1996/11/24/business/ted-don-t-fence-me-in-turner.html.

Field, Robert A. *Take Me out to the Crowd: Ted Turner and the Atlanta Braves*. Huntsville, AL: Strode Publishing, 1977.

Fimrite, Ron. "Bigwig Flips His Wig in Wigwam." *Sports Illustrated*, July 19, 1976. http://vault.sportsillustrated.cnn.com/vault/article/magazine/MAG 1091349/index.htm.

Fineman, Howard. "Why Ted Gave It Away." *Newsweek*, September 29, 1987. http://www.newsweek.com/id/97023/.

Flournoy, Don Michael, and Robert K. Stewart. *CNN: Making News in the Global Market*. Eastleigh, UK: University of Luton Press, 1997.

Fonda, Jane. *My Life So Far*. New York: Random House, 2005.

Garchik, Leah. "Fasten Your Seat Belt, It's Ted Turner." *San Francisco Chronicle*, November 27, 2008. http://www.sfgate.com/cgi-bin/article.cgi?f=/c/a/2008/11/27/DDF81469MK.DTL.

Goldberg, Robert, and Gerald Jay Goldberg. *Citizen Turner: The Wild Rise of an American Tycoon*. New York: Harcourt, Brace & Co., 1995.

Goodale, James C., and Rob Frieden. *All About Cable*. New York: Law Journal Press, 1981. Updated annually.

Greenwald, John, and John Moody. "Hands across the Cable." *TIME*, October 2, 1995. http://www.time.com/time/magazine/article/0,9171,983499,00.html.

Gross, Jane. "Cable Television: Boon or Bane for Sports?" *The New York Times*, June 17, 1979, Sports, S1.

Grover, Ronald. "AOL Time Warner Is Squandering a Key Asset—Ted Turner." *BusinessWeek*, May 12, 2000. http://www.businessweek.com/print/bwdaily/dnflash/may2000/nf00512e.htm?chan=db.

Gunther, Marc. "Ted Turner's Montana Adventure." *Fortune*, October 4, 2006. http://money.cnn.com/2006/10/03/news/economy/pluggedin_gunther_bison.fortune/index.htm.

Gunther, Marc. "Understanding AOL's Grand Unified Theory of the Media Cosmos." *Fortune*, January 8, 2001. http://money.cnn.com/magazines/fortune/fortune_archive/2001/01/08/294457/index.htm.

Hack, Richard. *Clash of the Titans: How the Unbridled Ambition of Ted Turner and Rupert Murdoch Has Created Global Empires That Control What We Read and Watch*. Beverly Hills, CA: New Millennium Press, 2003.

Hammel. Paul. "Turner 'Almost Done' Buying up Ranchland." *Omaha World-Herald*, February 7, 2008.

Harmon, Mark, and John Fryman. "Viewer Perceptions of CNN World Report: U.S v. International Students." *The Southwestern Communications Journal* 9 (1994): 83–90.

Henry, William A., III. "History as It Happens." *TIME*, January 6, 1992. http://www.time.com/time/magazine/article/0,9171,974614,00.html.

Henry, William A., III. "Shaking up the Networks." *TIME*, August 9, 1982. http://www.time.com/time/magazine/article/0,9171,925663,00.html.

Hillard, Robert L, and Michael C. Keith. *The Broadcast Century and Beyond*. Burlington, MA: Focal Point, 2005.

Hofmeister, Sallie. "Ted Turner Fumes as Merger Unfolds." *Los Angeles Times*, May 26, 2000. http://articles.latimes.com/2000/may/26/news/mn-34232.

Holson, Laura M. "Media Megadeal: The Deal; The Online Generation Courts the Old Guard." *The New York Times*, January 11, 2000. http://www.nytimes.com/2000/01/11/business/media-megadeal-the-deal-the-online-generation-courts-the-old-guard.html.

Jenkins, Nate. "Ted Turner's Land Purchases Raise Ranchers' Suspicions." The Associated Press, *The Boston Globe*, December 2, 2007. http://www.boston.com/news/nation/articles/2007/12/02/ted_turners_land_purchases_raise_ranchers_suspicions/.

Killing, Steve, and Doug Hunter. *Yacht Design Explained*. New York: Norton, 1998.

Kirkpatrick, Curry. "Going Real Strawwng." *Sports Illustrated*, August 21, 1978. http://vault.sportsillustrated.cnn.com/vault/article/magazine/MAG1093993/index.htm.

Kirkpatrick, David D. "AOL Reporting Further Losses; Turner Resigns." *The New York Times*, January 30, 2003. http://www.nytimes.com/2003/01/30/business/aol-reporting-further-losses-turner-resigns.html.

Kirkpatrick, David D. "Togetherness at AOL Time Warner Is Not High on Turner's Agenda." *The New York Times*, March 19, 2003. http://www.

nytimes.com/2003/03/19/business/togetherness-at-aol-time-warner-is-not-high-on-turner-s-agenda.html.

Kirkpatrick, David D. "What's $400 Million between Friends?" *The New York Times*, April 21, 2003. http://www.nytimes.com/2003/04/21/business/what-s-400-million-between-friends.html.

Klein, Alec. "Unconventional Transactions Boosted Sales." *Washington Post*, July 18, 2002. http://www.washingtonpost.com/ac2/wp-dyn/A21983–2002Jul17.

Kleinfield, N.R. "Making 'News On the Cheap' Pay Off." *The New York Times*, April 19, 1987. http://www.nytimes.com/1987/04/19business/making-news-on-the-cheap-pay-offhtml?sec=&spon=&&scp=2&sq=Making%20'News%20On%20The%20Cheap'%20Pay%20Off&st=cse.

Knights, Jack. "An Awesome Warning from the Sea." *Sports Illustrated*, April 27, 1979. http://vault.sportsillustrated.cnn.com/vault/article/magazine/MAG1095275/index.htm.

Koepp, Stephen. "Captain Outrageous Opens Fire." *TIME*, April 29, 1985. http://www.time.com/time/magazine/article/0,9171,1048325,00.html.

Lehrer, Jim. "Megamerger Masters: Steve Case and Gerald Levin." *Online NewsHour*, January 12, 2000. http://www.pbs.org/newshour/bb/business/jan-june00/aol_01–12.html.

Lehrer, Jim. "Troubled Marriage?" *Online NewsHour*, July 19, 2002. http://www.pbs.org/newshour/bb/business/july-dec02/aoltime_7–19.html.

Leonard, Andrew. "How the World Works: How to Save Doha with Soybeans." *Salon.com*, September 25, 2006. http://www.salon.com/tech/htww/2006/09/25/ted_turner/index.html.

Loomis, Carol J. "AOL+TWX=???" *Fortune*, February 7, 2000. http://money.cnn.com/magazines/fortune/fortune_archive/2000/02/07/272827/index.htm.

Loomis, Carol J. "AOL Time Warner's New Math." *Fortune*, February 4, 2002. http://money.cnn.com/magazines/fortune/fortune_archive/2002/02/04/317481/index.htm.

Lowe, Janet. *Ted Turner Speaks: Insight from the World's Greatest Maverick.* New York: John Wiley & Sons, 1999.

Mannes, George. "The Birth of Cable TV." *AmericanHeritage.com*. http://www.americanheritage.com/articles/magazine/it/1996/2/1996_2_42.shtml.

Marston, Red. "A Priority Fulfilled: Turner's Ocean Title." *The New York Times*, March 26, 1972, MB10.

Matthews, Jack. "Film Directors See Red over Ted Turner's Movie Tinting." *Los Angeles Times*, September 12, 1986. http://www.reelclassics.com/Articles/General/colorization-article.htm.

Mifflin, Lawrie. "Ted Turner Nonchalant about Not Being Chief." *The New York Times*, September 23, 1995. http://www.nytimes.com/1995/09/23/business/ted-turner-nonchalant-about-not-being-the-chief.html.

The Museum of Broadcast Communications. "The Financial Interest and Syndication Rules." http://www.museum.tv/archives/etv/F/htmlF/financialint/financialint.htm.

The Museum of Broadcast Communications. "United States: Cable Television." http://www.museum.tv/archives/etv/U/htmlU/unitedstatesc/unitedstatesc.htm.

Munk, Nina. *Fools Rush In: Steve Case, Jerry Levin, and the Unmaking of AOL Time Warner.* New York: HarperBusiness, 2004.

The New York Times. "Fastnet Search Comes to End." August 16, 1979, A17.

The New York Times. "Yachtsman Turner Purchases Braves." January 7, 1976, Sports, 59.

O'Connor, John J. "TV: The Early Days of 24-Hour News." *The New York Times*, June 5, 1980, Home Section, C23.

Okrent, Daniel "Happily Ever After?" *TIME*, January 24, 2000. http://www.time.com/time/magazine/article/0,9171,995889,00.html.

Paglin, Max D., ed., Joel Rosenbloom and James R. Hobson, co-eds. *The Communication Act: A Legislative History of the Major Amendments, 1934–1996.* Silver Spring, MD: Pike & Fischer, 1999.

Painton, Priscilla. "The Taming of Ted Turner." *TIME*, January 6, 1992. http://www.time.com/time/magazine/article/0,9171,974622,00.html.

Phinizy, Coles. "In the Wake of the Capsize Kid." *Sports Illustrated*, July 12, 1971. http://vault.sportsillustrated.cnn.com/vault/article/magazine/MAG1085063/index.htm.

Phinizy, Coles. "Sailing On A Sea Of Perplexity." *Sports Illustrated*, August 8, 1977. http://vault.sportsillustrated.cnn.com/vault/article/magazine/MAG1092674/index.htm.

Pike, Sid. *We Changed the World: Memoirs of a CNN Global Satellite Pioneer.* St. Paul, MN: Paragon House, 2005.

Range, Peter Ross. "Playboy Interview: Ted Turner." *Playboy*, August 1978, 67–90.

Rhode, David. "Ted Turner Plans a $1 Billion Gift for U.N. Agencies." *The New York Times*, September 19, 1997. http://www.nytimes.com/1997/09/19/world/ted-turner-plans-a-1-billion-gift-for-un-agencies.html.

Roberts, Johnnie L. "As Ted's World Turns." *Newsweek*, June 12, 2000. http://www.newsweek.com/id/85082/.

Rutenberg, Jim. "Media Talk: AOL Sees a Different Side of Time Warner." *The New York Times*, March 19, 2001. http://www.nytimes.com/2001/03/19/business/mediatalk-aol-sees-a-different-side-of-time-warner.html.

Schonfeld, Reese. *Me and Ted against the World: The Unauthorized Story of the Founding of CNN*. New York: Cliff Street, 2001.

Schwartz, Tony. "Turner Opens 2d Network in Cable-News War." *The New York Times*, January 4, 1982. http://www.nytimes.com/1982/01/04/arts/turner-opens-2d-network-in-cable-news-war.html.

Schwartz, Tony. "The TV News, Starring Ted Turner." *The New York Times*, May 25, 1980, Business & Finance, F1.

Schwartz, Tony. "Where Cable TV Stands after F.C.C. Deregulation." *The New York Times*, August 21, 1980, Home Section, C26.

Sellers, Patricia. "Gone With the Wind: Ted Turner is a Worried Man." *Fortune*, May 12, 2003. http://newsmine.org/content.php?ol=cabal-elite/secret-society/ted-turner-last-billion.txt.

Sherman, Stratford P. "Ted Turner: Back from the Brink." *Fortune*, July 7, 1986. http://money.cnn.com/magazines/fortune/fortune_archive/1986/07/07/67824/index.htm.

Skow, John. "Vicarious Is Not the Word." *TIME*, August 9, 1982. http://www.time.com/time/magazine/article/0,9171,925664,00.html.

Smith, Gary. "What Makes Ted Run?" *Sports Illustrated*, June 23, 1986. http://vault.sportsillustrated.cnn.com/vault/article/magazine/MAG1064962/index.htm.

Smith, Leslie, John W. Wright, and David H. Ostroff. *Perspectives on Radio and Television*. Mahwah, NJ: Lawrence Erlbaum Associates, 1998.

Smith, Sally Bedell. "CBS Criticizes Turner Views." *The New York Times*, May 3, 1985. http://www.nytimes.com/1985/05/03/business/cbs-criticizes-turner-views.html?scp=1&sq=CBS%20Criticizes%20Turner%20Views&st=cse.

Smith, Sally Bedell. "Turner Buys Sole Rival in Cable News Market." *The New York Times*, October 13, 1983. http://www.nytimes.com/1983/10/13/business/turner-buys-sole-rival-in-cable-news-market.html?scp=18&sq=Satellite%20News%20Channel%201983&st=cse.

Sterling, Christopher H., and John M Kittross. *Stay Tuned: A History of American Broadcasting*. Mahwah, NJ: Lawrence Erlbaum Associates, 2002.

Stuart, Reginald. "He's Getting Interference 1970–1981." *The New York Times*, September 13, 1981. http://www.nytimes.com/1981/09/13/business/hes-getting-interference-1970–1981.html.

Swisher, Kara, with Lisa Dickey. *There Must Be a Pony in Here Somewhere: The AOL Time Warner Debacle and the Quest for a Digital Future*. New York: Crown Business, 2003.

Taafe, William. "Goodwill, but Not a Very Good Show." *Sports Illustrated*, July 21, 1986. http://vault.sportsillustrated.cnn.com/vault/article/magazine/MAG1065048/index.htm.

TIME. "Cable TV: The Lure of Diversity." May 7, 1979. http://www.time.com/time/magazine/article/0,9171,920333,00.html.

TIME. "CBS Attacks." June 17, 1985. http://www.time.com/time/magazine/article/0,9171,959211,00.html.

TIME. "Person of the Year, 1991: Ted Turner." January 6, 1992. http://www.time.com/time/subscriber/personoftheyear/archive/stories/1991.html.

Turner, Ted. "Invest in Clean Energy." *Chicago Tribune*, January 4, 2009. http://archives.chicagotribune.com/2009/jan/04/opinion/chi-perspec-0104turnerjan04.

Turner, Ted. "My Beef with Big Media." *Washington Monthly*, July/August 2004. http://www.law.indiana.edu/fclj/pubs/v49/no1/lubinsky.html.

Turner, Ted, with Bill Burke. *Call Me Ted.* New York: Grand Central Publishing, 2008.

Turner, Ted, and Gary Jobson. *The Racing Edge.* New York: Simon and Schuster, 1979.

UN News Centre. "Ted Turner Receives Global Peace Award." April 20, 2005. http://www.un.org/apps/news/story.asp?NewsID=14031&Cr=disarmament&Cr1=.

Vaughan, Roger. *The Grand Gesture: Ted Turner, Mariner, and the America's Cup.* Boston: Little, Brown & Co., 1975.

Vaughan, Roger. *Ted Turner: The Man behind the Mouth.* Boston: Sail Books, 1978.

Vaughan, Roger. "Turner: Folk Hero Who's One of the Folk." *The New York Times*, December 24, 1978, Sports, S2.

Volkmer, Ingrid. *News in the Global Sphere: A Study of CNN and Its Impact on Global Communication.* Eastleigh, UK: John Libbey Publishing, 2004.

Weber, Harry R. "Turner Steps Down, Quietly." Associated Press, *The Boston Globe*, May 20, 2006. http://www.boston.com/business/technology/articles/2006/05/20/turner_steps_down_quietly/?rss_id=Boston+Globe+—+Business+News.

Wells, Alan, and Ernest A. Hakanen. *Mass Media and Society.* Greenwich, CT: Ablex Publishing, 1996.

West, Krista. "The Billionaire Conservationist." *Scientific American*, August 2002. http://www.scientificamerican.com/article.cfm?id=the-billionaire-conservat.

Whall, Hugh D. "Eagle on a Wild, Wet Flight." *Sports Illustrated*, March 16, 1970. http://vault.sportsillustrated.cnn.com/vault/article/magazine/MAG1083415/index.htm.

Whall, Hugh D. "The Eagle Was Plucked at Sea." *Sports Illustrated*, March 17, 1969. http://vault.sportsillustrated.cnn.com/vault/article/magazine/MAG1082190/index.htm.

Whall, Hugh D. "The Meanest Vamp at Sea." *Sports Illustrated*, March 28, 1966. http://vault.sportsillustrated.cnn.com/vault/article/magazine/MAG 1078345/index.htm.

Whittemore, Hank. *CNN, The Inside Story: How a Band of Mavericks Changed the Face of Television News*. Boston: Little, Brown & Co., 1990.

Williams, Christian. *Lead, Follow or Get out of the Way: The Story of Ted Turner*. New York: Times Books, 1981.

Wolff, Michael. "Happy New Media." *New York*, January 17, 2000. http://nymag.com/nymetro/news/media/columns/medialife/1837/.

Xavier, R. E. "Episode 4: The Birth of Cable Television." *Media Intell—Insights into Technology, Media, and the New Economy*. http://www.smallbizdr.net/2007/10/episode-4-birth-of-cable-television.html.

Zoglin, Richard, and Joseph J. Kane. "The Greening of Ted Turner." *TIME*, January 22, 1990. http://www.time.com/time/magazine/article/0,9171,969230,00.html.

WEB RESOURCES

Turner Related Web sites

Captain Planet Foundation. http://captainplanetfoundation.org/.

Nuclear Threat Initiative. http://www.nti.org/index.php.

Ted's Montana Grill. http://www.tedsmontanagrill.com/.

TedTurner.com. Good general site, excellent information on ranches. http://www.tedturner.com/enterprises/home.asp.

Turner Endangered Species Fund. http://www.tesf.org/turner/tesf/.

Turner Foundation, Inc. http://www.turnerfoundation.org/.

United Nations Foundation. http://www.unfoundation.org/.

Vermejo Park Ranch. Ecological Projects. http://www.vermejo.com/ecology.htm.

General Interest

Academy of Achievement. "Robert Edward (Ted) Turner Interview: Charismatic Visionary, Maverick Tycoon." October 20, 2007. Transcript: http://www.achievement.org/autodoc/page/tur0int-1.

Archive of American Television. Michael Rosen 8-part Interview with Ted Turner, June 12 and December 16, 1999. (Note instructions for accessing Part 3) http://www.youtube.com/view_play_list?p=663C40EC7C84B675.

Bronstein, Phil. "Ted Turner: The Legendary Maverick Tells All." Interview, The Commonwealth Club of California, San Francisco, November 19, 2008. http://fora.tv/2008/11/19/Ted_Turner_The_Legendary_Maverick_Tells_All.

Carson, Gerald (text), and Robert Reck (photography). "Slide Show: Ted Turner on His Armendaris Ranch Wild Animal Preserve, The Media Magnate Builds a Lodge in Tune with the Land." *Architectural Digest*, June 2008. http://www.architecturaldigest.com/homes/homes/2008/06/turner_slideshow?slide=1#globalNav.

Corazza, Ryan. Craig Sager Tells Us about Ted Turner and Jane Fonda's Weekend Tryst." *MOUTHPIECEblog*. http://www.mouthpiecesports.com/blog/2008/08/27/craig-sager-tells-us-about-ted-turner-and-jane-fondas-weekend-tryst/.

Cronkite, Walter. Report on America's Cup, Ted Turner. *60 Minutes*, 1977. http://www.cbsnews.com/video/watch/?id=4578655n.

Dobbs, Lou. Interview with Ted Turner, November 11, 2008. http://www.youtube.com/watch?v=wAQRdV0AyDU.

The Internet Movie Database. Turner Broadcasting System (TBS), filmography. http://www.imdb.com/company/co0005051/.

The Internet Movie Database. Turner Pictures, filmography. http://www.imdb.com/company/co0045447/.

Lamb, Brian. "Oral History Collection: 25th Anniversary Panel Discussion Satellite Programming." November 2000. http://www.cablecenter.org/education/library/oralHistoryDetails.cfm?id=308#transcript.

Lamont, Ned. "Ted Turner Looks at the World." Interview, The World Affairs Council of Connecticut, Hartford, April 7, 2009. http://fora.tv/2009/04/07/Ted_Turner_Looks_at_the_World.

Maxwell, Paul. "Oral History Collection: R. "Ted" E. Turner." Interview. *The Cable Center*, November 2001. http://www.cablecenter.org/education/library/oralHistoryDetails.cfm?id=179#interview.

Rose, Charlie. "A Conversation with Ted Turner." © Charlie Rose LLC, April 1, 2008. http://www.charlierose.com/view/interview/9019

Rose, Charlie. "An Hour With CNN Founder Ted Turner." © Charlie Rose LLC, July 23, 2004. http://www.charlierose.com/view/interview/1337.

Safer, Morley. "Ted Turner: Alone on the Range." *60 Minutes*, November 9, 2008. http://www.cbsnews.com/video/watch/?id=4586914n.

17 Update Early in the Morning: Quicktime clips. http://www.billtush.com/update.html.

Turner, Ted. Carl Sagan Interview, 1989.
    Part 1: http://www.youtube.com/watch?v=k2zMa3unSN8.
    Part 2: http://www.youtube.com/watch?v=acBqqe61WjQ.
    Part 3: http://www.youtube.com/watch?v=dj_MZ6i5Dr0.
    Part 4: http://www.youtube.com/watch?v=35EROe20kWI.
    Part 5: http://www.youtube.com/watch?v=6pqO1KFV0S8.

Turner, Ted. Fidel Castro Interview, 1990. http://www.youtube.com/watch?v= rvnUwvnvxgw&feature=related.

Turner, Ted. Speech at The National Press Club, October 10, 2006. http://www. publicradio.org/tools/media/player/noads/news/midday/2006/10/10_ midday2.smil.

Turner, Ted. Speech at the World Trade Organization Public Forum, Geneva, Switzerland, September 25, 2006. Document available at http://www. wto.org/english/forums_e/public_forum_e/session_25_num2_e.htm.

Turner, Ted. Transcript. Landon Lecture, Kansas State University, November 28, 2005. http://www.k-state.edu/media/newsreleases/landonlect/turn ertext1105.html.

WTCG/WTBS—25 Years of Bill Tush! http://www.youtube.com/watch?v= Qy8MTBxP7no.

Cable Regulation and Law

The Cable Communications Act of 1984, Public Law 98–549. October 30, 1984. http://www.publicaccess.org/cableact.html.

Cornell University Law School. "Supreme Court Collection: *Turner Broadcasting System, Inc. v. F.C.C.* (93–44), 512 U.S. 622 (1994)." http:// www.law.cornell.edu/supct/html/93–44.ZS.html.

Federal Communications Commission. Fact Sheet, Cable Television. http:// www.fcc.gov/mb/facts/csgen.html.

Geller, Henry. "Turner Broadcasting, the First Amendment, and the New Electronic Delivery Systems." 1 Mich. Telecomm. Tech. L. Rev. 1 (1995), available at http://www.mttlr.org/volone/geller_art.html#fnref6.

Home Box Office, Inc., Petitioner, v. Federal Communications Commission and United States of America, Respondents, Professional Baseball et al., Intervenors, 2 Media L. Rep. 1957; 185 U.S.App.D.C. 142; 2 Media L. Rep. 1561; 567 F.2d 9.

Lubinsky, Charles. "Reconsidering Retransmission Consent: An Examination of the Retransmission Consent Provision (47 U.S.C. § 325(b)) of the 1992 Cable Act." *Federal Communications Law Journal*, Volume 49, Number 1 (November 1996). http://www.law.indiana.edu/fclj/pubs/ v49/no1/lubinsky.html.

Price, Monroe E. "Red Lion and the Constitutionality of Regulation: A Conversation among the Justices." Communications and Society Program, *Aspen Institute*. http://staging.aspeninstitute.org/policy-work/commu nications-society/programs-topic/digital-broadcasting-public-interest/ red-lion-cons.

Text of Decision: http://altlaw.org/v1/cases/418780.

Turner Broadcasting System, Inc., et al. v. Federal Communications Commission et al. (95–992), 1997. http://caselaw.lp.findlaw.com/cgi-bin/getcase.pl?court=US&navby=case&vol=000&invol=95–992.

Turner Broadcasting System v. Federal Communications Commission. http://law.jrank.org/pages/12692/Turner-Broadcasting-System-v-Federal-Communications-Commission.html.

Warner, R. Matthew. "Reassessing Turner and Litigating the Must-Carry Law beyond a Facial Challenge." *Federal Communications Law Journal,* March, 2008. http://findarticles.com/p/articles/mi_hb3073/is_2_60/ai_n29431545/?tag=content;col1.

INDEX

Aaron, Hank (Henry), 70; and sale of WRET, 117

ABC (American Broadcasting Corporation), 114, 115, 118, 139, 179, 181, 194; and affiliate's Atlanta Hawks broadcasts, 47, 48; Capital (Cap) Cities' takeover of, 140; affiliate preemptions and WTCG, 47–48; and purchase of by Disney, 180. *See also* Satellite News Channels (SNC)

Abortion for Survival, 171

Academy Award Theater (WTCG), 47

Agricultural subsidies and tariffs, 207

Ailes, Roger, 183

Alan Cranston Peace Award, 206

Alison (Gelenitis), Betsy, 120n6

Amanpour, Christiane, on Turner, 213

American Eagle, 53–55; past history of, 53; Turner's farewell to, 55; 12-meters and ocean racing, 53–54

American Indian Movement (AIM), 77, 78

America Online (AOL): and Bertelsmann AG/AOL Europe purchase deal, 196, 197; history of, 189–90, 195; revenues and market capitalizations, 190; share prices of, 192 and Steve Case,

189; and *Washington Post* series, 197. *See also* AOL Time Warner, merger

America's Cup, 53; and Fastnet, 107; first American loss of, 121n23; history of, 56–57; 1970, 54–55; 1974, 56–71; 1980, 119–20; and second chances, 82. *See also* America's Cup, 1977; *Mariner*

America's Cup, 1977, 81–92; and Alan Bond, 88, 90–91; and amateurism, 91; and August trials, 84, 87; and *Australia*, 87, 88, 89, 90–91, 91–92; and Bailey Beach incident, 85–86, 92n5; and "Beat the Mouth" incident, 86–87; and Competition series, 89; and *Courageous*, 81–82, 83, 84, 86, 87, 88, 89, 90; and *Courageous* as second-class boat, 83; and *Courageous*'s crew, 83, 88; and *Courageous*'s sails, 83, 84, 86, 88; and June preliminaries, 84; and July trials, 86, 87; and *Mariner* debacle, 82; and media/public attention, 81, 85, 90, 91; and Noel Robins, 91–92; and NYYC, 88; and post-win, 90–91; and satellite receiver, 81; and *Sports Illustrated*, 83, 85, 88; Turner approached regarding, 81–82; and

Turner as underdog, 81, 83; and
Turner comment on sailing, 92; and
Turner invitation to White house,
88–89; and Turner on Australians,
91; and Turner referencing father,
88, 89, 91; and Turner's demeanor,
84, 85, 86, 90; and Turner's doubts,
82, 92; and Turner's skills, 82–83,
91–92; and win, 90; and "wives"
quote, 89–90; *See also* Doyle,
Robbie; Hood, Ted; Jobson, Gary;
Loomis, Alfred Lee, Jr.; North,
Lowell
Anan, Secretary General Kofi, 184
Anderson, John, and CNN presentation
of Reagan/Carter debate, 124
Andersson, Don, 49, 65
AOL Time Warner: advertising sales
and, 195; AOL dropped from company name, 198; and AOL e-mail,
195; AOL revenues and market
capitalizations, 190; and Bertelsmann AG/AOL Europe purchase
deal, 196, 197; and board vote
regarding, 190; and Bob Pittman,
191, 192, 197; Case and Levin comments on Turner, 192; Christiane
Amanpour on treatment of Turner,
213; "clicks and mortar," 191; and
debt, 196; and Dan Logan, 197; and
Dick Parsons, 191, 192, 196, 197,
198; and dotcom bubble, 191–92,
193; enthusiastic reception of, 191;
and executives' stock sales, 195; and
failure to meet growth targets, 195;
and failure to mesh, 195; FCC approval of, 193; and Gordy Crawford,
198; and Jamie Kellner, 194; and Jeff
Bewkes, 197; and Jerry Levin, 189,
190, 193, 195–96; and John Malone,
198; Ken Auletta and, 192; and Ken
Auletta quotes of Levin regarding
board, 195; and Levin's perceived
need of, 190; and $98.7 billion loss,

198; merger, 189–91, 212, 213; and
press-conference announcing, 191;
and SEC investigation, 197; and
share prices, 191, 192, 195, 197; and
Steve Case, 189, 192, 193, 196, 197,
198; structure of deal, 190, 193, 195;
and Terry McGuirk and reorganization, 194; Tom Johnson, on Turner,
199; and Turner, 189, 190, 195–96;
and Turner as vice-chairman, 190;
Turner at last board meeting, Atlanta, 199; and Turner comments
on, 191, 192; Turner leaves board,
199; and Turner's consultation
with confidants, 190, 200n2; and
Turner's emotional state, 194; and
Turner's holdings in new company,
190–91, 195; and Turner's off-the-
cuff comment controversies, 193–94,
196–97; and Turner's reaction to,
190, 191, 192; Turner stripped of
operational responsibility, 192; and
Turner's trust in Levin, 190; and
U.S economy, 191, 195; valuations
of deal, 190, 193; and *Washington
Post* series, 197; and World Championship Wrestling league financial
losses, 194–95; and Steve Case
Apple Computer, 211
Argentina, 203
Arledge, Roone, 118
Arnett, Peter, and Operation Desert
Storm (Persian Gulf War), 172
Atlanta Braves, 48, 50, 69–78, 119;
America's team, 77; appeal Kuhn's
decision on tampering charge, 75; as
bargain programming, 69; baseball
establishment reaction to Turner, 73;
and Bobby Cox, 77; and Bob Hope
promotions/publicity, 72–73; and
Bowie Kuhn, 74–75; and Cy Young
awards, 78; and divisional championships, 78; and firing of Donald
Davidson, 71; and Gary Matthews

controversy, 74–75; and Jane Fonda, 77–78; and Jimmy Carter, 75, 77, 88; John Malone and, 208; and Larry Foster, 78n2; Messersmith career with, 76–77, 78n2; and Native Americans/American Indian Movement (AIM), 77–78; opening game, 1976, 71; and player nicknames, 73; proposed sale of, 69; Rule 20 (e) invoked, 75; Terry McGuirk and, 70, 208; and the "tomahawk chop," 77–78; Turner announces purchase of, 70; Turner attempts to learn game, 70; Turner at baseball's winter meetings, 74; Turner at Los Angeles Hilton, 76; Turner meeting with Kuhn, 74; Turner as participant in promotions, 73; and Turner persona at games, 71, 72, 73; Turner promises changes, 70, 72; Turner purchases, 69–70; Turner serves as manager of, 75; Turner suspension for tampering, 74–75; ushering in baseball's free-agency era, 70–71; Will Sanders and, 70; and World Series, 77, 78

Atlanta-Fulton County Stadium, 71, 72, 77, 78

Atlanta Hawks, 47, 48, 153; and David McDavid, Atlanta Spirit, and TBS, 208; Turner purchase of, 76

Atlanta Spirit, 208

Atlanta Thrashers, 208

Attention Deficit Hyperactivity Disorder (ADHD), 35

Attorino, Edward, on TBS bid for CBS, 140–41

Auletta, Ken, 161; and AOL Time Warner, 192, 193, 195

Australia, considered move to, 39

Autobiographies, and Turner: Christian Williams's *Lead, Follow or Get out of the Way*, intended as, 22, 106; Simon & Schuster and, 111n20; Joe Klein and, 112n20. *See also Call Me Ted*

Avalon plantation, 156; and conservation, 203; and Turner/Fonda marriage, 160

Aziz, Tariq, 171–72

"Bailout" of Turner Broadcasting, 146–48; Bill Daniels and, 146, 147; cable partners and board seats, 147; and covenants of, 147; and implications of, 147–48; John Malone (TCI) and, 146–47; and possible conflicts on new board, 147; structure of deal, 147; Time Inc. and, 147; Turner fears of KNN, 147; Turner on first meeting of new board, 191; and Turner regrets on yielding veto power, 147

The Better World Society, 136; and Beijing conference of, 174; and documentaries, 136; and international board of, 136; and J. J. Ebaugh, 153

Bevins, Bill, and CBS takeover bid, 142; complaints regarding Schonfeld, 131; heart attack of, 147–48; hired as TBS CFO, 105; on implications of "bailout" of Turner Broadcasting, 147–48; and MGM purchase, 144; raiding petty cash, 133

Bibb, Porter, 21, 146

Big Sur, 161, 203

Bill and Melinda Gates Foundation, 185, 206, 207

Biofuels, 207

Bison (American Buffalo), 158, 160, 203, 204–5; and Native Americans, InterTribal Bison Cooperative (ITBC), 205; and North American Bison Cooperative (NABC), 204, 205; and Ted's Montana Grill, 204; world's largest private herd of, 204. *See also Ranches*

Blitzer, Wolf, 208

Boarding school, 3–4

Boesky, Ivan, 148n19

Bolero, 36

Bristol-Myers, 113–14

Brown, Jimmy, 6, 9, 34, 35, 151, 209,
    233; as best man, at Turner/Fonda
    marriage, 160; death of, 198; and
    Ed's suicide, 26; as sailing teacher, 7;
    as substitute father, 6, 37, 152

Brown, Lester (Worldwatch), 136

Brown University, 13–19, 209; and
    Brown Alumni Magazine, 197; and
    Classics, 16–18; and *The Daily
    Herald*, 17; description of Ted at, 13;
    Ed's letter, 17–18, 20n7; expulsion
    from, 18–19; and John Rowe Work-
    man, 16–17; study habits of, 14;
    suspension from, 15; Turner's induc-
    tion to Athletic Hall of Fame, 61;
    and Turner's 9/11 comments, 196–97

Buffet, Warren, 140, 206

Burke, Bill, and *Call Me Ted*, 208.
    See also Call Me Ted

Bush, President George H. W.: on
    CNN, 170; and Iraq, 172; and 1992
    election choices, 173

Bush, President George W., 33, 207

Cable television, 212; and advertising,
    66, 98, 103, 124; as agent of diver-
    sity, 67, 99, 105, 139; and AT&T
    terrestrial lines, 64; basic cable,
    66, 99, 212; and Bill Daniels, 135,
    138n31; and broadband, 190; and
    common carriers, 66; copyright fees
    and royalties, 48–49, 101, 103–4,
    133–34; and copyright violations,
    99; and distant signals, 48, 66,
    67, 99; growth of/penetration of,
    49, 96, 98, 99, 124, 139–40, 169,
    177; history of, 49; and microwave
    transmission, 49, 64, 66, 138n31;
    nation's first urban cable system,
    63; and Nielsen ratings, 96, 124;
    pay-TV, 64, 66, 96; and retransmis-
    sion consent/"must-carry," 99, 100,

101, 103, 111n19, 173, 177, 185n1;
    and satellite distribution, 63, 64, 65,
    66, 76, 98, 114; and subscriber fees,
    63, 66; 110n2; and "superstations,"
    66, 76, 99. *See also* CNN; "Fin-Syn";
    HBO; House Subcommittee on
    Communications; Levin, Jerry (Ger-
    ald); *Satcom I*; *Satcom III*, Southern
    Satellite Systems (SSS); Supersta-
    tion; Turner, Ted (Robert Edward
    Turner III), and the media

Cable Television Consumer Protec-
    tion and Competition Act of 1992,
    111n19, 177

Cal-40 boats, 37n8

Call Me Ted (autobiography), 16,
    20n11, 112n20, 162n20, 213; about,
    208–10; on AOL Time Warner
    merger, 190, 195; on "bailout" cable
    summit, 146–47; on CBS takeover
    attempt, 143; on failure of merger
    talks, 179; on Fastnet, 107; on Janie
    and second marriage, 152, 154; on
    J. J. Ebaugh, 153, 156; publication
    of, 208; reception of, 209–10 side-
    bars in, 200n1, 209, 210; and sister's
    illness/death, 22, 23

Captain Planet, 175n6; *and the Planeteers*,
    171; *The New Adventures of*, 173

Carlson, Curtis L., 29n8

Carter, Jimmy, 173; and Better World
    Society, 136; and Braves, 75, 88;
    and CNN presentation of Reagan
    debate, 124; and Panama Canal
    treaty dinner, 88–89; and tomahawk
    chop, 77

Cartoon Network: and *The New Adven-
    tures of Captain Planet*, 173; and new
    animation series, 173; and purchase
    of Hanna-Barbera, 173; and retrans-
    mission consent, 173

Castle Rock Entertainment (production
    studio): as producer of *Seinfeld*, 174;
    purchase of, 174

Castro, Fidel, 135, 157, 170; and CNN promotional spot, 129; and CNN signal 129; evaluation of CNN, 129; and Mariel boatlift, 123; Turner visiting, 129; urging a worldwide CNN, 130

CBS: and Benjamin Burton on costs associated with news, 118; Bob Wussler and, 116; and CBS Cable channel, 139; Daniel Schorr and, 102; and Gene Jankowski Senate testimony, 103–4; and Jesse Helms/ Fairness in Media targeting of, 139; merger talks with Turner, 139; sale to Westinghouse Electric, 143, 180, 186n8; and SNC contributing stations, 134; Turner's continued interest in, 179. See also CBS take-over bid

CBS Takeover bid, 140–43; approval of CBS stock repurchase plan and, 143; Bill Bevins and, 142; CBS letter to shareholders and, 141; CBS petitioning FCC to stop, 141–42; CBS quoting Daniel Schorr news-paper article, 142; CBS stock repurchase plan as roadblock to, 142–43; Change in perception of, 142; and E. F. Hutton, 140; initial commenting on, 140–41; questioning Turner's fitness to operate a network, 141; Mike Wallace comment on, 141; post-bid repercussions at CBS, 143; previous incendiary Turner quotes and, 141; and SEC approval of registration statement for, 142; structure of deal, 140; Thomas Wyman, CBS Chairman and, 141, 143; Turner financial loss associated with, 143; Turner demeanor during, 142; Walter Cronkite comment on, 141

Central Outdoor Advertising (Cincinnati), 3

Chance, Britton, 82, 83; and 1974 America's Cup, 57–58, 59, 60, 61

Channel 17, 81, 211; Andy Messersmith as, 73. See also Superstation (Channel 17); WJRJ (Channel 17); WTBS (Channel 17); WTCG (Channel 17)

CNN, 212, 214n6; and advertisers, 113–14, 124; and American journalism, 101; and attempted unionization of, 130; and Bill Lucas, 100; and bomb threat, 172; cable penetration and, 98, 139–40; as "Chaos News Network," 119; as "Chicken Noodle News," 119, 125, 170; and commentators, 102; as competition for networks, 99; and Compton Advertising report, 128; and Daniel Schorr, 101–2; 10th anniversary of, 170; doubts on success of, 118; and FCC, 114; and Fidel Castro, 129; financials of, 124, 133, 135, 140, 174; financing of, 98, 99, 103, 114, 117, 133; first proposed to NCTA, 98; first public mention of, 99; first words on, 119; gestation of idea for, 95–99, 110n2; growth of, 126, 132–33, 135 139–40; and Hank Aaron, 117; hiring of Tom (W. Thomas) Johnson Jr., 171; initial flubs of, 119; launch of, 118–19; lingering effects of SNC battle, 136; and Lou Dobbs, 113, 115; on news as rerun, 95; and National Cable Show, 1979 (Las Vegas), 100; and Native American themed programming, 78; and Omni Hotel purchase (CNN Center), 154; and "open newsroom" concept, 106; and Pan Am flight 759, 133; and planning for competition, 124; and "pool coverage" lawsuit, 125; and preemption of Brinks armored-car robbery, 128; press conference to announce, 101–2; and "randomonium," 119, 131; and RCA Americom, 115–16; and ratings of, 172; reacting to SNC, 133; and Reese Schonfeld, 96–97, 100, 101, 102, 106, 115, 116, 126, 130–31; relationship of with other news services, 115 128–29; as replacement of newspapers, 117–18; re-securing satellite for, 115–16, 117; and Roy Mehlman, 110n2; and satellite 98, 113–14, 115–16, 133; seen as underbudgeted, 118; and settlement with ABC/Westinghouse (SNC), 135; scheduled launch, 100; and "signoff" for, 118; staffing and on-air talent of, 114–15; subscriber fees, 98, 10–3, 126, 133; and substance of, 123; as synonym for news, 170; and Techwood Drive, 105–6, 114, 118; 10th anniversary of, 170; threat from SNC, 125–26; and Turner editorial on, 132; Turner on loss of satellite, 115–16; Turner's comments on, 113; Turner's hesitation, 98–99; Turner's initial vision of, 97; and Turner and news, 97, 101; 24-hour news, impracticality of, 96; Will Sanders and, 115; and WRET, 99 117

CNN Center: penthouse apartment at, 161; purchase of, 154

CNN, as international, 135, 151, 169, 170, 173, 174, 198, 212; CNN International, 137, 173; *International Hour*, 135; must-viewing for world leaders, 170; Turner outlaws "foreign" at TBS, 171; use of Soviet satellite, 169; *World Report*, 136–37. *See also* Iraq; 1991 Soviet coup attempt; Operation Desert Storm; Tiananmen Square

CNN NewsSource, 212; and idea for, 128; concerns over, 129; CNN Radio, 127

CNN, significant reportage in development of: death of John Lennon,

124; El Salvador, 129; fire at MGM Grand, 123–24; John Anderson and Presidential debate, 124; Mariel boatlift 123; Mt. St. Helens, 123; Reagan assassination attempt, 124–25, 132; Space Shuttle Challenger, 135; Titan II missile, 123; TWA Flight 847. *See also* Operation Desert Storm (Persian Gulf War); Tiananmen Square

CNN2/Headline News: announcement of, 127; as CNN Headline News, 134; and CNN NewsSource, 128–29; financials of, 127; financing of, 127, 133; launch of, 128; promotion of, 127, 128; as response to SNC, 126; securing transponder for, 126, 133; subscriber fees, 133; subscribers to, 133, 135. *See also* Satellite News Channels (SNC)

Coalition for Better Television (CBT), 128

Colorization, of films: 163–65; and artistic rights, France, 165; Bette Davis on, 164; business advantages of, 163, 165, 166; of *Casablanca*, 163; copyright and, 165; and cost of, 16; of *Dark Victory*, 164; of *Dr. Jekyll and Mr. Hyde* (1941), 163; of *42nd Street*, 164; George Romero on, 164; Ginger Rogers on, 164; history of, 163; of *It's a Wonderful Life*, 163, 164; Jimmy Stewart on, 164; of John Huston's, *The Asphalt Jungle*, 165; of *King Kong* (1934), 164; and MGM, 163; Martin Scorsese and, 166; and National Film Registry, 165; and plans for, 164; and process of, 165; as revival, 163, 164; Richard Corliss on, 164; Roger Ebert on, 165; Russell Baker on, 164; and state of technology, 164; and *The Aviator*, 166; Woody Allen on, 164; of *Yankee Doodle Dandy*, 163, 166. *See also*

Preservation and restoration, of films

Colorization (Inc.), 163, 163n1

Color Systems Technology, 163

Commercial communications satellites, Western Union, Westar satellites, 64, 65, 126 RCA Satcom satellites, 64, 65. *See also* RCA Americom; *Satcom I*; *Satcom III*

Common carrier, 66

Communications Act of 1934, 100, 117

Congressional Cup, 82–83

Conner, Dennis, 110, 121n23; and 1974 America's Cup, 58, 60, 61; and 1980 America's Cup, 119, 121n23; and Fastnet (1979), 110

Copyright fees. *See* Cable television, copyright fees and royalties; Turner Broadcasting Systems, copyright fees and royalties

Copyright Royalty Tribunal, 133–34

Coast Guard, 16, 19, 36

Courageous, 58–59; Britton Chance on Turner and, 61, 82; and Dennis Conner, 61; and 1974 America's Cup, 58–59, 61; and 1977 America's Cup, 81–82, 83, 84, 86, 87, 88, 89, 90; and 1980 America's Cup, 119–20; Olin Stephen and, 58–59

Cousteau, Jacques, 135

Cox, Bobby, 77

Cox Communications, 47, 48

Coxe, Tench, 42; and RCA Americom, 115, 116

Crawford, Gordy, and AOL Time Warner, 198, 200n2

Cronkite, Walter, 50, 84; on Turner's bid for CBS, 141

Crossfire, 131, 137n19

Cruise, Tom, 76

Culture wars, 212

Cyclothymia, bipolar disorder, 153–54

Dames, Peter, 14, 19, 32, 209; and Ed Turner on success, 25; and Turner Outdoor Advertising, 20

Daniels, Bill: and ABC/Westinghouse TBS deal, 135; and "cable summit," 146; as "The Father of Cable Television," 135, 138n31; on Turner and cable, 147

Daniels Cablevision v. FCC, 185n1

Derecktor, Bob, 55; and 1974 America's Cup, 58, 59, 60

DeSaix, Pierre, and *Mariner*, 58

Dillard, Jane (stepmother), 15, 16, 18, 22, 25, 27; marriage to Ed Turner, 16

Direct-response advertising, 46. *See also* Ginsu knives

Disney (The Walt Disney Company), purchase of Cap Cities/ABC, 180

Dobbs, Lou, 113, 115; on Turner's CNN editorial, 132

Dolan, Charles, and Cablevision Systems, 64; and HBO, 63–64; and nation's first urban cable system, 63 and possible satellite delivery of HBO, 64

"Dotcoms," "dotgones," "dotcompost," 191–92

Douglas, Mike, 131

Doyle, Robbie, 58, 83–84, 86, 88

Eagle. See *American Eagle*

Ebaugh, J. J. (Jeanette H.): about, 153; and *Atlanta* magazine article, 155; and Better World Society, 153; and home purchased for by Turner, 153; as influence on Ted's life, 153, 155; introduces Turner to fly-fishing, 155; and Janie Turner, 153, 154, 156; on lithium use by Turner, 154; meeting Turner, 153; and occult spirituality, 155–56; as proponent of therapy, 153; Turner moves in with, 154; and Turner's campaign to win her back, 154; as Turner's private pilot, 153

E. F. Hutton, 140

Fairness in Media, 139, 141

Falwell, Jerry, 128

Fastnet, 54; about, 106; Cowes Week, 107; Fastnet Rock, 108; Turner sets course record in, 55. *See also* Fastnet (1979)

Fastnet (1979), 106, 107; changing weather conditions of, 107, 107–8; and Christian Williams, 106; and conditions on *Tenacious*, 108; and Cowes Week, 107; early weather conditions of, 107; Gary Jobson and, 107, 108; and Irish Sea, 107, 108; and New York Yacht Club Challenge, 107; and Peter Bowker, 107, 108; and post-race Plymouth, 109; and prevailing waves, 108; and sails, 108; and smaller boats, 108; and Teddy Turner, 106; *Tenacious* and NYYC Challenge, 107; *Tenacious* as winner of, 109, 110; *Tenacious* finishes race, 108; *Tenacious* presumed lost, 109, 110; Tragic statistics of, 109–10; Turner as helmsman, 108; as Turner's "finest hour," 110; and Turner's post-race comments to media, 109, 110

Federal Communications Commission (FCC), 43, 49, 50, 66, 95, 139; and AOL Time Warner merger, 193, 195; and CBS takeover bid, 141, 143; and CNN, 114, 116, 117; *Daniels Cablevision v.*, 185n1; and differing rules for broadcast and pay cable, 66; and distant signals, 99–100; and regulatory changes of 1990s, 111n19, 177; and Southern Satellite/WTCG, 66–67, 76, 114; and Time-Warner/TBS merger, 181, 182; *Turner Broadcasting Inc. v.*, 185n1; Turner on, 101, 104; Turner petitioning, 125–26

Feeney, Chub (Charles Stoneham), 73, 75

Ferris, Charles, 104

Finley, Charles O., 73, 76, 79n3

"Fin-Syn" rules, relaxing of, 177

5.5-meter boats, 38n11; and Olympics competition, 36

5.5-meter Gold Cup, 54

5.5-meter Nationals, 55

5.5-meter World Championships, 54

Fonda, Jane, 4, 162n18, 183, 213; and additional Turner ranches, 160–61; announces retirement from film career, 159; and Asian trip, 161; as born-again Christian, 189; and domineering father, 157; and end of marriage to Turner, 189; on a dinner date with Turner, 159; and first call from Turner, 156; first date with Turner, 156–57; and fly fishing, 161; and international travel with Turner, 161; as "Hanoi Jane," 159; and "Home Sweet Homes" photo project, 161; and log home, 160; and marriage to Turner, 160; and Mikhail Gorbachev, 161; and mother's suicide, 157; opposing Turner's presidential ambitions, 173; and positive affects on Turner, 160; and public perceptions of relationship with Turner, 159; and reticence of, 158–59; and tomahawk chop, 77–78; and Tom Hayden, 156, 159; and Turner, 156–61, 190; on Turner and healing, 210; Turner as one of brother Peter's heroes, 156; and Turner, mutually smitten, 157; and Turner's bison herds, 158; and Turner's description of early life, 157; and Turner's familiarity with nature, 157, 161; and Turner's nightmare, 161; and Turner's rapprochement with his children, 159; and Turner's Ten Voluntary Initiatives, 158; and Turner unable to say "monogamous," 157; and visit with Turner to Montana ranch(s), 157–58; at wedding of Laura Lee Turner, 159–60

Fonda, Peter, 156, 157

Forbes 400 list, 184; Turner comments on, 184

Fox News Channel, 182–83, 193, 194; and Roger Ailes comment on Turner, 183; and Time Warner, 182–83; and Turner, 182–83

Free agency, baseball, 70–71

Freeman, Sandi, 131, 138n20

Gallatin National Forest, 205

Gandhi, Mahatma, 211

Gates, Bill: and Bill and Melinda Gates Foundation, 185, 206, 207; and talks with Turner, 179;

Gearon, Michael, Jr., 208

Geller, Henry, 103

General Outdoor Advertising, 1, 23, 27–28, 29n8, 34; Ed and purchase of, 23–25; Ted and purchase of, 23, 25, 26–27, 27–29

Georgia Military Academy, 5–6, 13

Gettysburg, 211

Ginsu knives, 140; as direct-response advertising, 46; sales of supporting CNN, 133

Global Leadership Award, 184

Global trade, 206–7

Global warming, 136, 185, 207

Gods and Generals, 211

Goldberg, Robert (co-author of Citizen Turner), on Time Warner purchase of Turner Broadcasting, 204

Gone With the Wind, 6–7; as debut of TNT, 170; as debut of Turner Classic Movies, 174; on deterioration of, by 1987, 166; on restoration of, 166. *See also* Rhett Butler

The Goodwill Games, 136, 154, 162n18; cancellation of, 198; as contributing to end of the Cold War, 136

Gorbachev, Mikhail, 157, 161; awarding Turner the Alan Cranston Peace Award, 206; on CNN coverage of coup attempt, 173; and dissolution of Soviet Union, 173; and 1991 Soviet coup attempt, 172, 173

Great Depression, 1

Hal Roach Studios, 163, 167n1

Hanna-Barbera Productions, Inc., 173; and MGM animation libraries, 173; purchase of, 173. *See also* Cartoon Network

Hayden, Tom, 156, 173

HBO (Home Box Office), 66, 181, 182, 192, 212; beginnings of, 63–64; Charles Dolan and, 63, 64; and contract with RCA Americom, 64; as "Green Channel," 63; initialing satellite cable, 64, 212; and Jimmy Ellis-Earnie Shavers boxing match, 63; and Muhammad Ali-Joe Frazier "Thrilla in Manilla," 64; and satellite delivery proof-of-concept, 63; and Sterling Manhattan Cable, 63; and Time, Inc., 63, 64; and 24-hour news, 96; and Westar satellites, 64; and Wilkes-Barre, Pennsylvania, 63–64

Helfrich, Bunky (Carl, Jr.), 11n12; as architect, 105, 106, 119; as crewmate, 7, 57, 119; and Fastnet reports, 110

Helfrich, Carl, 91

Helms, Jesse, 139, 141

Hinckley, John, 115, 132

Hinman, George (commodore), 56, 57, 58, 60

Hogan, Gerry, 46

Holliman, John, 172

Home Box Office. *See* HBO

Hood, Ted, 58, 81, 82; and *Independence*, 1977 America's Cup, 81–82, 84, 86, 87, 88; and sails, 81, 83, 84, 88

Hope, Bob, 72, 73

Hope plantation, 153, 156
House Subcommittee on Communications: 1976, 67–68, 100; 1979, 100–101, 105
Hunter, Jim "Catfish," 79n3

Inglis, Andy (RCA Americom), 115
Iraq: and Bernard Shaw interview with Saddam Hussein, 172; as contributing member of *World Report*, 171–72; and invasion of Kuwait, 171–72; Iraq War, 207. *See also* Operation Desert Storm (Persian Gulf War)
"I Was Cable When Cable Wasn't Cool," 130

Jackson, Jesse, 141, 142
Jankowski, Gene, 103, 104
Jobson, Gary: and America's Cup, 1977, 83, 84, 86, 88, 89; and America's Cup, 1977; post-win, 90, 91; on career with Turner, 120; and comment on Fastnet (1979), 110; and Fastnet (1979), 106, 107, 108; on Turner's "finest hour," 110
Johnson, Tom (W. Thomas), Jr.: hired as CEO of CNN, 171; and Iraqi invasion of Kuwait, 171; and Operation Desert Storm (Persian Gulf War), 172; and pen used for dissolution of Soviet Union, 173
Jordan, Hamilton, and drafting Turner as presidential candidate, 173
"Junk bonds," 140; and Michael Milken, 144; Turner on, 140

Karp, Russell (Teleprompter), 97
Kentucky Fried Chicken, 39
Kerkorian, Kirk, 143, 144, 146, 147, 149n19
King, Larry, 138n20
King, Martin Luther, Jr., 54, 211
Kinsley, Michael, 187n26
Kissinger, Henry, 123

Korea, DMZ, and environment of, 206; Turner proposal of DMZ "peace park"/UN World Heritage site, 206
Kuhn, Bowie, 74–75, 76, 85, 89; and House Subcommittee on Communications, 101
Kutcher, Ashton, 214n6

Ladendorff, Marcia, 131
Lamont, Ned, 212
Lear, Norman, 101
Levin, Jerry: and AOL Time Warner, 189, 190, 191, 193, 195–96; and CNN, 97; and death of son, 195; and Nick Nicholas, 196, 201n20; as president of HBO, 64: and satellite delivery proof-of-concept, 63; and Time Warner purchase of TBS, 180, 182; and Turner as best friend, 196; and Turner's "clitorized" comment, 185n5; and 24-hour news, 96
Lightnin', 55–56, 62n5
Lithium, use by Turner, 154, 160; and friends' evaluation of affects, 154; and presidential ambitions, 173
Loomis, Alfred Lee, Jr., 81–82, 86, 87, 90
Lotspeich school, 4
Lucas, Bill: death of, 100; first African American general manager in baseball, 100; as reminder of Turner's mortality, 155
Lurie, Bob, 74

Mahony City, Pennsylvania, 49
Malaria, 207
Malnutrition, 136
Malone, John: and AOL Time Warner, 192, 198, 200n2; and Atlanta Braves, 208; as board member of TBS, 171, 178; as libertarian, 180; and Rupert Murdoch, 180; and TBS "bailout" by cable industry, 146–47; and TCI veto power, 171, 178, 180;

and Time Warner purchase of TBS, 180, 181; and Time Warner shares, 181; on Turner within Time Warner, 181

Manhattan Cable, 63

Mariner, 56, 57, 82, 83; and Dennis Conner, 60, 61; design of, 58; elimination of, 61; problems with, 58–59; redesign of, 59–60; Turner dismissed as captain of, 60–61; Turner's performance with, 60; and *Valiant* (trial horse), 58, 59–60. *See also* America's Cup, 1974; Chance, Britton

Massachusetts Institute of Technology (MIT), 120n1

Mazo, Irwin, 25, 105, 209, 211; and General Outdoor reacquisition, 26, 27, 28, 29; and *Scylla*, 34, 35; and Turner on second marriage, 32; and Turner's goals, 211; and WJRJ acquisition, 42, 97; WRET and resignation of, 44

McCallie Military Academy (Chattanooga), 7–10, 13, 35, 40; and Holton Harris Oratorical Medal, 10; and stray animals, 156; Teddy and, 10; Turner looking back on, 10;

McClurkin, Lee, 44

McDavid, David, 208

McDonalds, 39

McGuirk, Terry, 11, 70, 98, 110, 114, 115, 194, 208

McIntosh, John, 7

Mehlman, Roy, 110n2

Mergers/partnerships explored, 174, 178; with Bill Gates/Microsoft, 179; *Call Me Ted* on, 179; with Gannett Newspapers, 146; with Jesse Helms/Fairness in Media for CBS, 139; with NBC, 178, 179; with Paramount, 179; with Rupert Murdoch, 146; with T. Boone Pickens for RCA/NBC, 139; with Time-Life, 146

Merry Jane, 6, 14, 23

Messersmith, Andy, 70–71; and baseball free agency, 70; career with Braves, 76–77, 78n2; as "Channel 17," 73; and Larry Foster, 78n2

MGM (Metro-Goldwyn, Mayer): as assuring programming availability, 144; Bill Bevins and, 144; changing consensus on, 146; and changing structure of deal, 144, 145; and film libraries, 144, 145, 146, 212; and "junk bonds," 145; initial general consensus on, 145, 146; and Kerkorian reacquisition of selected assets, 146; and Kirk Kerkorian, 143, 144, 146, 147, 149n19; MGM losses during planning of, 145; Michael Milken and, 144–45, 148n19; as more important than CBS purchase, 143; purchase, 144; resistance of board to, 144; and sale of selected assets, 146; Turner on, 145; and value of "content," 146

Microsoft: and talks with Turner, 179; and MSNBC, 182–83

Miklaszewski, Jim (James Allen), 129

Milken, Michael, 148n19; and Ivan Boesky, 148n19; as "king of junk bonds," 144; and MGM purchase, 144–45; racketeering and securities fraud charges against, 148n19; as Turner confidant, 200

Miller, Marvin, 76

Montana Department of Fish and Wildlife, 205

Murdoch, Rupert, 186n25, 207; on AOL Time Warner, 213; on CNN Tiananmen Square coverage, 169–70; and *Condor/Nirvana* and Sydney–Hobart, 182; embracing green technologies, 207; and feud with Turner, 182, 183; and Fox News Network, 182–83; and independent media ownership, 199; and interest in acquiring TBS, 180; and merger talks with Turner, 146; and *New York Post*, 183 Turner's comments on, 183, 207

"My Beef With Big Media," 198–99

NABC. *See* Bison
Naegele, Bob, 23–24, 25, 28, 29n8
National Association of Broadcast Electricians and Technicians (NABET), 125, 130
The National Audubon Society, 135
National Cable Broadcasters Association (NCBA), 134
National Cable Television Association (NCTA), 49, 98; and Bill Daniels, 138n31; 1973 convention, Anaheim, 63; and Robert L. Schmidt, 100; Turner's attendance of conventions, 65
National Labor Relations Board, 130
Native Americans, 77–78
NBC (National Broadcasting Corporation), 99, 116, 139; Atlanta affiliate preemptions and WTCG, 47; affiliate loses Braves to WTCG, 48; and CNBC, 170–71; Microsoft partnership with, in MSNBC, 179, 182–83, 194; and Time Warner veto power, 178–79; and Turner/T. Boone Pickens discussions on pursuing, 139; WRET becomes Charlotte affiliate of, 95
New Line Cinema (movie studio): film library of, 174; purchase of, 174; and Turner's approval of *The Lord of the Rings* cycle, 174
NewsSource. *See* CNN NewsSource
New York Yacht Club (NYYC), 54, 55, 56, 58–59, 88, 107; Turner's election to, 56
Nicholas, Nick, 196, 201n20
1984 Cable Communication and Competition Act, 169, 177

1991 Soviet coup attempt, 172–73; and CNN coverage of, 173
1976 Copyright Act, 99, 104, 134
Noroton Yacht Club, Connecticut, 20n3
North, Lowell, 81, 82, 84, 87; and anger of, 88; and *Enterprise*, 1977 America's Cup, 86, 87–88; and sails, 81, 83, 84, 88; Turner confrontation with, 84
Nothing But Nets, 214n6, 270
Nuclear arms control, 136
Nuclear Threat Initiative, 206; inspiration for, 193; mission of, 193; Sam Nunn and, 193
Nunn, Sam, 193
Nye, Judy Gayle (first wife), 18, 19, 21–22, 23, 32, 33, 209; divorce/reconciliation/end of marriage, 24, 31, 37n1; and Ed's advice to, 22; and fears for Ed, 25; and Laura Lee Turner (daughter), 23, 36, 36–37; marries Ted, 20; and Teddy Turner (son), 31, 36, 36–37; and sailing, 18, 21, 31, 33, 37n5
NYYC. *See* New York Yacht Club (NYYC)

Ogallala Aquifer, 205
Olympics boycotts, 136
O'Meara, Marty, 58
Operation Desert Storm (Persian Gulf War), 172; and bombing of Baghdad, 172; and Brent Scowcroft, 172; and CIA Director William Webster, 172; and CNN bomb threat related to, 172; as CNN's defining moment, 172; and major networks, 172
Outdoor Advertising Association of America (OAAA), 32

Paley, William (Bill), 143
Patterson, Houston, 8, 10
Paul White award, 170

Peterson, Russell (Audubon Society), 136

Perot, Ross, 173

Phelps, Michael, 35

Pike, Sidney, 45, 46

Pittman, Frank, 153–54

PlasTrend, 36, 45

Poverty, 207

Preservation and restoration, of films, 165–66; artistic judgments involved in, 166; of Gone With the Wind, 166; Martin Scorsese and, 166; and Sistine Chapel, 166

PTL Club, 49–50

Public schooling, 4, 6

Queen City Chevrolet, 1, 2

Radio, 39, 40–41; Turner disinterest in, 41

Ranches, 157, 160–61, 180; and acreage, 203, 205; and bison, 158, 160, 203, 204, 205; conservation and environmental aspects of, 157–58, 203, 204, 205; and controversies related to, 204–5; and easements, 203; as economically viable, 204; first purchase of, the Bar None, Montana, 156; and Jane Fonda, 157–58, 160; and Jerry Levin, 180, 192; and John Malone, 192; and mineral rights, 205; and Peter Fonda, 157; Peter Manigault and, 156; and Turner's increasing attention to, 183, 203

Rather, Dan, 97; and Fairness in Media, 139

RCA Americom: and loss of Satcom III, 115–16; and satellite earth stations, 65; and satellites, 64, 65, 95, 98, 115–16; and Turner exploration of satellite distribution, 65. See also Satcom I

Reagan, President Ronald: assassination attempt of, 124–25, 132; and CNN

presentation of Carter debate, 124; and El Salvador, 129

The Red Cross, 21

Reilly, Rick, 207

Reinhardt, Burt, 106; named CEO of CNN, 131; retirement of, 171

Retransmission consent. See Cable Television, retransmission consent/ "must carry"; Turner Broadcasting Systems, retransmission consent/ "must carry"

Reverse merger, 43

Rhett Butler, Gone With the Wind, 7, 11n11, 36

Rice, Harold, 95, 114

Robinson-Humphrey (investment bank): Lee Wilder of, on CBS takeover offer, 140; and WTCG and WRET, 43, 44

Roddey, Jim, 39–40, 40–41, 42, 97; initial impression of Ted, 40 resignation of, 44

Rose, Charlie, 194, 207

Rotary Club, 6, 21

Sager, Craig, 162n18

Sailing. See Turner, Ted (Robert Edward Turner III), and sailing; individual events; individual boats

St. Philips Island, purchase of, 106

Sanders, Will, 44–45, 66, 70, 115; leaves TBS, 105

San Francisco Chronicle, 210, 211

Satcom I, 76, 95, 115, 116, 117, 126

Satcom III, 98; launch and loss of, 113. See also RCA Americom, and loss of Satcom III

Satellite distribution of cable television, proof-of-concept, 63

Satellite News Channels (SNC): and ABC's reticence with news, 127, 134; advantages over CNN, 126–27; approaches Reese Schonfeld, 134–35; and Bill Daniels, 135; as CNN competition, 125, 126, 135;

and CNN's advantages over, 126; CNN2 as Turner response to, 126; and contributing stations, 134; final signoff of, 135; financial losses at, 134; launch of, 132–33; and no subscription fee, 126, 133; and Pan Am Flight 759, 133; partners in, 125; plans for, 125–26; and satellites, 126; and settlement with TBS, 135; slogan for, 126; subscribers, 132, 134, 135; and Turner Broadcasting anti-trust lawsuit, 134; Turner on, 127

Savannah yacht club, 6, 7, 9

Save the Children, 185

Schmidt, Elliot, 8

Schonfeld, Reese, 96, 101, 115, 116, 119, 126, 129, 130–31, 212; at announcement of CNN, 102; approached by ABC/Westinghouse (SNC), 134–35; and Bill Bevins, 131; and Fastnet reports, 110; firing of, 131; and first impressions of Ted, 65, 96; and How to Win Friends and Influence People, 131; and ITNA (Independent Television News Association, 96, 100; and Marcia Ladendorff, 131; and Mike Douglas, 131; and National Cable show, 1979 (Las Vegas), 100; and "open newsroom" concept, 106; reaction to being fired, 131; recalling 1974 visit with Ted Turner at WTCG, 64–65; and Sandi Freeman, 131; signs contract with Turner, 10; staff reaction to firing of, 132; and Turner, 130; Turner on management style of, 132; upset at preemption of Brinks armored-car robbery coverage, 128

Schorr, Daniel, 101–2; at announcement of CNN, 102; CNN rebuttal commentary regarding Turner's editorial, 132; and concerns regarding Turner, 102; and earlier career, 102; and Fastnet reports, 110; and newspaper article quoted by CBS, 142; and resignation from CBS, 102; and unique contact of, 102

Scientific Atlanta, 64; and satellite delivery proof-of-concept, 63; Turner purchase of earth station from, 65. See also Topol, Sid

Scorsese, Martin, 166

Scylla, 34–35

17 Update Early in the Morning, 50–51, 95, 111n13

Seydel, J. Rutherford (son-in-law), 208

Seymour, Frances Ford (mother of Jane Fonda), 157

Shaw, Bernard, 119; and interview with Saddam Hussein, 172; and Operation Desert Storm, 172; and Reagan assassination attempt, 124–25; and Tiananmen Square, 169. See also Shaw, Bernard (retirement party)

Shaw, Bernard (retirement party), 193–94; Brit Hume (Fox News Network) and, 193–94; New York Post and, 194; and Turner Ash Wednesday comment, 193; Turner's official comments at, 194

Showbiz Today, 51

Sicking, Henry (maternal great-grandfather), 2

Silver Hill (rehabilitation center), and Ed Turner, 24–25, 26

60 Minutes, 141; and 1977 America's Cup, 84

Slate 60, top 60 philanthropists list, 187n26

Solar power, 207

Southern Ocean Racing Conference (SORC), 34, 35, 35–36, 53–55, 56, 57, 115

Southern One-Ton Championships, 55–56

Southern Satellite Systems, 66; and FCC, 66, 67

Sports Illustrated, 15, 20n4, 35, 53–54, 83, 85, 89, 146, 207

Stephens, Olin, 57, 58, 58–59, 121n23

Sterling Manhattan Cable. *See* Manhattan Cable

Subcommittee on Communications of the Senate Committee on Commerce, Science, and Transportation, 103, 105; and Gene Jankowski, 103, 104; and Henry Geller, 103–4, 104; Turner's appearance before, 103, 104, 105

Sumner, Mississippi, 1–2, 3; and Turner connection with nature, 4, 156

Superstation (Channel 17), 78, 95, 113, 162n18, 212; and *Abortion for Survival*, 171; as agent of diversity, 101; claims of copyright violations, 99, 100–101; direct-response ads on, supporting CNN, 133; and environmental programming, 135; financials of, 127, 140; growth of, 99, 127, 139–40; and *Portraits of America*, 135; programming changes on, 99, 135, 171; and "Turner Time," 124. *See also* Turner Broadcasting Systems (TBS); WTBS (Channel 17), WTCG (Channel 17)

Taxi Driver, as harmful media, 67; and John Hinckley's infatuation with Jodie Foster, 125; Turner CNN editorial on, 132

Taylor, Ed, 66, 115; and Western Union, meeting with Turner, 65. *See also* Southern Satellite Systems (SSS)

Ted's Montana Grill, 204; and George McKerrow Jr., 204; and the Green Restaurant Revolution, 204; and the North American Bison Cooperative (NABC), 204, 205

Ted Turner debates. *See Crossfire*

Teleprompter, 98, 125–26; and satellite delivery proof-of-concept, 63

Television (TV), allure of, 39, 42–43; VHF (Very High Frequency), 41, 42 *See also* UHF (Ultra-High Frequency) television

Telsat Canada, *Anik I*, 63

Tenacious, and Fastnet (1979), 106–7, 108, 109, 110

"Think Different," 211

Tiananmen Square, 169–70; Bernard Shaw and, 169; Rupert Murdoch on, 169–70; and Turner's later statement on, 174n1

Time Inc.: and "bailout" of TBS, 147; and CNN, 97; and HBO, Charles Dolan, 63, 64; and Jerry Levin, 24-hour news, 96; and Warner Communications merger, 181

TIME magazine, Man of the Year, 213

Time Warner: as board partner of TBS, 178; and debt of, 178, 181–82; and failures with "new media," 190; and Fox News Channel, 182–83; and Mayor Rudolph Giuliani, 183; and MSNBC, 182–83; and New York City cable Franchise and Concession Review, 183; and TBS veto power, 178; and Turner on being "clitorized" by, 178; and Turner's focus on share price, 184; and Turner trying to free himself from as TBS board member, 178; as world's largest media company 181. *See also* Levin, Jerry (Gerald)

Tisch, Laurence, 143

TNT (Turner Network Television), *Gone With the Wind* as debut of, 170; launch of 170; and programming of, 170; and revenues from, 170

Topol, Sid, 65; and satellite delivery proof-of-concept, 63; and Reese Schonfeld 1974 visit with, 64; and 1974 Ted Turner meeting, 64–65. *See also* Scientific Atlanta

Transatlantic race, 36, 54

Turner, Beau (Beauregard) (son), and Atlanta Spirit, 208; birth of, 36;

Turner, Ed (no relation), 114, 115; and "flyaway" transmitters, 136

Turner, Ed (Robert Edward Jr.) (father), 1–3, 17–18, 20, 22, 24–25, 33;

abandonment and beatings of Ted, 3–4, 5–6, 7–8, 209–10; birth and family history of, 1–2; and Central Outdoor Advertising, 3, 5; and child-rearing, 209; and discipline, 4, 8, 9, 14; divorce of Florence, 14; doubting worth of his success, 25; expanding his business to Savannah, 5; excessive drinking of, 3, 6; and General Outdoor Advertising purchase, 23–25; and Great Depression, 2–3, 26; inability to accept success, 25; "insecurity breeds success," 7; and Jane Dillard (second wife), 15, 16, 18; and Jimmy Brown, 6, 26; to Judy Nye, on "the provider," 22; and letter to Ted, 209; marries Florence, 2; and Mary Jean's illness/death, 9, 22, 23, 26, 210; and the *Merry Jane*, 6, 14, 23; and Millsaps College, 2–3; and Mrs. Sicking's hotel, 2–3; net worth of, 27; and Peter Dames, 20; and phone call to Bob Naegele, 25; and Queen City Chevrolet, 2; and religion, 2, 23; as salesman, 21; on setting goals, 24; and Silver Hill rehabilitation center, 24–25; suicide of, 25–26; and Ted, 3, 209; at Ted's first wedding, 20; and Turner Outdoor Advertising, 3, 4, 5, 23–24, 25–26; and ultraconservative politics, 7; and upward mobility, 7; vow to parents, 2; and womanizing, 3

Turner, Florence Rooney (mother), 1, 2, 3, 9, 14, 22, 25–26, 27, 146; and call to Curtis L. Carlson, 29n8; death of fiancé, 3; divorce from Ed, 14; Ed as husband, 3, 6, 9; Ed's suicide, 25–26; marries Ed, 2; and Mary Jean, 3, 9, 14, 23; meeting Ed, 2; and religion, 2–3; Ted's treasure, 9

Turner, Jane (Janie) Smith (second wife), 32, 154; and Beauregard Turner (son), 36; as butt of Turner's

humor, 152; and children, 151; demands marriage counseling, 152; dependence on Jimmy Brown, 151, 152; and divorce, 154; emotional state of, 37; friends describing state of after divorce, 154; as good, conservative Southern wife, 152, 153; and Goodwill Games, 154; and J. J. Ebaugh, 153, 154; mental state during marriage, 153; and 1977 America's Cup, 85, 86, 90; and 1968 dinner with Roger Vaughan and wife Possum, 152; and Rhett Turner (son), 36; and Sarah Jean (Jennie) Turner (daughter), 37; on Turner during courtship, 34; and Turner's extramarital affairs, 153; as stepmother, 37, 152

Turner, Judy Gayle (first wife). *See* Nye, Judy Gayle

Turner, Mary Jean (sister), 6, 14, 26; apparent nickname, 210; birth of, 3; death of, 23; illness of, 9; and *Merry Jane*, 6, 14

Turner, Rhett (son), birth of, 36

Turner, Robert Edward (paternal grandfather), 1–2

Turner, Ted (Robert Edward Turner III): abandonment and beatings of, 3–4, 5–6, 7–8, 209–10; and abundance of J's, 210; as American icon, 92; birth of, 1; as Charlemagne, 211; and commercials, 45–46; and debating, 9–10; and debt, 32, 38; and diagnosis of bipolar disorder, 153–54, 160; and drive for success, 8, 27, 33, 151; ethics of, 8; exhaustion of, 169, 180; as father, 23, 36, 37, 47, 106, 151, 152, 155, 159; father's suicide, 25–26, 27; and 53rd birthday, 160; and first marriage of, 20, 21–22, 23, 24; first word, 3; and General Outdoor Advertising purchase, 23, 25, 26–27, 27–29; goals and accomplishments,

211–12; as "glorious asshole," 57; honesty and cornerstone values of, 57; and human failings, 210; image of, 33; and Jane Fonda, 77–78, 156–61, 162n18, 183, 189; as Jiminy Cricket, 211; and J. J. Ebaugh 153, 154, 155 as husband, 21–22, 23, 31, 32, 106, 151, 152, 159, 161; as largest individual landowner, 205; landholdings of, 203; and lithium, 154, 160, 173; and marriage counseling, 152; as motivator, 31–32, 33, 35, 72 net worth, 184, 206; nicknames for, 7, 35, 37, 86, 91; personal heroes, 8, 16, 211; personal frugality of, 71, 182; and personal morality, 210; and presidential ambitions, 92, 173, 211; priorities of, 152, 183; and purchase of first ranch, 156 rambunctious nature of, 3, 4, 8, 13, 14–15; and regrets for second marriage, 154; as salesman, 21, 46; and satellite distribution, 211; and self-reflection, 210–11; and sister's illness/death, 9, 23, 210; and stepmother, 15–16; and taxidermy, 6; and Teddy's accident, 154–55; and his Ten Voluntary Initiatives, 158, 162n20; and Turner ethos, 46–47; viewed as traitor by UHF broadcasters, 68. See also Nye, Judy Gayle; Turner, Ted (Robert Edward Turner III), and the environment; Turner, Ted (Robert Edward Turner III), and the media; Turner, Ted (Robert Edward Turner III), and philanthropy;; Turner, Ted (Robert Edward Turner III), and religion; Turner, Ted (Robert Edward Turner III), and sailing

Turner, Ted (Robert Edward Turner III), and the environment: and bison, 204; conservation projects on ranches/plantations, 203–204, 205; and grandparents' farm (Sumner,

MS), 4, 156; Global Sustainable Tourism Criteria (GSTC), 208; global warming, 136,185, 207; The Green Restaurant Revolution, 204; and his Ten Voluntary initiatives, 158, 162n20; and Jacques Cousteau/ Cousteau Society, 135; and J. J. Ebaugh, 153; knowledge of, 157, 161; Korean demilitarized zone (DMZ), 206; and McCallie, 8; The National Audubon Society, 135; and National Geographic, 135; and overpopulation, 207: and Savannah, 6, 7. See also The Better World Society; Captain Planet; The Turner Endangered Species Fund; The Turner Foundation; The UN Foundation

Turner, Ted (Robert Edward Turner III), and the media: and basic cable, 66, 99, 170, 212; Cable, and Turner programming, as alternative, 46–47, 67, 96, 99, 101, 104–5, 139; and Coalition for Better Television/Donald Wildmon, 128; deficiencies of network news, 104–5, 128; destruction of American values, 67, 127, 128, 212; House Subcommittee on Communications: 67–68, 100–101, 105; House subcommittee on violence on television, 128; immorality of, 139; and Jerry Falwell, 128; lobbying for cable, 134, 151; mindlessness of network programming, 101, 104, 105; "My Beef With Big Media" 198–99; network executives as traitors, 132; as mind pollutants, 125; seeing his future in cable, 67, 100; Subcommittee on Communications of the Senate Committee on Commerce, Science, and Transportation, 103, 104, 105; sex in, 128, 210, 212; TIME, Man of the Year, 213; and Turner ethos, 46–47; violence in, 46–47, 67, 101, 128, 132, 212. See also Taxi Driver

Turner, Ted (Robert Edward Turner III), and philanthropy: 183, 184, 187n26, 212; Kutcher, Ashton, 214n6. *See also individual foundations*

Turner, Ted (Robert Edward Turner III), and politics: changing views of, 171, 183; early leanings, 14; Fidel Castro and, 129–30; as "global citizen," 135; at World Trade Organization, 206–7

Turner, Ted (Robert Edward Turner III), and religion: 9–10, 22–23

Turner, Ted (Robert Edward Turner III), selected comments of: on Avondale public school, 4; on being fired, 212–13; on being irrelevant, 213; on being $2 billion in debt, 146; on boarding school, 3–4; to Bowie Kuhn, 75; on conscience, 210; on early days as CEO, 32; on early WTCG and WRET, 44; on Fidel Castro, 129–30; on Georgia Military Academy, 5; on land acquisition, 205; on landholdings, 205; to Levin, 196; on *Mariner* experience, 60; on *Mariner* group, 59; to Mike Wallace on 9/11 comment, 197; on Murdoch, 182, 183; on news, 95; on nightmare, 161; on NYYC, 88; on Ponzi scheme, 33; on praise from father, 23; on professionalism in sailing, 92; on regrets regarding second marriage, 154; on risky business, 45; on sailing schedule, 54; on *17 Update*, 101; on sister's illness, 9; to *60 Minutes* on Lowell North, 84; on SNC threat, 127; on solar power, 207; on switching boats, 90–91; on United States, 171; on wasting resources, 41 on winning America's Cup, 91

Turner, Ted (Robert Edward Turner III), and sailing: 7, 8, 10, 13, 15, 16, 18, 21, 23, 33, 34–36, 53–61, 62n5; 106–8, 119–20; and computerization of, 120 and having never liked, 120 and Jobson summing up career with, 120; and professionalism/commercialism of, 120; and "retirement" from, 120; as ship's captain, 57; as source of Murdoch feud, 182; Turner's "finest hour" in; 110. *See also individual events; individual boats*

Turner, Teddy (Robert Edward Turner IV) (son): accident in Moscow, 154–55; birth of, 31, 36, 36–37; and Fastnet (1979), 106; and Jimmy Brown, 37; and mother (Judy Nye), 36, 37; and stepmother (Janie), 37, 152; and Time Warner purchase of TBS, 182; on Turner as father, 37, 152, 155

Turner Broadcasting Inc. v. FCC, 185n1

Turner Broadcasting Systems (TBS): 116; and advertising sales, 126, 133; and antitrust lawsuit filed by, 134; and "bailout" of by cable industry, 146–48; and colorization, of films, 163, 164, 165, 166; and David Mc-David lawsuit, 208; and debt, 142, 145–46; and empire, 33, 43, 48, 105, 183; and Financial News Network (FNN), 170–71; financials of, 124, 127, 133, 135, 140, 174, 181–82; future threatened by structure of MGM deal, 145; and Ginsu knives, 133; and Goodwill Games, 136; growth of, 169, 174, 177; and MGM purchase, 143–46; and 1984 Cable Communication and Competition Act, 169, 177; outlaws the term "foreign," 171; and post-"bailout" control of, 169, 170, 174, 177, 178, 179; and preservation and restoration, of films, 165–66; promotion/marketing of, 127; and retransmission consent/"must-carry," 177; and Techwood Drive headquarters, 105, 114, 118, 134, 153; and Time Warner purchase of, 180–82; and Tom

Todd, 128; Turner considers sale of, 178; and Turner's concerns over regulatory environment, 17–78; Turner practically living at, 153; within 24 hours of losing electricity, 133. *See also* Turner Communications Group

Turner Broadcasting Systems, sale of, to Time Warner: consummation of deal, 181; factors in Turner's agreeing to sell, 179–80; and John Malone (TCI), 180, 181; and outsider doubts about, 180; and press-conference announcing, 181; proposal of, 180; Time Warner's perceived advantages of, 181–82; Turner on, 181; Turner's compensation for, 181; Turner's role within Time Warner, 181, 182; valuation of deal, 180

Turner Classic Movies (TCM): launch of, 174; and *Gone With the Wind* as debut, 174

Turner Communications Group: 41; financials of, 42, 44, 45; publicly traded, 43 reverse merger of, 43; and name change to Turner Broadcasting Systems, 120n1. *See also* Turner Broadcasting Systems (TBS)

The Turner Endangered Species Fund, 203

The Turner Foundation, 159

Turner Garlington, Jennie (Sarah Jean) (daughter), birth of, 37; and daughter's illness, 193

Turner Network Television. *See* TNT (Turner Network Television)

Turner Outdoor Advertising: and Ed Turner, 3, 4, 5, 23–24, 25–26; and Ted Turner, 9, 18, 19, 20, 21, 23, 27, 31–32, 32–33, 34

Turner Productions: and Native American themes, 78

Turner Publishing, 171

Turner Seydel, Laura Lee (daughter): birth of, 23, 36, 36–37; and Jimmy

Brown, 37; marriage of, 159–60; and mother (Judy Nye), 36, 37, 160; on naming of, 37; and stepmother (Janie), 37, 152

TUSH, 51

Tush, Bill, 50–51, 95, 102

Twitter, 214n6

UHF (Ultra-High Frequency) Television, 41–42, 43, 45–46, 66; Turner commercial on installing a UHF antenna, 45; Turner on, 96

UNICEF, 136

United Nations (UN), 184–85, 206, 207; and Turner's $1 billion pledge to, 184, 206; and unpaid dues of U.S., 184, 193

The UN Foundation, 184–85, 206, 207; and international board of, 184; and mission of, 184–85; as vital resource, 185; Tim Wirth and, 68, 184, 185

U.S. Naval Academy, 13

U.S Yachtsman of the Year award, 55, 56, 114, 120n6

Vamp X, 35–36

Van Deerlin, Lionel, 100, 111n19

Van Ness, Legaré, 57, 59; on *Mariner* design, 59; on Turner plans for news, 95

Vaughan, Roger, 5, 37, 37n1, 37n5, 95; description of Turner at Brown, 13; and 1977 America's Cup, 86, 92; and a 1968 dinner party at the Turners', 152; on Turner as ship's captain, 57

Veeck, Bill, 72

Wallace, Mike, and Turner on 9/11 comment, 197

Walson, John, 49

WAPO (Chattanooga radio station), purchase of, 39–40; rechristened WGOW, 41

Washington Monthly, 198–99

Watergate, 85

WATL (Atlanta UHF station), closing of, 45; as competition of WTCG, 43, 43–44; *The Now Explosion*, 45

Watson, George, 114–15, 123

Westinghouse Electric (Group W), 117, 143; and ABC partnership in SNC, 125; and purchase of CBS, 180; and Teleprompter, 125–26

WGOW (radio station). *See* WAPO

Wickersham, Liz, 154

Wilder, Lee, 140

Wildmon, Dennis, 128

Williams, Christian, 4, 22, 34, 40; and Fastnet (1979), 106; and Turner "autobiography," 111n20

Williams, Mary Alice, 115

Williams, R. T., 46

Wirth, Tim, 67–68

WJRJ, Channel 17 (Atlanta UHF station), 41–43; opposition to purchase of, 42 rechristened WTCG, 43; Turner intrigued by, 42–43

Workman, John Rowe, 16–17

World Affairs Council, Connecticut, 212–13

World Ocean Racing Championship (WORC), 54, 55; Turner wins, 55

World One-Ton Championships, 56

World Trade Organization, 206–7

WRET (Charlotte UHF station): "begathon" of, 45; growth of, 48; holdup in sale of, 117; Jim and Tammy Faye Bakker and, 49–50; Mazo's resignation over purchase of, 44; as NBC affiliate, 95; religious atmosphere of, 49–50; sale of negotiated, with Westinghouse Electric, 105; sale of pursued, as CNN financing, 99; sale to Westinghouse approved, 117; Turner on, 44

Wright, Gene, 46

WTBS: name change from WTCG, 120n1. *See* Superstation

WTCG (Channel 17), 43, 96, 100; and Atlanta Braves, 48, 69; and Atlanta Hawks, 48; and FCC, 66–67; financials of, 44, 48, 49, 69; growth of, 97; initial satellite transmission of, 76; name change to WTBS, 120n1; NBC Preemptions and, 47–48; programming, 44, 47–48; satellite delivery of, gestation of idea, 64–66; *17 Update Early in the Morning*, 50–51, 95; staff reaction to idea of CNN, 97–98; as "superstation," 66; *Television/Radio Age*, 49; "Thank you" celebration of, 45; 24-hour programming of, 43, 101; "Watch This Channel Grow," 48; and wrestling, 48. *See also* Superstation

Wussler, Bob (Robert), 120; and CBS, 116

Wyman, Thomas, 141, 143; TBS bid for CBS as threat to country, 141

Yachtsman of the Year award. *See* U. S. Yachtsman of the Year award

Yeltsin, Boris, 172–73; on CNN coverage of 1991 Soviet coup attempt, 173

Y-Flyer Nationals, 33

Young Republicans' Club, 32

About the Author

MICHAEL O'CONNOR, a long-time print and electronic publishing professional with 25 years of experience in writing and editing, has brought to publication dozens of award-winning reference, science, technical, and medical projects. Early in his career he served as a television production trainee at Ted Estabrook's Exploring Post 1, creating shows aired on Manhattan Cable. This is his first book.